2.00 PM

# Ragtime

# Ragtime
## A Musical and Cultural History

Edward A. Berlin

UNIVERSITY OF CALIFORNIA PRESS
BERKELEY · LOS ANGELES · LONDON

University of California Press
Berkeley and Los Angeles, California
University of California Press, Ltd.
London, England
Copyright © 1980 by
The Regents of the University of California
ISBN 0-520-03671-9
Library of Congress Catalog Card Number: 78-51759
Printed in the United States of America


1  2  3  4  5  6  7  8  9

To
Andrée, Michèle,
Stephanie, and Kim

# Contents

# List of Plates

# List of Examples

# Acknowledgments

I have been fortunate in the writing of this book to have had the advice and encouragement of numerous friends and colleagues. The earliest version of the manuscript was a doctoral dissertation, completed at the City University of New York under the able and sympathetic supervision of H. Wiley Hitchcock. Additional members of the dissertation committee, all of whom were most diligent with constructive criticism, were William B. Kimmel, Eileen Southern, Leo Kraft, Sherman Van Solkema, and Richard Jackson, the last-named also being of invaluable service as the head of the American music section of the New York Public Library. Subsequent readers who aided with their comments were Michael Leavitt and William J. Schafer.

For generously sharing the resources of their private ragtime libraries, as well as for their stimulating conversation, I am indebted to David Jasen, and to the ever-scintillating Max Morath, the ragtime performer who, more than any other, has achieved a balance between scholarship and entertainment.

John Hasse, currently working on his own dissertation on ragtime, has demonstrated an uncanny ability to locate the rarest of materials and, living up to the highest ideals of scholarship, has unselfishly shared these with me. To Vera Brodsky Lawrence I am indebted for the inspiration of her work on the Scott Joplin edition, and for giving me some guidance through the murky realm of sheet-music copyrights.

I am grateful to Alain Hénon, my editor at the University of California Press, for his encouragement and faith in my project, and to my excellent copyeditor Jane-Ellen Long, who, in addition to working tirelessly on details that strayed into inconsistency, enlightened me on some of the workings within the record industry.

Most of all, it is to my wife Andrée de Plata that I owe gratitude, for her patience, her reading of a seemingly endless stream of revisions, and her valiant attempts to attune a musician's ear to the cadences of language.

# Preface

The resurrection of ragtime in the 1970s is a phenomenon unprecedented in America's musical history; never before has a long-buried style been so widely and eagerly embraced by a mass public. For some this has been, at least partially, a nostalgic trip to the "simplicity and charm" of the past, but for the majority, indifferent or oblivious to ragtime's historicity, this enthusiastic reception has been in response to the same musical qualities that so intrigued Americans seventy years ago: ragtime's direct melodic and harmonic message, its irresistible, foot-tapping, rhythmic impulse.

At the time of this writing, the ragtime fervor has peaked; it is no longer in (and on) the air so unremittingly as it was three and four years ago; it is no longer in such incessant demand. But neither is it returning to its former niche of historical obscurity. Madison Avenue ad agencies continue to milk ragtime for its cheerful ebullience; piano (also harpsichord and organ) recitalists are still "daring" to program Joplin, Scott, and Lamb in the rarified company of Chopin, Mozart, and Scarlatti. And although many of those whose conviction and actions brought about the revival—among those most prominent, Joshua Rifkin, William Bolcomb, Vera Brodsky Lawrence, Gunther Schuller—are now occupied with new concerns, others—Max Morath, Rudi Blesh, and the small coterie of dedicated, hard-line ragtimers who kept the music alive during its leaner years—remain faithful to the cause, and are now buttressed by a greatly enlarged corps of fans and scholars who are both demanding and bringing to ragtime studies a new intensity and perspective.

Much of the literature that has accompanied and followed the ragtime revival has been blatantly exploitative, works promising to fulfill the thirst for information created by the revival but offering only reruns of earlier writings, works which have the further pernicious effect of uncritically perpetuating—often in defiance of simple logic—worn-out myths and unsupported truisms.

One can, of course, also find among recent literature a few works of true merit, sincere efforts that reflect original research and insight. The main emphasis in both categories, though, has been on personalities, especially on Scott Joplin—the revival's main focus—and others touched by his influence. This emphasis, in itself unobjectionable, has brought to light what may be the best in ragtime and has stimulated investigation into peripheral areas. What the critical reader misses, and what is available in the scholarship of most other styles, is substantive discussion, in musical terms, of the genre and its evolution, and of its position in the panorama of American music and culture. It is with a recognition of these deficiencies that the present book was begun.

Initially, my intent was to make a stylistic study, to take a broad look at the scope of ragtime music and to fill in the background required for a historical understanding and evaluation of the music. To this end I examined over 1,000 piano rags, analyzing each piece individually and statistically, as well as an uncounted number of vocal rags and other related music. From this accumulated data emerged the course of ragtime's evolution and its relationship to other music of the period.

A major question that emerged in the course of this musical survey was how to determine what music could reasonably be considered ragtime. Along with the hundreds of unproblematic examples that possess the musical traits of ragtime (or more properly, my conception at that time of what these traits should have been) and are clearly labeled as such, are numerous pieces that, while failing to match these criteria, could not automatically be discarded: works that display ragtime characteristics but are without the proper label; works designated as rags but lacking the expected musical traits; works that have neither the expected traits nor a specific label, but which were apparently considered by contemporaries to be rags. In an attempt to sort out these various categories and to learn how ragtime was viewed sixty to eighty years ago (and disregarding the advice of a prominent ragtime authority who insists that the public of that time had no understanding of ragtime), I consulted the books, magazines, and newspapers of the period. The abundance and breadth of literature was totally unanticipated: hundreds of articles discussed ragtime in relation to a broad scope of musical, aesthetic, and social issues. My original search for a working definition of ragtime was almost dwarfed as I became immersed in the conflicts of its day, concerning ragtime's origins, racial content, relevance to American music, innovative features, potential for "artistic" development, effects on cultural, moral, and physical well-being, and the like. What had begun as a preliminary, minor investigation gradually assumed major proportions, adding perspective to an understanding of the music as well as significant insights into aesthetic and sociological issues transcending the immediate concerns of ragtime.

The realization of how greatly the original conceptions of ragtime differ from those of the present day prompted yet another area of investigation. This inquiry, the final third of the study, traces commentary to the present in an effort to detect the reasons for the altered attitudes and the means by which these changes were effected.

This book presents views that differ markedly from those expressed in other histories of ragtime, and it will undoubtedly disturb a few partisans who find their cherished beliefs without support. My intent has been to permit the investigation to unfold without prejudice, to reflect the available evidence and documents, and to depict, as closely as possible, what actually *was* rather than what some wish might have been. I do not expect (or even desire) complete agreement with my ideas, and I readily admit the plausibility of alternative interpretations of some of the data. But I do hope, most fervently, that my efforts will help remove ragtime studies from the domain of vague intuition and romantic fantasy, and direct it toward a path of greater critical scrutiny.

# Part One

# The Ragtime Era: Perceptions of the Music

In 1974, seventy-two years after its publication, Scott Joplin's piano rag *The Entertainer* swept the country, reaching the number three spot in *Billboard's* survey of best-selling recorded singles. Promoted by the award-winning film score for *The Sting*, this piece led the return of ragtime to a prominence in American popular culture unequaled since the first two decades of the century.

The present interest does not quite parallel the original ragtime phenomenon, for the musical emphasis has shifted. Had *Billboard* made a survey of favorite rags in 1902, the list probably would have included *Mister Johnson Turn Me Loose*, *All Coons Look Alike to Me*, *My Coal Black Lady*, *Hello! Ma Baby*, and *Under the Bamboo Tree*. All songs! Today, in contrast, ragtime is generally thought of as piano music, especially that of Scott Joplin, Joe Lamb, James Scott, and a few others. While such recorded ensemble versions as *The Red Back Book* have demonstrated how vibrant ragtime can be in other media,[1] the keyboard remains at the center of the present-day conception of the genre.

Clearly, if the contemporaries of that past period perceived ragtime as primarily a vocal form, then ours is an altered view. Nor is the view of ragtime as predominantly a music for piano held only by an uninformed lay public; it is expressed also in respected studies of American music:

It is noteworthy that from the time of its origin rag music seems to have been associated primarily with the piano.[2]

. . . ragtime is essentially music for the piano. Ragtime may be described as the application of systematic syncopation to piano playing and composition.[3]

Even ragtime specialists, unquestionably familiar with the ragtime song, tend to deny its legitimacy. It is not considered at all in the discography *Recorded Ragtime, 1897–1958*,[4] and in *Rags and Ragtime* the term "ragtime song" is called "a contradiction in terms."[5]

In contrast, writings from the ragtime era—the years from about 1896 to 1920—reveal far less interest in ragtime as piano music. In a sampling of 230 ragtime-related articles and books from that period, only 21 refer to piano music, with a mere 16 citing specific piano rags. The number of items referring to ragtime played by bands or instrumental ensembles is smaller— 15—but ragtime songs have a higher representation—40. While the remaining writings make no reference to performing media, the contexts in most clearly imply that the concern is with songs.

These statistics underline an important requirement for a comprehensive historical study of ragtime: since piano ragtime accounted for only a small part, perhaps less than 10 percent, of what the music's contemporaries understood by the term "ragtime," it is necessary to consider the other forms as well. Only in this way can piano ragtime be perceived in a valid historical and cultural perspective. Such consideration, while broadening the scope of our study, does not detract from the significance of the piano music, which remains the focus of this book. Vocal and piano ragtime are, for the most part, two different types of music: the former belongs in the realm of popular song, while the latter is a unique body of instrumental music which by virtue of its rhythmic impulse and historical influence is most properly considered within the sphere of instrumental jazz. These two categories, despite their differences, are not mutually exclusive; there are important overlappings between the two, overlappings that become apparent when viewed in the broad context advocated here.

Part One of the present study examines how the contemporaries of the ragtime era perceived the various aspects of ragtime. The main issues considered are: (1) the contemporary understanding and identification of ragtime; (2) the contemporary conception of the origins of both the music and the term; and (3) the reactions to the music and the underlying causes of these reactions.

## Notes

1. Angel S-36060.

2. Eileen Southern, *The Music of Black Americans: A History* (New York: W. W. Norton, 1971), p. 312.

3. Gilbert Chase, *America's Music from the Pilgrims to the Present* (2d ed., rev., New York: McGraw-Hill, 1966), p. 434.

4. David A. Jasen, *Recorded Ragtime, 1897–1958* (Hamden, Conn.: Archon Books, Shoe String Press, 1973).

5. David A. Jasen and Trebor Jay Tichenor, *Rags and Ragtime* (New York: Seabury Press, 1978), p. 7.

# CHAPTER I

# The Scope of Ragtime

### Ragtime as Popular Song

The earliest kind of popular song identified as ragtime is the "coon song," a Negro dialect song frequently, but not always, of an offensively denigrating nature.[1] Although the coon song had a long prior existence in the American minstrel and vaudeville traditions, in the 1890s it acquired the additional label of "ragtime."

> "Rag time" is a term applied to the peculiar, broken rhythmic features of the popular "coon song."[2]

> A hopper is fitted onto the press and into it are poured jerky note groups by the million, "coon poetry" by the ream, colored inks by the ton, and out of the other end of the press comes a flood of "rag-time" abominations, that sweeps over the country.[3]

The coon songs which are cited most often (indicating a degree of popularity and currency) are Ernest Hogan's *All Coons Look Alike to Me* (1896), Joseph Howard and Ida Emerson's *Hello! Ma Baby* (1899), and Theodore Metz's *A Hot Time in the Old Town* (1896).[4]

By 1906 the popularity of the more flagrantly abusive form of coon song had faded, but popular vocal music retained the ragtime label. Some song hits, such as Lewis Muir's *Waiting for the Robert E. Lee* (1912), still presented Southern imagery, but even songs totally devoid of regional or racial implications, such as *Alexander's Ragtime Band* (1911) and *Everybody's Doin' It* (1911), fell within the scope of ragtime. This deracialization of ragtime songs was, in fact, viewed by James Weldon Johnson (1871–1938), a prominent writer on black culture, as a theft from the black man:

> The first of the so-called Ragtime songs to be published were actually Negro secular folk songs that were set down by white men, who affixed their own names as composers. In fact, before the Negro succeeded fully in establishing his title as creator of his secular music the form was taken away from him and made national instead of racial. It has been developed into the distinct musical idiom by which America expresses itself popularly, and by which it is known universally. For a long while the vocal form was almost absolutely divorced from the Negro; the separation being brought about largely through the elimination of dialect from the texts of the songs.[5]

A controversial article appearing in the London *Times* includes a rhythmic analysis of *Waiting for the Robert E. Lee* and cites as other examples of ragtime *Oh, You Beautiful Doll, Going Back to Dixie,* and *How Are You Miss Rag-Time?*[6] Although the article was widely quoted and discussed, both in praise and criticism,[7] there was no disagreement on the choice of music cited as ragtime. Similarly, in a pair of articles by Hiram K. Moderwell, a prominent music critic, ragtime is portrayed almost exclusively in its vocal forms:

> I remember hearing a negro quartet singing "Waiting for the Robert E. Lee," in a café, and I felt my blood thumping in time, my muscles twitching to the rhythm. . . .
> I think of the rollicking fun of "The International Rag," the playful delicacy of "Everybody's Doing It," the bristling laziness of "Waiting for the Robert E. Lee," the sensual poignancy of "La Seduction" tango, and the tender pathos of "The Memphis Blues."[8]

In proposing that ragtime be taken out of the cafés and put into the concert halls, he writes:

> I firmly believe that a ragtime programme, well organized and well sung, would be delightful and stimulating to the best audience the community could muster.[9]

The novelist, critic, and essayist Carl Van Vechten (1880–1964), while disputing the advisability of some of Moderwell's proposals, nevertheless agrees that ragtime is vocal music.[10] And composer-educator Daniel Gregory Mason (1873–1953), who vehemently opposes most of Moderwell's views on this subject, has no qualms about accepting such songs as *Everybody's Doin' It* and *Memphis Blues* (1912) as ragtime:

> Suppose . . . we examine in some detail a typical example of ragtime such as "The Memphis Blues" . . . [11]

As songs were the most conspicuous species of ragtime, it follows that songwriters were the most conspicuous composers. This assumption is confirmed by the literature of the time, for those named as ragtime composers were almost invariably songwriters (some exceptions will be discussed in Chapters Four and Nine). Some of the most frequently mentioned were Irving Berlin (b. 1888), George M. Cohan (1878–1942), Louis Hirsch (1887–1924), Lewis F. Muir (1884–1950), and Jean Schwartz (1878–1956). Irving Berlin, who did not attain prominence with his ragtime songs until 1911, even claimed a part in the genesis of ragtime:

> I believe that such songs of mine as "Alexander's Ragtime Band," "That Mysterious Rag," "Ragtime Violin," "I Want To Be in Dixie," and "Take a Little Tip from Father" virtually started the ragime mania in America.[12]

It has been suggested in recent years that the popular understanding of ragtime today is not what it was when the music was being created, but the thesis has not met with general acceptance. In a letter to the Ragtime Society newsletter in 1965, one who was apparently present during the early days of ragtime expressed his perplexity over the present trend of emphasizing a particular kind of piano ragtime and ignoring vocal ragtime:

> . . . we who were around when "Boom de Ay" was discovered in Babe Connor's place in St. Louis as the nineties started up, and when the "Hot Time" tune took words and entered the ragtime-song race . . . await enlightenment as to just what it is about a specimen of syncopation that makes it "classic ragtime," while countless of the world's favorite old ragtime numbers apparently go rejected by the modernists.[13]

Perhaps the vocal ragtime mentioned above is not on the same musical level as the best in piano ragtime. Quite possibly only a few ragtime enthusiasts today would be interested in these songs. But ignoring the fact that this music was considered ragtime conceals the historical truth and inevitably leads to serious misinterpretations. Whereas the restricted interpretation of ragtime suffices for the needs of today's entertainment, for a true historical and critical view of the subject a broader perspective must prevail.

### The Ragtime Band

The predominance of vocal music in early writings on ragtime is revealed not only in the relatively high proportion of articles devoted exclusively to songs, but also in the frequent linking of vocal with instrumental ragtime. Although ragtime songs seem to have made their initial impact upon the musical stage, they were played as well by dance, march, and concert bands:

> Probably the majority of our readers are aware that the most popular music of the day is that known as "rag-time." . . . From New York to California and from the great lakes to the gulf ragtime music of all styles is the rage. Look at the ballroom programmes for the past season and we find rag-time and other "coon" melodies introduced into every dance where it is practicable.[14]

> [John Philip Sousa] was as usual liberal with his encores consisting of his own marches and ragtime ballads.[15]

> [In New Orleans, around 1905] many of the tunes played by the small marching bands were popular ragtime songs, not classic rags such as those composed by Joplin.[16]

Even when they were not direct adaptations of existing songs, instrumental rags were frequently thought of as derivatives of the vocal medium:

> The craze for "coon" songs, as they are familiarly known, began about three years ago, and shows little sign of abatement at the present time. Not content with "rag-time" songs, marches, two-steps, and even waltzes have been subjected to this syncopated style of treatment, in order to appease the seemingly insatiable thirst for that peculiar rhythmic effect produced by successive irregular accent.[17]

The song-to-instrument route was not one-sided; the process was also reversed as original instrumental rags such as Kerry Mills' dance hit *At a Georgia Campmeeting* (1897) were reissued in alternate versions with words. In addition, many early instrumental rag publications include a vocal chorus. Because of such developments, original instrumental pieces and adaptations from songs frequently merged into one body of ragtime literature.

An important phase of ragtime ensemble performance—

important because it reflects on the origins of both ragtime and jazz—is the improvised syncopation, or "ragging," of existing pieces. By its very nature the music is not notated, and no contemporaneous recordings have been discovered, but the style is known today through later re-creations made by musicians from the period, such as those recorded by ragtime-jazz musician Bunk Johnson (1879–1949) in the mid-1940s, and through descriptions. Johnson has related how hymns were transformed by turn-of-the-century New Orleans funeral bands,[18] and Jelly Roll Morton (1855–1941) has similarly depicted the ragging of Sousa marches,[19] a popular practice described also by black poet-song lyricist Paul Laurence Dunbar (1872–1906):

But hit's Sousa played in ragtime, an' hit's Rastus on Parade,
W'en de colo'd ban' comes ma'chin' down de street.[20]

Although much ensemble ragtime was published and copyrighted in piano editions, it is evident that in at least some cases the composers intended the music for band performance. On the cover of William Krell's *Mississippi Rag* (1897), the earliest identified piano score using the term "rag" in its title, is a banner proclaiming: "The First Rag-Time Two Step Ever Written, and First Played by Krell's Orchestra, Chicago." In another case, an unusual bass line in Arthur Pryor's *A Coon Band Contest* (1899) is identified as "trombone solo" (Example I–1).

EXAMPLE I–1. Arthur Pryor, *A Coon Band Contest* (Arthur Pryor, 1899), C 2–6.*

Trombone Solo.

*The designation C 2–6 means: third formal section, or strain, measures 2–6. The formal designs of instrumental rags are discussed in Chapter Five.

The prominence of bands in early nonvocal ragtime recordings also testifies to the importance of this medium,[21] as do the advertisements for band arrangements in some popularly oriented music magazines. One such periodical that devoted considerable space to band advertisements was *Metronome*. During 1897 *Metronome* printed numerous announcements of cakewalk marches, two-steps, schottisches, polkas, waltzes, and band arrangements of coon songs. The first advertisement in this magazine to specify "ragtime" appeared in the January 1898 issue, and by the following year such notices were commonplace. Ragtime advertisements continued to appear in substantial quantities until early 1916, when the demand for this music in the ballroom was reduced. (The other dances being advertised in 1916 were one-steps, tangos, fox and turkey trots, waltzes, and maxixes.) In the November 1916 issue the category of ragtime was eliminated. Although the word "rag" continued to appear occasionally in titles, such pieces were not necessarily considered rags; Eubie Blake's *Bugle Call Rag* (1916), for instance, was labeled a fox trot.

### Ragtime for Other Instrumental Combinations

The media for ragtime were not restricted to piano, song, and band. The instrumental diversity included some combinations which seem exotic today. The cover of the piano publication of Theodore Morse's *Coontown Capers* (1897), for instance, lists the availability of fifteen different arrangements, including orchestra; brass band; violin and piano; banjo; zither; and two mandolins, guitar, and piano. Similarly, the cover of Abe Holzmann's *Bunch o' Blackberries* (1899) advertises: "Published also for all instruments including Mandolin, Guitar, Banjo, Orchestra, Band, Etc."

Recordings of the period reveal this same diversity. While the listings in Jasen's *Recorded Ragtime* do not specify the medium, some clues to the instruments of frequently recorded artists are given on pages 7–10 of the introduction, and additional identification is occasionally supplied by the name of the performing group, such as "Murray's Ragtime Banjo Quartet."[22] Thus it is possible to detect some of the instrumental variety that was represented on recordings: two accordion performances (1914, 1915) of *Hungarian Rag*, a marimba-band version (1916) of *Dill Pickles*, three piccolo solos (1900–1902) on *Rag Time Skedaddle*, a xylophone recording (1912) of *Red Pepper*. Similarly, among the 8,000 listings in Koenigsberg's *Edison Cylinder Records*, are many of rags played on "exotic" instrumental combinations.

The relative position of piano ragtime is considered more thoroughly in Chapter Four. For the present it is sufficient to observe that with such an abundance and variety of instrumental and vocal versions of ragtime, the piano genre did not have the prominence it enjoys today.

## Syncopation

At the core of the contemporary understanding of ragtime, regardless of medium, was syncopation. The question "What is ragtime?" was asked throughout the period, and almost invariably explanations included a statement about syncopation:

> So rag-time music is, simply, syncopated rhythm maddened into a desperate iterativeness; a rhythm overdone, to please the present public music taste.[23]

> Rag-time is merely a common form of syncopation in which the rhythm is distorted in order to produce a more or less ragged, hysterical effect.[24]

> RAG TIME. A modern term, of American origin, signifying, in the first instance, broken rhythm in melody, especially a sort of continuous syncopation.[25]

> "Rag-Time," then may be said to be a strongly syncopated melody superimposed on a strictly regular accompaniment, and it is the combination of these two rhythms that gives "rag-time" its character.[26]

> Ragtime music is chiefly a matter of rhythm and not much a matter of melody or fine harmony. It is based almost exclusively upon syncopated time.[27]

Not satisfied simply with designating syncopation as the defining feature of ragtime, Hiram Moderwell, who as a frequent contributor of music articles to *New Republic* and other periodicals should have known better, attributes an exaggerated significance to the rhythms of ragtime:

> It [ragtime] has carried the complexities of the rhythmic subdivision of the measure to a point never before reached in the history of music.[28]

Irving Berlin reverses the relationship between ragtime and syncopation as he says, not that ragtime is a form of syncopation, but that "Syncopation is nothing but another name for ragtime." From this false premise, he compounds his error by concluding that "the old masters" also wrote ragtime, but "in a stiff and stilted way."[29]

The implication, evident in many of these articles, that the term "ragtime" refers directly to the ragged rhythmic quality of syncopation is occasionally spelled out explicitly. An editorial referring to compositions "written *in* what is contemptuously called 'rag time'"[30] clearly designates ragtime as a rhythmic process as well as a genre. The word is also used as a synonym for syncopation: "in American slang to 'rag' a melody is to syncopate a normally regular tune."[31] "Strictly speaking, to rag a tune means to destroy its rhythm and tempo and substitute for the 2–4 or 4–4 time a syncopated rhythm."[32] An article on ragtime performance specifies that the pianist must have the ability "to syncopate (rag) the tones."[33]

The term "rag" is thus seen to be a noun, identifying a type of music; a verb, referring to the process of syncopation; and an adjective, modifying "time," that is, "ragged time." Etymologically, the hyphenated form used in the earlier articles (rag-time) and the rarer two-word form (rag time) also suggest adjectival origins.

The assumption of ragtime's being characterized primarily by a syncopated rhythm was so widespread that few writers questioned this connection. One who did was music critic and biographer Francis Toye (1883–1964). Noting the absence of syncopation in some pieces identified as ragtime, he commented:

> I do not think that rag-time can be defined as rhythm at all. True it has a characteristic rhythm and usually a syncopated one. But not invariably. The popular "Hitchy-Koo" and "Dixie," for instance, are hardly syncopated, yet it were pure pedantry not to class them as rag-time.[34]

Another writer, giving similar reasons, tried to separate the concept of ragtime from syncopation:

> Perhaps the best way to define ragtime and prove that it and syncopation are not necessarily analogous will be to go to the bottom of things and summon up some actual illustration. . . .
>
> "For Me and My Gal" is typically ragtime, yet it is practically free of syncopation—to be exact, there are just three measures of syncopated melody. . . . The most striking example of ragtime music came out a few years ago in Irving Berlin's song "Alexander's Ragtime Band." . . .
>
> What made this song so popular? It was not syncopation, for there is no syncopation at all in the chorus, which is the most pleasing part of the song.[35]

These articles, however, are exceptions, and reflect the general tendency by 1911 to include in the ragtime category almost any rhythmical, popular music. At least one commentator protested against this extension of the term "ragtime," suggesting that its application be restricted to syncopated music:

> "Ragtime" . . . has become a most comprehensive word in recent years, and at least with a certain class of musicians who should know better, it means pretty nearly anything not under the head of *serious* or classical music.
>
> If the rhythmic element predominates or is at all prominent it is "ragtime," no matter whether a single instance of syncopation occurs in the music or not. . . .
>
> The writer, for one, is in favor of restricting the word ragtime to its original definition, as meaning that time or rhythm in which the dominating characteristic feature is syncopation.[36]

This protest reveals a recognition, by 1913, of the process that was already divesting ragtime of its most definitive feature. Of this process, more will be said later.

### Ragtime Dance

From its earliest days ragtime has been associated with dancing. Performers who sang ragtime lyrics on the minstrel stage also danced to its rhythms. As the music moved to the ballroom, syncopated ragtime marches, two-steps, and cakewalks co-existed with unsyncopated versions of the same steps. In some instances the dances themselves acquired the ragtime label. Throughout the period there are references to specific steps being "rags" and to "ragging" being a style of dancing.[37] More often, though, dances were simply associated with ragtime music without appropriating the name. While almost any duple- or quadruple-metered step could be executed to the music, some dances had an especially close affiliation with ragtime.

Ragtime sheet music, which frequently lists the "appropriate" dances, is an important source of information on ragtime ballroom styles; a year-by-year survey of the sheet music clearly reveals the gradual changes in fashions.

The dances named on the earliest ragtime sheet music are the cakewalk, march, and two-step. (As with the word "ragtime," there is no orthographical consistency; "cakewalk" and "two-step" appear also as "cake walk," "cake-walk," "two step," and "twostep.") An indication of the lack of musical distinction made between these dances is that all, or any combination, may be listed on a single piece of music: *The Rag-Time Sports. Cake Walk-March and Two Step* (1899); *Rag Time Society. Characteristic March &*

*Two Step* (1899); or *Africana. A Rag-Time Classic. Characteristic March Two-Step and Cakewalk* (1903). Sometimes another
dance, such as the polka, is also included: *The Honolulu Cake
Walk. Ragtime March* (1899) "Can also be used as: Two-Step,
Polka or Cake-Walk."[38]

The first of these three main dances to disappear from the
sheet music was the cakewalk, which died out by 1904. The
march began to decline in 1908, and the two-step in 1911; both
dances, though, lingered on until the mid-1910s.

In the second decade of the century new dances were cited
on ragtime sheet music, but without the persistence of the earlier
steps. The turkey trot had a short life, from about 1912 to 1914;
the one-step and fox trot were both prominent by 1913, the
former lasting until 1917, the latter having an unmatched longev-
ity.[39] The slow drag was mentioned throughout the entire ragtime
period, but never in significant numbers.

With less consistency many other dances were associated
with ragtime. The vocal version of Scott Joplin's *Ragtime Dance*
is particularly interesting for its inventory of dances,[40] some of
which do not appear in other sources. It is possible that these less
familiar dances had a restricted circulation and were known
primarily in the black communities. The dances mentioned are
the "rag time dance," "cake walk prance," "slow drag," "worlds
fair dance," "clean up dance," "Jennie Cooler dance," "rag two
step," "back step prance," "dude walk," "stop time," and "Sedidus
walk."

Despite the variety of dance names appearing in Joplin's
piece, almost all of the music retains the same rhythmic character. Only the "stop time" and "Sedidus walk" use music of a different style—"stop-time" music, which appears infrequently in
published ragtime.[41] It was not until the second decade of the
century, with the appearance of the fox trot, that a major
ragtime-related dance was again linked with music of a differ-
entiated character. As is demonstrated in Chapter Eight, the
rhythmic patterns associated with the fox trot tended to replace
the accepted modes of ragtime syncopation, and this process ultimately led to the disintegration of ragtime as a distinctive musical type.

### Jazz and the Close of the Ragtime Era

It was with the advent of the "jazz age," shortly before 1920,
that the ragtime era came to a close. The end came gradually, as

characteristics of ragtime were absorbed by jazz; for a while the two terms were freely interchanged. At last, supplanted by a newer wave of syncopation, ragtime ceased to be the emissary of American popular culture.

Jazz, like ragtime, originally embraced a much broader musical and social spectrum than is accorded to it by present-day thought. In publications of the late 1910s and early twenties jazz was typified not by the figures who are today considered the main exponents of that time (such as Louis Armstrong, Jelly Roll Morton, Fletcher Henderson, and Bix Beiderbecke), but by popular band leaders and songwriters (Paul Whiteman, Irving Berlin, Victor Herbert)—and by ballroom dance.

Many writers used the terms ragtime and jazz almost synonymously:

> Oldtimers such as "Alexander's Ragtime Band" . . . and "Maple Leaf Rag" began to establish a conventional form for jazz. . . .
> For purposes of this discussion we will omit the waltz, which is not jazz, and the so-called "ballad." Just how is the typical "rag" built?[42]

A report on Roger-Ducasse's *Epithalme* discusses the composer's use of "ragtime rhythms" as "evidence of the valuable use to which the European craze for jazz can be put."[43] A discussion of jazz describes the "ragtime pianist" in terms that apply equally to the jazz pianist: "The real ragtime pianist is a composer as well as performer. That is, he can take a tune and reharmonize it if necessary, judiciously introduce innovations, alter the rhythm."[44] In describing "fly-drumming," a ballroom drum technique, one writer suggests that the distinction between jazz and ragtime is in name only: "A decade past it was called 'ragging' while today we call it 'jazzing.' "[45]

There were some who objected to the word "jazz," preferring to retain the older "ragtime": "The Rag-time movement would have been the better style, but the word 'Jazz' has passed into at least two languages."[46] Others favored the term "jazz," even applying it to music clearly falling within the ragtime era and sphere: "Ragtime was the name employed by Mason and Moderwell; jazz was the thing they were discussing."[47] While disagreeing over the more appropriate terminology, these two writers implicitly concur in assuming no substantive distinction between ragtime and jazz.

Some commentators of the time also tried to identify the

characteristics of jazz, and while the intent was not necessarily to contrast it with ragtime, the descriptions and affiliations of jazz often served to differentiate it from the earlier style. One such association was with new dances, especially the fox trot:

> The latest international word seems to be "jazz." It is used almost exclusively in British papers to describe the kind of music dancing—particularly dancing—imported from America. . . . While society once "ragged," they now "jazz."[48]

> Jazz, in brief, is a compound of (a) the fox-trot rhythm, a four-four measure (*alla breve*) with a double accent, and (b) a syncopated melody over this rhythm.[49]

Jazz is also typified by certain unique instrumental effects:

> Jazz, strictly speaking, is instrumental effects, the principal one being the grotesque treatment of the portamento, especially in the wind instruments. The professor of jazz . . . calls these effects "smears." The writer first heard jazz performed by trombone-players in some of the marching bands. . . . Afterward the ingenious players of the popular music discovered how to produce these wailing, sliding tones on other instruments.[50]

The most common and fundamental view was that jazz was a later and more complicated phase in the development of syncopated music. While some writers continued to think of jazz and ragtime as the same phenomenon going under two labels, others considered jazz as the maturation of the earlier style:

> "Jazz" . . . is Ragtime raised to the Nth power.[51]

> Rag had been mainly a thing of rhythm, of syncopation. . . . Jazz is rag-time, plus orchestral polyphony; it is the combination, in the popular current, of melody, rhythm, harmony, and counter-point.[52]

> Ragtime has definitely become jazz—ragtime never died, it grew up.[53]

Much of the argument seems to be reducible to a matter of semantics. What is important is that accompanying the stylistic evolution of ragtime in the late 1910s was a shift away from the term "ragtime" and toward "jazz." By 1924 it could be confidently written that jazz "is the symbol, the byword for a great many elements in the spirit of the time—as far as America is concerned it is actually our characteristic expression."[54]

Contemporaneous sheet music and changes in musical style

(discussed in Chapter Eight) confirm the observations made by the writers quoted above. By the late 1910s the number of compositions identified as rags had declined substantially and the stylistic traits that had previously characterized ragtime had blurred. Some aspects of ragtime were retained by later forms, but the evolution in style and terminology made it a thing of the past: the ragtime era came to a close.

## Notes

1. Some coon-song lyrics are quoted in Chapter Three.

2. "Questions and Answers," *Etude* 16 (October 1898): 285.

3. W. F. Gates, "Ethiopian Syncopation—The Decline of Ragtime," *Musician* 7 (October 1902): 341.

4. Although the well-known chorus of this last piece does not usually bear the coon-song or ragtime label today, the lyrics are in Negro dialect, the music of the verse is syncopated in the manner of ragtime, and it is referred to as ragtime in the literature of its day. See Charles R. Sherlock, "From Breakdown to Ragtime," *Cosmopolitan* (October 1901): 639; Lester Walton, "Music and the Stage: President Bans Ragtime," *New York Age*, 6 February 1908, p. 10; and "'A Hot Time' Is War Song," *American Musician and Art Journal* 24 (14 February 1908): 4. It is significant that these three publications concur on the categorization of *Hot Time*, for they cover a broad spectrum of opinion: *Cosmopolitan* was a general-interest magazine, *New York Age* a leading Negro newspaper, and *American Musician and Art Journal* a periodical concerned primarily with band music.

5. James Weldon Johnson, Introduction to *The Second Book of Negro Spirituals* (New York: Viking Press, 1926), pp. 16–17.

6. "Rag-Time," *Times* (London), 8 February 1913, p. 11.

7. Reprinted in full in *Boston Symphony Orchestra Programmes* 32 (19 February 1913): 1186–96. Quoted and discussed in "Sees National Music Created by Rag-Time," *New York*

*Times*, 9 February 1913, sec. 4, p. 5; "Ragtime as Source of National Music," *Musical America* 17 (15 February 1913): 37; "Philosophizing Rag-Time," *Literary Digest* (15 March 1913): 574–75; Francis Toye, "Ragtime: The New Tarantism," *English Review* (March 1913): 656; Daniel Gregory Mason, "Folk-Song and American Music," *Musical Quarterly* 4 (July 1918): 324–25; "Flays Rag-Time as Not Reflecting Americanism," *Musical America* 28 (20 July 1918): 22.

8. Hiram K. Moderwell, "Ragtime," *New Republic* (16 October 1915): 285.

9. Hiram K. Moderwell, "A Modest Proposal," *Seven Arts* 2 (July 1917): 371.

10. Carl Van Vechten, "Communications," *Seven Arts* 2 (September 1917): 669–70.

11. Daniel Gregory Mason, "Concerning Ragtime," *New Music Review and Church Music Review* 17 (March 1918): 114.

12. Irving Berlin and Justus Dickinson, "Words and Music," *Green Book Magazine* (July 1915): 104–105.

13. Russ Cole, untitled letter, *Ragtime Society* 4 (March/April 1965): 19–20. As Cole's letter suggests, the songs *Ta-ra-ra Boom-de-ay!* (1891) and *A Hot Time in the Old Town* have been traced to Babe Connor's, a Negro brothel in St. Louis: they both appeared there around 1891. The actual origins of the songs are uncertain, as each is enmeshed in conflicting stories and claims. One version dates *Ta-ra-ra Boom-de-ay!* as far back as 1854 or even earlier—see Edward R. Winn, "'Ragging' the Popular

Song-Hits," *Melody* 2 (May 1918): 8; Isaac Goldberg, *Tin Pan Alley: A Chronicle of the American Popular Music Racket*, (New York: John Day, 1930), pp. 113–17, 165–67. The term "classic ragtime," discussed in Chapter Ten, is a designation applied to the piano rags of Scott Joplin and a few others.

14. W. H. Amstead, "'Rag-Time': The Music of the Hour," *Metronome* 15 (May 1899): 4. Amstead was the editor of *Metronome*.

15. "Sousa at the Hippodrome," *New York Times*, 15 January 1906, p. 9.

16. George W. Kay, "Reminiscing in Ragtime: An Interview with Roy Carew," *Jazz Journal* 17 (November 1964): 9. This is a statement by Roy Carew (1884–1967), a pioneering figure in ragtime research, recalling his experiences in New Orleans during the first decade of the twentieth century. Carew is discussed further in Chapter Nine.

17. R. M. Stults, "Something about the Popular Music of Today," *Etude* 18 (March 1900): 97. Stults was a successful composer of sentimental popular songs.

18. Marshall W. Stearns, *The Story of Jazz* (London: Oxford University Press, 1956), p. 61.

19. Alan Lomax, *Mister Jelly Roll: The Fortunes of Jelly Roll Morton, New Orleans Creole and "Inventor of Jazz"* (New York: Duell, Sloan and Pearse, 1950; 2d ed. Berkeley, Ca.: University of California Press, 1973), pp. 12–13.

20. Paul Laurence Dunbar, "The Colored Band" in *Lyrics of Love and Laughter* (New York: Dodd, Mead, 1903), stanza 3, lines 3–4. This poem was set to music by J. Rosamond Johnson (1873–1954) in 1901; see James Weldon Johnson, *Along This Way* (New York: Viking Press, 1933), p. 161.

21. The most thorough discography of ragtime recordings on 78 r.p.m. discs is David Jasen's *Recorded Ragtime, 1897–1958* (Hamden, Conn.: Archon Books, Shoe String Press, 1973). Additional ragtime recordings are listed in James R. Smart, *The Sousa Band: A Discography* (Washington, D.C.: Library of Congress, 1970), and in Allen Koenigsberg, *Edison Cylinder Records, 1889–1912; with an Illustrated History of the Phonograph* (New York: Stellar Productions, 1969).

22. Jasen, *Recorded Ragtime*, p. 51.

23. C. Crozat Converse, "Rag-Time Music," *Etude* 17 (June 1899): 185. Converse (1832–1918) was a composer of religious and patriotic American music.

24. A. J. Goodrich, "Syncopated Rhythm vs. 'Rag-Time,'" *Musician* 6 (November 1901): 336. Goodrich (1847–1920) was an eminent theorist and academician.

25. *Grove's Dictionary of Music and Musicians* (New York: Macmillan, 1908), s.v. "Rag Time," by Frank Kidson.

26. "Rag-Time," *Times* (London).

27. Leo Oehmler, "'Ragtime': A Pernicious Evil and Enemy of True Art," *Musical Observer* 11 (September 1914): 14.

28. Moderwell, "Ragtime."

29. Frederick James Smith, "Irving Berlin and Modern Ragtime," *New York Dramatic Mirror*, 14 January 1914, p. 38.

30. "Music for Piers and Parks," *New York Times*, 29 May 1902, p. 8 (my emphasis).

31. "Rag-Time," *Times* (London).

32. "'To Jazz' or 'To Rag,'" *Literary Digest* (6 May 1922): 37. Quoted here is Paul Whiteman (1890–1967), a commercially successful band leader, "popularizer" of jazz, and self-acclaimed "King of Jazz."

33. Edward R. Winn, "Ragtime Piano Playing: A Practical Course of Instruction for Pianists," *Tuneful Yankee* 1 (January 1917): 42.

34. Toye, "Ragtime," p. 654.

35. Harold Hubbs, "What Is Ragtime?" *Outlook* (27 February 1918): 345.

36. Myron A. Bickford, "Something about Ragtime," *Cadenza* 20 (September 1913): 13.

37. Virgil Thomson, "Jazz," *American Mercury* (August 1924): 465; Rupert Hughes, "A Eulogy of Ragtime," *Musical Record*, No. 447 (1 April 1899): 158; "Canon Newboldt's Warning," *New York Times*, 26 August 1913, p. 8; Ernest Ansermet, "Sur un orchestre nègre," *Revue romande* 3 (15 October 1919): 10; "The Origin of Ragtime," *New York Times*, 23 March 1924, sec. 9, p. 2. Composer Virgil Thomson (b. 1896) and conductor Ernest Ansermet (1883–1969) are well-known figures in concert music. Rupert Hughes (1872–1956) was a novelist, a dramatist, and a respected writer on musical subjects.

38. The distinction between subtitle and description is also treated inconsistently. The practice in this book is to consider any dance label as part of the subtitle unless it is clearly presented as a description, in which case it will be transcribed as in the last citation.

39. The fox trot of that time, though, was not the indiscriminate shuffle commonly called "fox trot" today; note the instructions printed in *Christensen's Ragtime Review* 1 (March 1915): 8:

How To Dance the Fox Trot

The fox trot resembles the onestep, but is a slightly faster dance and is quite easy to learn. The exaggerated movements of the shoulders and arms, characteristic of the turkey trot, the things that made it capable of vulgarity, are absent from the fox trot. Here are the four figures of this dance:

Fig. 1.—Four slow steps, four running steps and four running steps turning. Repeat four times.

Fig. 2.—Two slow grapevines and four running steps. Repeat four times.

Fig. 3.—One polka step and rest: four running steps. Repeat four times.

Fig. 4.—Four wigwags, then three steps to each side.

40. There are two versions of this piece, both published by Stark Music, St. Louis, Mo. The earlier publication (1902) has lyrics simulating calls as they might be heard at a country dance, and parenthetical instructions specifying when each new step is to begin. The later version (1906), subtitled a "Stop-Time Two Step," is without lyrics, and indicates only once— for the "stop-time"—where a step is to begin.

41. The main characteristics of "stop-time" are heavy accents, frequent rests, and a stereotyped cadential pattern:

42. Don Knowlton, "The Anatomy of Jazz," *Harper's Magazine* (April 1926): 578–79.

43. "Ducasse Uses Ragtime in New Tone Poem," *Musical America* 37 (10 March 1923): 15.

44. William J. Morgan, "A Defense of Jazz and Ragtime," *Melody* 6 (September 1922): 5.

45. Carl E. Gardner, "Ragging and Jazzing," *Metronome* 35 (October/November 1919): 34.

46. Clive Bell, "Plus de jazz," *New Republic* (21 September 1921): 93.

47. Goldberg, *Tin Pan Alley*, p. 252. Critic Hiram K. Moderwell and composer Daniel Gregory Mason were on opposing sides of a heated controversy that raged over ragtime during the second decade of the century; see Chapter Three.

48. "A Negro Explains Jazz," *Literary Digest* (26 April 1919): 28; reprinted in Eileen Southern, ed., *Readings in Black American Music* (New York: W. W. Norton, 1971), p. 224.

49. Thomson, "Jazz," p. 465. See also Aaron Copland, "Jazz Structure and Influence on Modern Music," *Modern Music* 4 (January/February 1927): 10.

50. W. J. Henderson, "Ragtime, Jazz, and High Art," *Scribner's Magazine* (February 1925): 202. Henderson (1855–1937) was a music critic for the *New York Times* and *New York*

*Sun*, and author of many books on music. See also Thomson, "Jazz," p. 466, and Gilbert Seldes, *The Seven Lively Arts* (New York: Harper and Bros., 1924; rev. ed., New York: Sagamore Press, 1957), pp. 85–96.

51. Rupert Hughes, "Will Ragtime Turn to Symphonic Poems?" *Etude* 38 (May 1920): 305.

52. Carl Engel, "Jazz: A Musical Discussion," *Atlantic Monthly* (August 1922): 186. At the time this article appeared, Engel (1883–1944) was Head of the Music Division at the Library of Congress.

53. Goldberg, *Tin Pan Alley*, p. 251.

54. Seldes, *Seven Lively Arts*, p. 83.

# CHAPTER II

# Örigins and Early Manifestations

Ragtime was a new musical experience for most Americans in the late 1890s, and fascination with the music extended to curiosity about its origins. There were many commentators willing to minister to this interest; literature from the period provides a great variety of explanations as to where, when, and how the music developed, became popular, and acquired its name. Some of these accounts have the ring of truth; others border on fantasy. All the reports, though, provide us with additional insight into how contemporaries of the period considered the music.

## Origins of the Music

### RACIAL ORIGINS

Whether referring to vocal or instrumental ragtime, almost all commentators expressed the view that the originators of this syncopated music were black. Many even assumed that the music was a direct import from Africa. One composer announced that a popular coon song that he had written was simply an adaptation of an African melody,[1] and the celebrated music scholar and journalist Henry Edward Krehbiel (1854–1923) claimed to perceive similarities between ragtime and the African music he had heard some years earlier at the 1893 Chicago World's Fair (officially known as the World's Columbian Exposition).[2]

More frequently, ragtime's descent was traced to indigenous American Negro musical styles—plantation spirituals and work songs, "boisterous merry-making," banjo strumming, "patting juba"—and to the popular imitation and caricature of Negro music, minstrelsy.[3] One might therefore expect these forerunners to be heavily and prominently syncopated, but contemporary transcriptions generally fail to support this expectation. The 1867 publication of *Slave Songs of the United States*,[4] for instance, includes a few pieces with "ragtime" syncopations, but hardly on a sufficient scale to sustain a thesis of derivation. Tracing the origins of rhythmically prominent ragtime back to the purely rhythmic practice of "patting juba"—a dance accompaniment with a variety of rhythmic sounds produced by foot-tapping, hand-clapping, and slapping parts of the body[5]—is a natural and attractive hypothesis, and was suggested as early as 1899 by Rupert Hughes:

> The division of one of the beats into two short notes [in ragtime] is perhaps traceable to the hand-clapping; every American is familiar with the way the darkey pats his hands with two quick slaps alternating with the time-beating of the foot. Something like this effect is seen in the Bolero and in the accompaniment to the Polonaise. The so-called "snap" may be traced to the quick slap of the heel and toe of the foot in sharp succession.[6]

There is some slight evidence of what Hughes describes, but it is not quite contemporary, coming twenty-seven years later. In a 1926 re-creation of a traditional Negro dance piece, *Come On, Eph!*, blues pioneer W. C. Handy (1873–1958) depicted syncopated patterns employing voice, hands, and feet (Example II–1a), but his re-creation of *Juba* is totally unsyncopated (Example II–1b).[7]

EXAMPLE II-1. Rhythms in W. C. Handy re-creations: (a) *Come On, Eph!*; (b) *Juba*.

(a) Voice
    Hands on alternate thighs
    Shuffle and scrape alternately
    with feet

(b) Voice
    Hands { on alternate thighs
               clap
    Tap feet

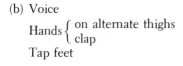

While it is difficult to document ragtime's roots in these genres, the lack of specific notated evidence does not in itself preclude the validity of these claims. There was undoubtedly more than one style of patting juba; Handy's and Dett's unsyncopated versions are not necessarily representative. And in view of the abundant testimony of the syncopated nature of black music, it is likely that many unsyncopated transcriptions are simply not faithful to the performed music. In at least one case a direct comparison can be made between a published, unsyncopated version of a popular minstrel piece and a syncopated transcription of an actual performance. The transcription is by composer Charles Ives (1874–1954) and is given in his *Memos* to illustrate his memories of "black-faced comedians . . . ragging their songs" in Danbury and New Haven, Connecticut, around 1893–1894 (Example II–2).[8]

EXAMPLE II-2. Irving Jones, *I'm Livin' Easy* (New York: F. A. Mills, 1899), opening of chorus: (a) published version; (b) Ives's transcription.

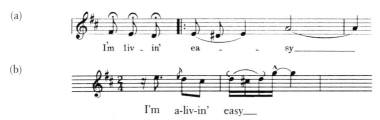

(a)

I'm  liv - in'     ea     -     -     sy____

(b)

I'm    a-liv-in'  easy___

Had other transcribers possessed some of Ives's skill, the historical record might be clearer on the precise relationship between ragtime and earlier black music. The shortage of verifying performance transcriptions, though, does not negate the testimony of contemporaries, and there are earlier published sources (presented in Chapter Six) that support the link between ragtime syncopation and Afro-American music.

The history of black music in America is too complex and varied to be blanketed by a single musical gesture, but there is probably some poetic (as opposed to literal) truth in Scott Joplin's statement that "There has been ragtime music in America ever since the Negro race has been here."[9]

PIANO ORIGINS

Commentary on piano ragtime accounts for only a small portion of ragtime literature, but several sources connect the piano with the origins or early appearances of the genre. A description in James Weldon Johnson's novel *The Autobiography of an Ex-Colored Man*[10] specifically attributes ragtime's genesis to pianists, making the ragtime song a derivative of the piano style:

> This was rag-time music, then a novelty in New York, and just growing to be a rage, which has not yet subsided. It was originated in the questionable resorts about Memphis and St. Louis by Negro piano-players who knew no more of the theory of music than they did of the theory of the universe, but were guided by natural musical instinct and talent. It made its way to Chicago, where it was popular for some time before it reached New York. These players often improvised crude, and, at times, vulgar words to fit the melodies. This was the beginning of the rag-time song.[11]

The piano is also central to the various accounts of Ben Harney (1871–1938) and his role in the early development of ragtime:

> Mr. Ben Harney is believed to have been the first Caucasian to translate ragtime to the piano. He learned it from a negro whose songs he accompanied and made it the rage of Chicago and the West before it was heard in the East.[12]

> Ben Harney, a white man who had a fine negro shouting voice, probably did more to popularize ragtime than any other person. Harney, who was playing in Louisville, heard the new music, and grew so adept at it that he came to New York and appeared in the Weber and Fields Music Hall. Of course ragtime may have appeared here before Harney; there were numbers of wandering musicians playing in saloons and cafés in those days; but credit is due him because he played in a first-class theatre before any other ragtime exponent.[13]

Harney (who was actually a black man passing for white) apparently took his reputation as originator, or original popularizer, of ragtime quite seriously.[14] In 1918, in response to rival assertions—most notably those of minstrel dancer Jim McIntyre, who claimed to have introduced ragtime to Tony Pastor's Theatre in New York in 1879—Harney offered to leave the profession and forfeit one hundred dollars if anyone could submit a rag predating his own ragtime songs, the earliest being *You've Been a Good Old Wagon but You've Done Broke Down* (1895) and *Mister Johnson Turn Me Loose* (1896).[15] Presumably, no one claimed the award.

Harney's prominence in early piano ragtime was established entirely through his performance career. Although he published several successful ragtime songs, he issued no original piano rags. Even his *Ragtime Instructor* (1897), the first piano ragtime instruction manual, consists entirely of song transcriptions. It is clear, then, that his piano style had roots in the popular song style of the day, and he represented a fusion of vocal and piano ragging.

## GEOGRAPHIC ORIGINS

Ragtime was most generally assumed to have been born in "the South," in some heavily black-populated area, but by the early 1890s the ragtime idea (in music, if not in name) must have been known in many areas of the United States: Charles Ives heard it in minstrel shows in Danbury, Connecticut, before 1892,[16] and popular sheet-music already hints at it by the late 1880s (see Example VI–5). The city of Chicago, though, and specifically the vicinity of the 1893 World's Fair in Chicago, seems to have been the site of the initial unveiling of ragtime to a mass public and the beginning of its popularity. These associations are made repeatedly by commentators:

> The negroes of the South employed it [syncopation] in the banjo accompaniments to their songs, but not until the "midways" of our recent expositions stimulated general appreciation of Oriental rhythms did "rag-time" find supporters throughout the country.

> The [coon song and ragtime] fad had its origin along about 1893, the year of the Chicago World's Fair.

> It has been said that "rag-time" first appeared in our music-halls about the time of the Chicago World's Fair.

> The work [on the first published ragtime arrangements] was begun in Chicago, which still echoed with the joyousness of the World's Fair of 1893.[17]

Precisely what occurred at the Fair in terms of ragtime, or of some embryonic form, is elusive. Blesh and Janis assert that Joplin and hundreds of other itinerant pianists converged upon the Fair, givings ragtime a strong impetus,[18] and while they provide no documentation, there is some evidence that notable pianists—perhaps including Ben Harney—took part in "contests" in Chicago during this period.[19] Specific contemporary comment on these activities, though, is lacking (or at least has not been discovered). Although Africans were invited to participate in the Fair and received considerable attention in the press, Afro-Americans were allowed only a minimal role.[20] If any ragtime exhibitions occurred on the fairgrounds they were without official sanction and were therefore "officially" ignored; should they have occurred outside the fairgrounds, they probably would have been viewed as the activities of lower-class, socially unacceptable Negros in establishments of questionable reputation. It is therefore understandable (though unfortunate) that respectable newspapers and magazines failed to record these events.

## Origins of the Term

The source of that peculiar word "ragtime" was another issue that evoked considerable speculation. Some of the theories offered seem reasonable; others strain credulity.

Precisely when the word "ragtime," or some recognizable variant or ancestor, was first used is yet to be discovered. Blesh and Janis propose an article from 1886 in which the rhythm of a Negro dance music is described as "ragged":

> The bamboula still roars and rattles, twangs, contorts, and tumbles in terrible earnest. . . . Will they dance nothing else? Ah!—the music changes. The rhythm stretches out heathenish and ragged.[21]

The musical example corresponding to the description of the "ragged" rhythm, though, does not present ragtime rhythms (Example II–3a). Ironically, the preceding bamboula, which is mentioned before the rhythm becomes "ragged," is illustrated by music more closely resembling ragtime (Example II–3b). While it

EXAMPLE II-3. Illustrations from Cable, "The Dance in Place Congo": (a) page 526; (b) page 525.

(a)

En  bas  hé,  en   bas hé, Paren bas  yé  pé-lé-lé moin, yé pé-lé-lé, Counjaille

(b)

Vo - yez ce mu - let la, Mi - ché Bain - jo, comme il est in - so - lent

is intriguing to speculate that Cable's use of the term may be related in some way to the eventual blossoming of the word "ragtime," that his use may have reflected a common and widespread manner of describing Negro dance rhythms, additional supportive evidence is lacking.

Another article cited by Blesh and Janis attributes the first written use of the term "ragtime" to an unidentified journalist:

> This branch of music was later named "rag time" by a white newspaper critic who was not aware that he had discovered a name for it even after other writers and the public had taken the name and used it.[22]

However, without knowing where or when this journalist used the term, the claim cannot be evaluated.

Despite the indication that some form of ragtime made an appearance at or around the 1893 Chicago World's Fair, there is no evidence that the term was at that time attached to the musical style. The earliest authenticated application of the words "rag" and "ragtime" is on several coon-song editions from 1896, published by M. Witmark (New York and Chicago). Appended to Ernest Hogan's song *All Coons Look Alike to Me* is an optional arrangement of the chorus, labeled: "Choice Chorus, with Negro 'Rag' Accompaniment Arr. by Max Hoffmann"; a similar statement and arrangement by Hoffmann is included in the publication of W. T. Jefferson's *My Coal Black Lady* (see Example IV–1). Also, on the cover of Ben Harney's *You've Been a Good Old Wagon but You've Done Broke Down* appears the banner: "Original Introducer to the Stage of the Now Popular 'Rag Time' in Ethiopian Song."[23] By the following year, 1897, many published songs and instrumental pieces bore these labels. The preface to the song *Syncopated Sandy* (1897)—perhaps the earliest printed discussion of ragtime—suggests that the term is derived from a description of the characteristic syncopation:

Rag-Time
As Illustrated in "Syncopated Sandy"

> The authors and publishers in presenting "Syncopated Sandy" to the public, have succeeded in illustrating for the first time the absolute theory of the now famous "RAG-TIME" music, which originated with the negroes and is characteristic of their people. The negroe in playing the piano, strikes the keys with the same time and measure that he taps the floor with his heels and toes in dancing, thereby obtaining a peculiarly accented time effect which he terms "RAG-TIME."[24]

The suggestion of this preface, that the word "rag-time" is an outgrowth of attempts to describe the syncopated rhythm, is supported by other writers as well:

"Where did the term 'Ragtime' originate?" It originated in the South at a darkey dance! . . .
One of the dusky dancers stepped up to the first fiddler and asked him to repeat the dance.
"Which one?"
"Oh, the one that had sort of a ragged time to it, a sort of rag-time piece."[25]

Etymological roots were also proposed. A librarian at the Library of Congress sought to connect "rag" with Indian "raga,"[26] while Rupert Hughes found Romanic derivations:

The negroes call their clog-dancing "ragging," and the dance a "rag." There is a Spanish verb, *raer*, "to scrape," and a French naval term *ragué*, "scraped," both doubtless from the Latin *rado*— and in such direction the etymologists may find peace, for the dance is highly shuffling.[27]

Far less sober is the account tracing ragtime to Shake Ragtown, a supposed mid-nineteenth century village outside Saint Louis. The Shake Raggers, as the inhabitants were known, often had dances, the music being provided by a single musician,

. . . a left-handed fiddler, a Frenchman named Tebeau, whose musical proficiency was limited to three tunes . . . ; to make up for his lack of music and to give variety to his performance he would also sing the tune and keep time by pounding on the floor with his heavy boots. . . .
It was not long before the shake ragger's dances became known all over St. Louis, and the left-handed fiddler Tebeau was called upon to preside at more pretentious affairs. Musicians soon imitated him. . . . Tebeau's ragtime extended along its [the Mississippi River's] length and spread up and down its tributaries until it became known all over the country.[28]

The ambiguity of the word "rag," referring equally to the music, to the clothing worn by its black exponents (taking a stereotyped view), and to the rag-picking vocation, produced puns in titles and on covers: *Rag-a-Muffin Rag, Ragged Rastus, Rag Pickers Rag, Rags to Burn, Original Rags*—"Picked by Scott Joplin"—(cover depicting a Negro rag-picker), *Harlem Rag* and *Rag Medley* (both with covers showing ragged clothing on clotheslines), and the like. Inevitably, this equivocation suggested derivations of the word as well:

> "Rag-time" originated in the South, where bands of colored musicians first played it. These bands are not usually organized, not uniformed, being volunteer affairs. The colored race is extremely imitative, and all playing mostly "by ear," any mistake or peculiarity made by one band, which happens to take their fancy, is readily taken by all the others.
>
> This music got its name from the rough appearance of the bands, which are called rag-bands, and the music rag-music, or "rag-time" music.[29]

Another Ben Harney story also associates the term's origin with clothing. Attending a Negro party in a suburb of Louisville, Harney tried to imitate at the piano the rhythm he heard being produced on two banjos. One of the banjoists then approached Harney and inquired:

> "Marsa Ben, wha' am yo' playin' dar? Dat am de funniest kin' ob tune I'se ebber heerd."
>
> "I don't know what it is myself," replied Harney, in an off-hand way. "I suppose if I had a dress suit on like some of these actors at the show, I might give it a nice, fashionable name. But as it is I can't think of any name in these rags and you will have to let it go at that."

The following week Harney was at another party in the same neighborhood, and the banjoist announced to the guests:

> "Ladies an' ge'men. Marsa Ben Harney has got some ob de most peculiarist kin' ob music dat I ebber heerd afo'. An' I'se beg yo' kin' 'dulgence for' t' hyar it. I'se don' know de name ob de tune, but it am de lobliest I'se ebber heerd."
>
> Ben thought the remark very funny and replied, "What do you mean, Jasper? That music I played in those rags last week?"
>
> "Yes," returned Jasper, enthusiastically, "dat rag-time music."[30]

Of the various derivations of the term, those tracing the name to condition of dress and to places are too implausible for serious consideration. Etymological derivations, too, though interesting, are not convincing. Dance may be a source of ragtime rhythms, but it does not appear to have supplied the name. Overwhelmingly, the evidence points to the simplest and most direct explanation: the ragged quality of the syncopated rhythm.

## Notes

1. Unidentified article from the Chicago Chronicle, 1897, as quoted in Rudi Blesh and Harriet Janis, They All Played Ragtime (4th ed., rev., New York: Oak Publications, 1971), p. 150.

2. Henry Edward Krehbiel, Afro-American Folksongs: A Study in Racial and National Music (New York: G. Schirmer, 1914), pp. 60–68.

3. Krehbiel, Afro-American Folksongs, pp. v, 48; Natalie Curtis, "The Negro's Contribution to the Music of America," Craftsman (15 March 1913): 662; Rupert Hughes, "A Eulogy of Rag-Time," Musical Record, no. 447 (1 April 1899): 158; Chárles R. Sherlock, "From Breakdown to Ragtime," Cosmopolitan (October 1901): 639; George W. Kay, "Reminiscing in Ragtime: An Interview with Roy Carew," Jazz Journal 17 (November 1964): 8; Russ Cole, untitled letter, Ragtime Society 4 (March/April 1965): 20.

4. William Francis Allen, Charles Pickford Ware, Lucy McKin Garrison, eds., Slave Songs of the United States (New York: A. Simpson, 1867).

5. See descriptions in Eileen Southern, The Music of Black Americans: A History (W. W. Norton, 1971), pp. 53, 99, 168–69.

6. Hughes, "A Eulogy of Rag-Time," p. 158.

7. Permission to quote Handy's music denied. See Come on, Eph!, and Juba in W. C. Handy, ed., with Abbe Niles, Blues: An Anthology (Albert & Charles Boni, 1926; rev. by Jerry Silverman, New York: Collier Books, 1972), pp. 52–53, 204. R. Nathaniel Dett's version of juba is also unsyncopated: see his "Dance (Juba)," in In the Bottoms (Chicago: Clayton F. Summy, 1913); reprinted in The Collected Piano Works of R. Nathaniel Dett (Evanston, Ill.: Summy-Birchard, 1973).

8. Charles E. Ives, Memos, ed. John Kirkpatrick (New York: W. W. Norton, 1972), p. 56. The date of 1899 on the song publication need not reflect unfavorably on Ives's memory or veracity, for it was not uncommon for songs to circulate among professionals prior to publication (Charles Trevathan's Bully Song and Ben Harney's Mr. Johnson Turn Me Loose are examples); the list of twenty-nine minstrel singers or teams cited on the cover suggests that this is the case. Also, the differences in rhythm and key in the two examples support the thesis that Ives knew the piece from performance rather than from publication.

9. "Theatrical Comment," New York Age, 3 April 1913, p. 6.

10. Originally published anonymously (Boston: Sherman, French, 1912); reprinted with the author's name (New York: Alfred A. Knopf, 1927); reprinted in Three Negro Classics (New York: Avon Books, Discus Books, 1965), pp. 391–511.

11. Johnson, Ex-Colored Man, chap. 6. Although this passage is from a work of fiction, its serious consideration as a historical document is justified. Johnson (1871–1938) was a widely accomplished individual whose activities spanned the various provinces of education, law, international diplomacy, literature, music, musical theater, history, journalism, and race relations. In the first decade of the twentieth century he was intimately connected with the creation of ragtime songs, collaborating as a lyricist with his brother J. Rosamond Johnson (1873–1954)—educated at the New England Conservatory of Music—and Bob Cole (1863–1911) in writing some of the most successful songs and Negro musical comedies for the New York stage. In the above novel music, and especially ragtime, is assigned a decisive role. In following years, Johnson wrote several important nonfictional studies of Afro-American history, music, and culture. His allusions to ragtime, then, should be judged not as fantasy but as the considered opinions of an able and articulate black man who had devoted much

of his life to the revelation and furtherance of black culture.

12. Hughes, "A Eulogy of Ragtime," p. 159.

13. "The Origin of Ragtime," *New York Times*, 23 March 1924, sec. 9, p. 2.

14. That Harney was actually black is the assertion of ragtime pianist and songwriter Eubie Blake (b. 1883); see Alex Wilder, *American Popular Song: The Great Innovators, 1900–1950* (New York: Oxford University Press, 1972), p. 9. A photograph of Harney is reproduced in Blesh and Janis, *They All Played Ragtime*, following p. 80.

15. "Again the Origin of Ragtime," *Melody* 2 (December 1918): 4.

16. Ives, *Memos*, p. 56.

17. Respectively: "Questions and Answers," *Etude* 16 (December 1898): 349; "'Coon Songs' on the Wane," *American Musician and Art Journal* 22 (12 June 1906): 26a; Curtis "The Negro's Contribution," p. 662; Isidore Witmark and Isaac Goldberg, *The Story of the House of Witmark: From Ragtime to Swingtime* (New York: Lee Furman, 1939), p. 169.

18. Blesh and Janis, *They All Played Ragtime*, pp. 18, 41. The "Worlds Fair Dance" in Joplin's *Ragtime Dance* might refer to the Chicago Exposition, but any of several later fairs may have provided this name.

19. Roy J. Carew, "Shephard N. Edmonds," *Record Changer* (December 1947): 14.

20. Eugene Levy, *James Weldon Johnson: Black Leader, Black Voice* (Chicago: University of Chicago Press, 1973), pp. 39–40.

21. George W. Cable, "The Dance in Place Congo," *Century Magazine* (February 1886): 525. Quoted in Blesh and Janis, *They All Played Ragtime*, p. 83.

22. Unidentified article from *Stage* (September 1904), as quoted in Blesh and Janis, *They All Played Ragtime*, p. 103.

23. The copyright registrations for these songs are dated, respectively, 3 August 1896, 23 November 1896, and 5 August 1896. *You've Been a Good Old Wagon* had a prior publication, in 1895, by a different publisher (Louisville, Ky.: Greenup Music), without the ragtime banner.

24. Ned Wayburn and Stanley Whiting, *Syncopated Sandy* (New York: Broder and Schlam, 1897), p. 2; see Example IV–1 below. Some time later, Wayburn asserted that this was the first rag introduced to Broadway; see "The Father of Ragtime Has Another Big Idea," *New York Times*, 12 September 1915, sec. 6, p. 3.

25. Leo Oehmler, "Ragtime: A Pernicious Evil and Enemy of True Art" *Musical Observer* 11 (September 1914): 14.

26. "A Ragtime Communication," *Musical Courier* 40 (30 May 1900): 20.

27. Hughes, "A Eulogy of Rag-Time," p. 158.

28. "Origin of Rag-Time," *Metronome* 17 (August 1901): 7.

29. "Questions and Answers," *Etude* 18 (February 1900): 52.

30. "Origin of Rag Time," *Musician* 6 (September 1901): 227.

CHAPTER III

# The Ragtime Debate

Ragtime's emergence in the 1890s coincided with new technical means of mass music communication—recordings and
piano rolls—and a vastly expanded publishing industry. Growing
in mutually beneficial ways, these developments combined to
alter drastically the nature and scope of popular culture; whereas
regionalism continued (and continues) to exist, it became possible
to introduce trends on a nationwide basis, creating a degree of
national homogeneity.

Many of the nation's cultural leaders looked on with horror
as ragtime, the first recipient of the new music technology, en-
gulfed the nation. They had envisioned the country's musical life
"maturing" along the supposedly well-ordered lines of European
musical academicism. Instead, they witnessed the intrusion of a
music that stemmed not from Europe but from Africa, a music
that represented to them not the civilization and spiritual nobility
of European art but its very antithesis—the sensual depravity of
African savagery, embodied in the despised American Negro.

Reacting to what they perceived as a threat to "good music,"
fearing that Bach and Beethoven might be replaced by Botsford
and Berlin, and, moreover, attributing youthful rebellion to "unwholesome" Negro influences filtered through the new popular
music, these self-appointed protectors of public taste and morals
lashed out against ragtime with unreserved virulence. Undaunted, the music's supporters counterattacked, presenting
ragtime as a positive, innovative force and as the long-awaited
symbol of American cultural independence. Thus, within well-
defined positions, ensued the great ragtime debate.

*Ragtime Texts*

There was one major objection to ragtime on which opponents and many supporters agreed; the song texts—especially in the earliest examples of the style—were in exceedingly poor taste:

> Unfortunately, the words to which it [ragtime] is allied are usually decidedly vulgar, so that its present great favor is somewhat to be deplored.[1]

The reasons for the complaints are obvious; many of the early songs—the coon songs—make the basest appeals to racial bigotry, using caricatured, stereotyped ridicule and brutally coarse language. As described by one writer, in announcing the demise of the coon song:

> Nearly all of them were written around the ornery, lazy, "nigger" type of the negro, who was everlastingly having trouble of some kind with his "gal."[2]

Another, also celebrating the decline of this genre, depicted it as "the crude and rough 'coon' song that tells about razors, chickens and pork pies."[3] Emphasizing that his distaste for coon songs was not a blanket condemnation of all ragtime, he added:

> While the "rag" dance is always a fairly welcome addition to modern music—such as the "Maple Leaf," the new "Buxton Rag" and other odd affairs, still these are a far cry to the acrobatic, tough, darky shout.[4]

Generally, the themes of coon-song lyrics can be summarized as: violence (especially with a razor), dishonesty, greed, gambling, shiftlessness, cowardliness, and sexual promiscuity.[5] A few samples of notable early ragtime songs illustrate these points:

May Irwin's "Bully" Song

> Have yo' heard about dat bully dat's just come to town
> He's round among de niggers a-layin' their bodies down
> I'm lookin' for dat bully and he must be found.
>
> . . . . . . . . . . . . . . . . . . . . . . . . . . . . . . . . . . . . . . . . . .
>
> I was sandin' down the Mobile Buck just to cut a shine
> Some coon across my smeller swiped a watermellon rin'
> I drawed my steel dat gemmen for to fin'
> I riz up like a black cloud and took a look aroun'
> There was dat new bully standin' on the ground
> I've been lookin' for you nigger and I've got you found.
> Razors 'gun a flyin', niggers 'gun to squawk.[6]

### My Coal Black Lady

[Chorus]
This coal black lady, She is my baby,
You cannot blame me, No! no! no!
'Case I love her, so! so! so!
Her color's shady, But she's a lady,
Don't trifle with my coal black lady.

[Verse 2]
I'se particular to mention,
That it is my great intention
For to carve that yaller coon,
That tries to win this girl of mine,
This little coal black valentine,
My razor'll seal his doom.[7]

### Mister Johnson Turn Me Loose

[Verse 1]
T'other eb'ning when eb'rything was still, Oh! babe,
De moon was climbin' down behind de hill, Oh! babe,
T'ough eb'ry body was a sound asleep,
But a old man a Johnson was a on his beat, Oh! babe.
I went down into a nigger crap game,
Where de coons were a gambling wid a might and main,
T'ought I'd be a sport and be dead game,
I gambled my money and I wasn't to blame,
One nigger's point was a little, a Joe,
Bettin' six bits t'a quarter he could make the four.
He made dat point but he made no more,
Just den Johnson jump'd through de door.

[Chorus]
Oh! Mister Johnson turn me loose,
Got no money but a good excuse,
Oh! Mister Johnson, I'll be good,
Oh! Mister Johnson turn me loose,
Don't take me to de calaboose,
Oh! Mister Johnson, I'll be good.

[Verse 2]
. . . . . . . . . . . . . . . . . . . . . . . . . . . . . . . . . . . . . . . . . . . . . .
A big black coon was a lookin' fer chickens,
When a great big bulldog got to raisin' de dickens,
De coon got higher, de chicken got nigher,
Just den Johnson opened up fire.

[Chorus 2]
    I got no chance for to be turned loose
    Got no chance for a good excuse
    Oh! Mister Johnson, I'll be good,
    And now he's playin' seben eleben
    Way up yonder in de nigger heab'n,
    Oh! Mister Johnson, made him good.[8]

### Do Your Honey Do

[Verse 1]
    What am de use for to tarry and toil,
    And to save up all your dough,
    When you feel in your bones,
    Dat de gal dat you love,
    Is another big nigger's beau,
    And the cheek of dat wench
    For to come around and say,
    Dis here love you nebber can share,
    I've another big coon,
    He am de star o' my soul,
    Now do him if you dare.

[Chorus]
    And I done him, cause I loved her
    I carved him long, I carved him deep,
    Yes I done him, Does you believe me,
    And I put that coon to sleep. . . . [9]

There were some who were willing to find positive features to such lyrics. Rupert Hughes, for example, praised Ernest Hogan (Reuben Crowders, 1865–1909) for "his exceedingly ingenious satire on his own race, 'All Coons Look Alike to Me.'"[10] While this song is not quite as offensive as those quoted above, other individuals sensitive to the mockery inherent in the title viewed it less generously. When black singers J. Rosamond Johnson and Bob Cole performed it, uneasy about using the word "coon," they habitually substituted the word "boys," thereby removing much of the piece's racially denigrating quality.[11] Because of the embarrassment he caused others of his race, Hogan came to regret having been responsible for bringing this song before the public,[12] a song he actually did not originate, but had appropriated from a Chicago saloon pianist. Ironically, Hogan's contribution to the song was to make the words more socially acceptable, "coons" replacing the original "pimps."[13]

After the first few years of the twentieth century, the most flagrantly abusive lyrics were put aside and replaced by texts of greater acceptability to a broad spectrum of the American public. James Weldon Johnson, for instance, although he favored dialect lyrics as a valuable part of the Afro-American heritage, avoided the rough, razor-wielding bully and other demeaning stereotypes in his own lyrics; instead, he depicted situations and characters with which his white audience could sympathize, and even identify (see his words for *Under the Bamboo Tree*, page 37 below). As the trend toward milder lyrics continued, instances of criticism directed toward song texts accordingly declined. While later songs were also occasionally accused of vulgarity, the specific objections are not clear. Scott Joplin, for example, who was not averse to writing coon lyrics of a gentler sort (as in his song *The Ragtime Dance*), as late as 1913 voiced a complaint against ragtime song texts:

> I have often sat in theatres and listened to beautiful ragtime melodies set to almost vulgar words as a song, and I have wondered why some composers will continue to make the public hate ragtime melodies because the melodies are set to such bad words.
> I have often heard people say after they heard a ragtime song, "I like the music, but I don't like the words." And most people who say they do not like ragtime have reference to the words and not the music.
> If someone were to put vulgar words to a strain of Beethoven's beautiful Symphonies, people would begin saying: "I don't like Beethoven Symphonies." So it is the unwholesome words and not the ragtime melodies that many people hate.[14]

A writer for the London *Times* was less inclined to attack later ragtime lyrics. Quoting the text of *Waiting for the Robert E. Lee* (1912):

> Way down on the levee in old Alabamy
> There's daddy and mammy
> There's Ephraim and Sammy
> On a moonlight night you can find them all,[15]

and citing other songs with equally innocuous words, he defended the texts and praised the settings, demonstrating the rhythmic compatibility of words and music.[16]

Hiram Moderwell, a fervent supporter of ragtime, acknowledged that "The words, also, too often have the chief vice of vulgarity," but failed to demonstrate this "vice." Instead, he pointed out that "ragtime words have at least one artistic quality of the highest rank. They fit the music like a glove."[17] In a later article he came out with a more forthright defense; comparing the words of *I Love a Piano* with the saccharine lyrics of an unnamed American art song, he asked which a "healthy people" should prefer. His conclusion suggests that charges of vulgarity may be directed against nothing more objectionable than ordinary American, or New York, slang.[18] (As he pointed out elsewhere in the article, labeling these words as "vulgar" is hardly a criticism at all, signifying simply that they are of "the people.")[19]

Regardless of how the question of vulgarity was viewed, ragtime songs became a part of the American landscape, and as such were reflected in other areas of culture. The song *Under the Bamboo Tree* (1902), for instance, was echoed outside the sphere of ragtime on at least two occasions. The song itself represents a notable departure from the usual coon song, as it relates, in sympathetic language, the courtship of a maid of "dusky shade" by a "Zulu from Matabooloo":

> If you lak-a-me, lak I lak-a-you
> And we lak-a-both the same,
> I lak-a say, this very day,
> I lak-a-change your name;
> 'Cause I love-a-you and love-a-you true
> And if you-a love-a-me,
> One live as two, two live as one
> Under the bamboo tree.[20]

This song's prominence is apparent in its adaptations beyond the musical stage. At Yale University, *Under the Bamboo Tree* was parodied for a victory song:

> Oh, I'd like to win, And you'd like to win
> We'd both like to win the same.
> But we'd like to say This very day
> Yale's going to win this game.[21]

*Under the Bamboo Tree* is also the obvious source for a minstrel scene in T. S. Eliot's "Fragment of an Agon":

### SONG BY WAUCHOPE AND HORSFALL
### SWARTS AS TAMBO. SNOW AS BONES

> Under the bamboo
> Bamboo bamboo
> Under the bamboo tree

> Two live as one
> One live as two
> Two live as three
> Under the bam
> Under the boo
> Under the bamboo tree.[22]

Another song that caught Eliot's attention is *That Shakespearian Rag*, from the Ziegfeld Follies of 1912. The words

> That Shakespearian Rag,
> Most intelligent, very elegant[23]

are transferred to lines 128–30 of Eliot's *The Waste Land* (1922), "Shakespearian" undergoing an amusing syncopation in the process:

> O O O O that Shakespeherian Rag—
> It's so elegant
> So intelligent.[24]

The use of ragtime lyrics in both popular and high culture reflects the pervasiveness of this genre and underlines the increased public acceptability of the non-abusive texts. In spite of the elimination of the offensive lyrics, however, criticism of ragtime continued and even intensified. The reasons for such criticisms, therefore, must lie beyond a consideration of the words.

### Lowering of Musical Tastes

Throughout the entire period, many of the promoters of "good music" expressed apprehension and fear that they were being replaced. From the earliest days there were warnings that ragtime was debasing musical tastes and occupying a position in the hearts of the public which rightfully belonged to "the great masters":

> Pass along the streets of any large city of a summer evening when the windows are open and take note of what music you hear being played. It is no longer the great masters, or the lesser classicists — nor even the "Salon-componisten" that used to be prime favorites with the boarding-school misses. Not a bit of it! It is "rag time."

> Louis Blumenberg, the 'cello-virtuoso, reports to us that ragtime—a rag-weed of music—has grown up everywhere in the Union and that its vicious influences are highly detrimental to the cause of good music.

It can not be denied that the lower types of "rag-time"—and the bulk of it—has done much to lower the musical taste and standard of the whole musical public, irrespective of color.[25]

Some commentators denied that ragtime could injure the cause of "legitimate" music; among them was the respected art composer Arthur Farwell (1872–1952). In a series of articles in the otherwise stuffy *Musical America*,[26] Farwell rejected the thesis of an antagonism between popular and art music. Instead, he maintained that the two are completely different, noncomparable and noncompeting entities, separated by a distinct psychological boundary:

> The mistake has been in supposing that there is an unbroken scale of musical excellence, for all music, and that popular music pertains to the lower, and artistic to the higher degrees of this scale. . . . Popular and artistic music each live in their own right in their own world, and such a thing as opposition between them, in themselves, does not exist since they can never meet at the same level.[27]

He described three types of music lovers: the Apache, the Mollycoddle, and the Highbrow. The Apache perceives music as physical stimulus, a stimulus generated by popular music and expressed in dance. The Mollycoddle seeks music for the sensation of sound and the creation of mood and sentiment; music, for him, is a diffuse atmosphere. The Highbrow has less interest in the actual sound than in the development of a "musical thought." Farwell refused to criticize any of these types (although his choice of the term "mollycoddle" has a judgmental flavor), saying that despite the separate character of each of the three musical processes, an individual may pass from one to another.[28] Citing himself as an example, he admitted that, although basically a Highbrow, he was capable of Apache functioning; "I often catch my foot in the act of appreciating it [ragtime] when my higher nature is off guard."[29]

Despite this occasional crossing over, the inherent distinctiveness separating ragtime (Apache) from art music (Highbrow) is such that the existence of one cannot interfere with appreciation of the other. Further, noting that serious composers have often enriched their art through judicious use of popular materials, he argued that popular music is even "necessary as a permanent subsoil for musical-art growth."[30]

Whatever tempering effect Farwell's reasoning and prestige

may have brought to the controversy was countered by others of equal or greater prominence in the music world. Karl Muck, imported from Germany to conduct the Boston Symphony Orchestra, denounced ragtime as a poison that destroys the musical tastes of the young,[31] and Daniel Gregory Mason—composer, educator, and member of America's most illustrious musical family—warned against ragtime's insidious, seductive powers:

> When we consider that the formula of ragtime is essentially "two thrills a beat" we cannot but realize that its power of jading the attention for less highly galvanized stimuli is fraught with danger for our appreciation of simpler, sincerer, more thoughtful music.[32]

After witnessing debate on this issue for almost two decades, the *Musical Courier* reviewed the arguments:

> Is ragtime a crime? Does it debase musical tastes? Does it keep the public from buying good music? Is it debauching our children and spoiling them as future concert goers? Would symphony fare better in this country if ragtime were suppressed? Would more songs and piano pieces by MacDowell be bought if there were fewer compositions by Irving Berlin for sale?[33]

The article concludes against these positions, but those who viewed ragtime as an intruder were not inclined to be swayed by reason. Fervently believing ragtime to be the enemy of true art and "good music," they unleashed an unrelenting attack.

### The Attack

The main lines of the offensive against ragtime were: (1) ridicule; (2) appeals to racial bias; (3) prophecies of doom; (4) attempts at repression; and (5) suggestions of moral, intellectual, and physical dangers. Reactions to anti-ragtime criticism became especially evident in the second decade of the century as prominent publications praised the music. In response to such acclaim, additional negative arguments were formulated.

The first two categories of attack, ridicule and appeals to racial bias, are apparent in criticisms already cited. References to ragtime as "rag-weed," as the outgrowth of mistakes perpetuated by disheveled Negro bands, as a rhythmic "distortion," and as a "debased" style are all obvious manifestations of ridicule, some with touches of bigotry. The racial aspect was most apparent in the early days of the style, when ragtime's racial character was most pronounced, but even as late as 1924 a writer expressed his objection to the music on the premise that "the negro is a modernized savage."[34] Such racial animosity seems to have been an underlying reason for much of the antagonism expressed toward the music.

PROPHECIES OF DOOM

One approach used to combat ragtime was to deny its significance by suggesting that it was merely a passing fad. In the beginning, at least, such a hypothesis was certainly believable, and was stated even by some of those sympathetic to the style.[35] As time elapsed, however, the insistence upon an imminent extinction became more and more hollow and ludicrous:

[January 1900]
Thank the Lord they [ragtime pieces] have passed the meridian and are now on the wane.

[January 1900]
. . . the day of "coon songs," Negro "Cake Walk" and the "Rag Tag Time" song and dance is fast drawing to a close, and . . . we are coming to a line of more dignified and artistic music.

[March 1900]
Rag-time is simply having its day. It will be forgotten as a craze in a few years.

[July 1901]
Rag-time has passed the zenith of its popularity, musicians say, and they are now anxious to lay out the corpse.

[July 1912]
The Chicago (Ill.) *Herald* says that, at last the music publishers have turned their thumbs down on rag-time.

[February 1918]
It is gratifying to observe that this one-time doubtful feature [rag-time syncopation] is gradually losing favor and promises to be eventually overcome.[36]

A positive and aggressive alternative to waiting for the natural passing of ragtime was to ban it in some way. This step was actually attempted by the American Federation of Musicians at the National Meeting in 1901. The musicians "swore to play no rag-time, and to do all in their power to counteract the pernicious influence exerted by 'Mr. Johnson,' 'My Rag-Time Lady' and others of the negro school."[37]

While the musicians' union was obviously unable to enforce a ban, there were others who could effectively prohibit ragtime within a more restricted jurisdiction. Thus, the Commissioner of

Docks in New York City, concerned about educating "the popular taste," excluded ragtime from the free summer pier concerts,[38] and the Superintendent of Vacation Schools in New York similarly banned ragtime from school music-programs.[39]

Such restricted acts, though, could hardly satisfy those who perceived ragtime as a direct and immediate threat, and calls were made for outright extermination:

> White men also perpetuate so-called music under the name "ragtime," representing it to be characteristic of Negro music. This is also a libelous insult. The typical Negro would blush to own acquaintance with the vicious trash put forth under Ethiopian titles. If the Negro Music Journal can only do a little missionary work among us, and help to banish this epidemic it will go down in history as one of the greatest musical benefactors of the age.
>
> Let us take a united stand against the Ragtime Evil as we would against bad literature, and horrors of war or intemperance and other socially destructive evils.
>
> In Christian homes, where purity of morals are stressed, ragtime should find no resting place.
>
> Avaunt with ragtime rot! Let us purge America and the Divine Art of Music from this polluting nuisance.[40]

Arthur Farwell had made the point that it would be senseless to eliminate ragtime without having something "equally practical and sympathetic" available for the masses;[41] he was not actually calling for a replacement, but simply illustrating the futility of contemplating an injunction. Other writers, not sharing Farwell's appreciation of the absurd, suggested that collections of folk music be made to replace ragtime. Typically, reflecting conditions that led composer Charles Ives to condemn music educators, critics, and tastemakers as "old ladies of both sexes," it was proposed that "The pioneer work here described is recommended as fitting for the women's clubs."[42]

That efforts to ban ragtime were themselves doomed to failure, that the articulation of such positions was often ludicrously self-deluding, does not detract from the significance of these considerations being formulated and seriously proposed by influential segments of the music world. Revealed in the passionate denunciations and calls for eradication are the real anxieties of those who felt threatened by what was incomprehensible to them: the proximity of a music falling slightly outside the academic tradition, and the dynamics of popular music.

## WARNINGS OF HARMFUL EFFECTS

Another line of attack attributed various unwholesome properties and effects to ragtime: its basic degeneracy, its offenses against civilized moral values, against the intellect, and against the body.

One sin imputed to ragtime was its tendency toward the extreme: it was accused of abusing the accepted virtue of moderation and instilling like inclinations in youth:

> This craze was a unique example of an exaggerated use of a musical idiom that in itself is not only a lawful means of musical expression, but one that, used in reasonable moderation and in proper surroundings, is full of beauty and interest, namely, the feature of Syncopation. . . .
>
> [Ragtime] creates in the minds of the young a distaste for that which is more staid and solid.
>
> Strictly speaking, I believe there is but one well-founded theoretical objection to ragtime, and that is the occasional excessive use of its peculiar type of syncopation . . . when taken to excess it over-stimulates; it irritates.[43]

Ragtime, it was warned, was also incapable of fulfilling essential functions assigned to music by prevailing aesthetic theories — the functions of intellectual enlightenment and spiritual exaltation. The resulting vacuum was considered a danger both to the individual and to the country as a whole:

> How can we regard this invasion of vulgarity in music other than as a national calamity, in so far as the mental attainments of the nation are concerned? . . .
>
> This cheap, trashy stuff could not elevate even the most degraded minds, nor could it possibly urge any one to greater effort in the acquisition of culture in any phase.
>
> There is no element of intellectuality in the enjoyment of ragtime. It savors too much of the primeval conception of music, whose basis was a rhythm that appealed to the physical rather than to the mental senses.[44]

Aside from the dangers to the spiritual and mental qualities of humanity, it was warned that ragtime was also making incursions upon conventional morality; it was asserted that the music was "symbolic of the primitive morality and perceptible moral limitations of the negro type," and that, through its influence,

"America is falling prey to the collective soul of the negro."[45] Another writer, commenting on ragtime's power "to lower moral standards," claimed that the inspiration for its "restless rhythm and suggestive words" comes from the brothel, and that the music is regularly found "in the dens of vice and in the vilest of cabarets," along with "sporting papers and salacious novels."[46]

Another approach used to discredit ragtime was to use unpleasant similes, those of drunkenness and disease, for example:

> The counters of the music stores are loaded with this virulent poison which, in the form of a malarious epidemic, is finding its way into the homes and brains of the youth to such an extent as to arouse one's suspicions of their sanity.
>
> The country is awakening to the real harm these "coon songs" and "rag-time" are doing. . . . It is an evil music that has crept into the homes and hearts of our American people regardless of race, and must be wiped out as other bad and dangerous epidemics have been exterminated.
>
> A person once inoculated with the ragtime-fever is like one addicted to strong drink!
>
> Ragtime is syncopation gone mad, and its victims, in my opinion, can only be treated successfully like the dog with rabies, namely, with a dose of lead.[47]

Denunciations were not limited to association and allusion. Ragtime's "unnatural rhythms" were also accused of having detrimental effects on pianistic technique[48] and even upon the body, mind, and nervous system. Maintaining that a healthy organism requires a steady pulse, pseudo-medical terminology and references to Plato were used to argue that ragtime syncopation disrupts normal heart rhythms and interferes with the motor centers of the brain and nervous system.[49]

## The Counterattack

Ragtime's proponents were quite as outspoken as its critics. Ragtime, they claimed, was liked by most people, including European royalty and some notable European musicians; its rhythms were distinctive, unique, and innovative; it was the only music characteristically American; it had the potential of further development in classical music and should form the basis of a national school of composition.

RAGTIME'S POPULARITY

Some of ragtime's partisans based a defensive argument on the music's popularity. In the London *Times*, for example, it was asserted that ragtime musicians are the one type of musical artist that the American public "is disposed to idolize and enrich," and that ragtime thereby meets some of the essential qualifications for a viable art.[50] Hiram Moderwell estimated that ragtime "is in the affections of some 10,000,000 or more Americans,"[51] and critic Olin Downes (1886–1955) found ragtime's popularity an indication of its worth:

> As for "rag-time," its wide acceptance by the people can only be accepted as proof that it finds an echo in their hearts. And what finds an echo in the hearts of the people I refuse to believe to be wholly insincere, superficial or meretricious. "Rag-time" in its best estate is for me one of our most precious musical assets.[52]

The obvious counterargument, that public taste is not a valid criterion for artistic quality, was not long in coming.[53] But ragtime proponents also appealed to the American inclination to defer to European tastes, suggesting that Europeans in general, and some particularly prominent individuals, liked ragtime. Composer-bandmaster John Philip Sousa (1854–1932) reported that European royalty liked ragtime: "King Edward VII of Great Britain, William of Prussia, German Emperor, and Nicholas II, Czar of All the Russias, have accorded it their approval, confess that they like it."[54] The widely traveled James Weldon Johnson referred to ragtime's "world-conquering influence" and to its popularity in Europe,[55] Natalie Curtis recounted the dramatic impression it made on an eminent European conductor,[56] Moderwell related the delight expressed by such prominent visiting composers as Ernest Bloch and Percy Grainger,[57] and *Current Opinion* reported that composer "Stravinsky collects examples of it with assiduity."[58] Stravinsky's views were expressed more fully in a *New York Tribune* article:

> I know little about American music except that of the music halls, but I consider that unrivaled. It is veritable art, and I never can get enough of it to satisfy me. I am convinced of the absolute truth of utterance in that form of American art. . . . God forbid that you Americans should compose symphonies and fugues.[59]

With these statements and reports ragtime enthusiasts could claim the support of the supposedly more sensitive and highly developed tastes of accepted representatives of European culture. A method dear to the critics of ragtime—appeal to the authority of the leaders of "legitimate" music—had, in effect, been turned against them.

## RAGTIME AS INNOVATION

Supporters further argued that ragtime demanded the attention of music lovers because it was something uniquely new, innovative, and possessing a technical validity of high order. On one point, at least, there was a surprising concurrence of opinion among many proponents and critics. The rhythm was perceived as having a remarkably powerful effect, and was described, with some consistency, as possessing a "swing" or "tingle":

> It has a powerfully stimulating effect, setting the nerves and muscles tingling with excitement.

> It certainly has a swing to it that sends one's blood tingling. . . .

> There is a certain sway and swing, a certain indescribable, sensuous something appealing and suggestive about the ring and melody, the rhythm and versification of this music.

> You simply can't resist it. I remember hearing a negro quartet singing "Waiting for the Robert E. Lee," in a café, and I felt my blood thumping in time, my muscles twitching to the rhythm.

> Suddenly I discovered that my legs were in a condition of great excitement. They twitched as though charged with electricity and betrayed a considerable and rather dangerous desire to jerk me from my seat. The rhythm of the music, which had seemed so unnatural at first, was beginning to exert its influence over me. It wasn't that feeling of ease in the joints of the feet and toes which might be caused by a Strauss waltz, no, much more energetic, material, independent as though one encountered a balking horse, which it is absolutely impossible to master.[60]

There were some detractors, though, who denied that ragtime had any unique qualities, claiming that "the great masters" used the same figurations. Commenting on the stated opinions of some noted musicians, one magazine reported that ragtime

> came from the great maestros of the earth. Wagner lapsed into it much after the manner of statesmen who sometimes get tired and drop into versification. Mozart also had moments of fatigue or exuberance, when he dashed off a few notes in the measure of the

cake-walk melody . . . and so have Bach and Beethoven yielded to
the impulse to put their thoughts into sharps and flats that would
be appreciated in music hall circles. . . .

The song from "Carmen," "Love Is a Wild Bird," is one of the
best examples of rag-time in modern music. In the overture to
"Don Juan" by Mozart and in some compositions of Bach we have
good examples of syncopation.[61]

A distinguished academician, intent upon denying any possible
originality to ragtime composers, cited examples of ragtime in
Beethoven, and claimed the actual sources of this popular American music to be the sarabande, bolero, habanera, Scottish and
English folk songs, and, ironically, Southern plantation songs.
Above all, he maintained that the most important source for ragtime "plagiarists" was the Hungarian csárdás.[62]

C. Crozat Converse (1832–1918), an American composer of
religious and patriotic music, was more sympathetic to ragtime
and turned the observation of its "respectable genesis" into a positive argument. Quoting examples of "ragtime" from Beethoven
(*Leonora* Overtures numbers 2 and 3, first allegro theme), Haydn
(Op. 76, no. 3, second movement, variation 2), and Gregorian
chant (!), he concluded that American ragtime, in sharing certain
rhythmic similarities with great masterpieces, must also have
merit. He also prophesied that ragtime's worth would someday be
recognized, and that future music historians would study it,
finding it bound in volumes in public libraries.[63]

Other defenders were equally undaunted by comparisons
with foreign dance and folk music, claiming that despite certain
resemblances in notation, ragtime was unlike other music:

The first half of a rag-measure often resembles the Habanera,
♪♪♩♪ But though I am fairly familiar with the music of the
Spanish races on this continent, I must say that rag-time bears
them only the faintest possible resemblance in letter and spirit.

The "Habanêra" . . . is strangely similar in rhythm to the commonest form of ragtime.
Whether this is a coincidence or an actual importation is impossible to tell; it matters little, for they are altogether unlike in spirit.
Unless set against the unvarying, even bass ragtime is not ragtime.[64]

The suggestion that classical composers had a prior claim to
syncopation did not disturb Irving Berlin. While admitting that

"the old masters" used ragtime syncopation, Berlin viewed their work as "stiff and stilted," lacking the grace and euphony of modern music.[65] Moderwell, though, denied that the syncopation of classical music was the same as that of ragtime:

> The schools have their reply. "Ragtime is not new," they say. "It is merely syncopation, which was used by Haydn and Mozart, Beethoven and Brahms, and is good, like any other musical material, when used well." But they are wrong. Ragtime is not "merely syncopation." . . . Ragtime has its flavor that no definition can imprison. No one would take the syncopation of a Haydn symphony to be American ragtime. "Certainly not," replies the indignant musician. Nor the syncopation of any recognized composer. But if this is so, then ragtime *is* new.[66]

Moderwell did not simply stop with a defense. He asserted further that ragtime should be of musical interest to the academician:

> But ragtime is also "good" in the more austere sense of the professional critic. I cannot understand how a trained musician can overlook its purely technical elements of interest. It has carried the complexities of the rhythmic subdivision of the measure to a point never before reached in the history of music. It has established subtle conflicting rhythms to a degree never before attempted in any popular or folk-music, and rarely enough in art-music. . . . It has gone far beyond most other popular music in the freedom of inner voices (yes, I mean polyphony) and of harmonic modulation.[67]

These "technical elements of interest" were discussed and elaborated upon by several others. Arthur Farwell, speaking at a convention of dancing teachers, presented analyses to demonstrate that ragtime was "a distinct and highly developed kind of music,"[68] and written analyses appeared elsewhere attesting to "rhythmical subtleties [that] can only be paralleled in the motets of the early contrapuntists"[69] and rhythms that were "the realization of varieties' wildest dreams."[70]

The strongest attack on ragtime's claim to value as an innovative force came from composer Daniel Gregory Mason, whose primary target, along with ragtime, was Moderwell:

> Suppose . . . we examine in some detail a typical example of ragtime such as "The Memphis Blues" of which he [Moderwell] assures us that "In sheer melodic beauty, in the vividness of its characterization, in the deftness of its polyphony and structure, this song deserves to rank among the best of our time.

Quoting the first four measures of the second strain of *Memphis Blues*, Mason finds nothing but "trivial, poverty-stricken, thread-bare conventionality." Then, approaching the rhythmic dimension, he questions

> the contention of the champions of ragtime that its type of synco-pation is capable of great variety, and even makes possible effects elsewhere unknown, a contention in support of which some of them have even challenged comparison of it with the rhythmic vigors of Beethoven and Schumann.

Accepting the challenge, Mason demonstrates with musical quotations the more varied and imaginative use of syncopation in Schumann's *Faschingsschwank* and in the finale of his Piano Concerto.[71]

It was apparently in response to Mason's demonstration that Charles Ives wrote: "To examine ragtime rhythms and the synco-pations of Schumann and Brahms seems to the writer to show how much alike they are not."[72] In other ways as well Mason's arguments falter, for he was not really discussing the same music as that praised by his opponents. Moderwell repeatedly referred to actual *performances*; Mason, in turn, would consult a printed score. In failing to consider how popular-music performers tend to deviate from the score, Mason overlooked the intrinsic nature of the music.

RAGTIME AS AMERICAN MUSIC

Another defense claimed a uniquely American character for ragtime. At a time when it was generally acknowledged that American art music was a poor copy of European models, rag-time was championed as the only music with a sufficiently in-digenous character to reflect American society.

Such claims did not go unchallenged. When John Philip Sousa announced after a successful European tour that "Rag-time is an established feature of American music; it will never die," the *Music Trade Review* commented: "Sousa's views on the permanency of 'ragtime' . . . will hardly meet with the approba-tion of sincere workers in the advancement of American music." The writer readily admitted American inferiority in music, plac-ing the blame on the youthfulness of the nation, and assured readers that "when the republic of the United States has existed as many centuries as the kingdom of England, it may produce composers as learned as Sir C. H. Parry or Sir Frederick Bridge." But ragtime, he cautioned, should not in any case be considered a significant feature of American music, because it is not of American origin:

> We are unable to say who "invented" ragtime, but it is much older than America. When Columbus was battling with the court of Ferdinand and Isabella, the Bohemian gypsies of Hungaria were playing ragtime in its rudimentary form, and Scotch mothers in the Highlands were singing their babes to sleep with it. . . . It "growed" and "growed" from the rudimentary form of the Hungarian and Scot till it became the exaggerated thing which is now supposed to be a lifelike reproduction of the negro song, but is nothing of the sort. The same trick of throwing the accent into unexpected places was practiced long before the negro took it up, and he employed it in his slave songs just as the older races had before him.[73]

A similar response came from the editor of *Musical America* after he received the report that Theodore Roosevelt had announced, in an address to Negro students:

> There are but two chances for the development of schools of American music and of American singing, and these will come, one from the colored people and one from the vanishing Indian folk.

Again, denial of American heritage became the method of excluding black music from a part in national expression:

> The so-called negro melodies, even if they be original with the colored race, cannot be considered as American, for the negro is a product of Africa, and not of America.[74]

Despite such detractions, by the second decade of the century ragtime was repeatedly characterized as uniquely and distinctively American:

> In Europe the United States is popularly known better by rag-time than by anything else it has produced in a generation. In Paris they call it American music.

> Now of the character of "rag-time" there can be no doubt—it is absolutely characteristic of its inventors—from nowhere but the United States could such music have sprung.

> Our children dance, our people sing, even our soldiers march to "rag-time." . . . This bizarre and fascinating music with its hide-and-seek accent has not only swept over the United States, but it has also captured Europe, where it is rightly known as "American Music," and is taken quite seriously as typical of this country.[75]

The strongest call for the recognition of ragtime as the characteristic musical idiom of the United States came in 1915 from Hiram Moderwell. Referring to it as "the one original and indigenous type of music of the American people," and the "folk-music of the American city," he concluded:

> As you walk up and down the streets of an American city you feel in its jerk and rattle a personality different from that of any European capital. This is American. It is our lives, and it helps to form our characters and conditions our mode of action. It should have expression in art, simply because any people must express itself if it is to know itself. No European music can or possibly could express this American personality. Ragtime I believe does express it. It is to-day the one true American music.[76]

Moderwell's article was carefully scrutinized in current periodicals, various facets being summarized, supported or criticized. Daniel Gregory Mason, a major opponent of Moderwell's views, often addressed himself to the subject of Americanism in music, and although he was willing to allow that a certain degree, or type, of American character is expressed in ragtime, he emphasized that this was a limited view:

> Here is a music, local and piquantly idiomatic, and undeniably representative of a certain aspect of American character—our restlessness, our insatiable nervous activity, our thoughtless superficial "optimism," our fondness for "hustling," our carelessness of whither, how, or why we are moving if only we can "keep on the move." If . . . there was nothing more solid, sweet or wise in America than this galvanic twitching, then indeed rag-time would be our perfect music. But every true American knows that, on the contrary, this is not our virtue but our vice, not our strength but our weakness, and that such a picture of us as it presents is not a portrait but a caricature.[77]

Using Moderwell's portrayal of the American character of ragtime as a point of departure, Charles L. Buchanan, in two essays both entitled "Ragtime and American Music,"[78] argued against the nationalist view. Buchanan was not opposed to ragtime; on the contrary, he considered it "rattling good fun," possessing "inherent, irresistible charm."[79] To avert the squandering and loss of the American musical heritage, he even proposed a foundation to preserve ragtime.[80] He had a fundamental disagreement with Moderwell, however, in that he emphatically denied to music the capacity of expressing nationality:

A "people" does not create its own art; its art is created for it by a unique thing called genius. From a poetic standpoint it is all very pretty to think of a people winding their common joys, fears, hopes and sorrows into beautiful verse and song, but, as a matter of cold fact, if art had to depend upon this sort of thing there would be precious little art in the world today. Art is ninety-nine times out of a hundred the record of one man's emotions, nothing more, nothing less. . . .

Let us ask ourselves when and where music began to express the personality of people and of cities? Furthermore, is "jerk and rattle" all we have to offer in the way of a national personality? Does ragtime conclusively sum up our American temperament? . . .

The fundamental error committed by these writers on nationality in art is the assumption that art expresses and must express nationality. Will they never learn that art is a personal matter, that art is only incidentally concerned with nationality, and is in no way, shape or form under obligation to represent the character of a nation?[81]

Despite such arguments as Buchanan's, the conviction that ragtime was characteristically American was undiminished. In England, one reflection of this opinion appeared in a poem in the magazine *Punch*, in which American soldiers are referred to as "raggers."[82] In the United States, an article examining the support for ragtime reported: "Indeed, ragtime, its champions say, reflects the soul of the American people."[83] Lyrically expressing a firm conviction of their generation, the Gershwin brothers in 1918 put this widely held sentiment into song: *The Real American Folk Song (Is a Rag)*.

## RAGTIME AS A SOURCE FOR CLASSICAL MUSIC
## AND A BASIS FOR NATIONAL STYLE

Taking the premise of the American character of ragtime one step further, some commentators suggested that in ragtime a basis of an American school of composition had at last been found.

One of the major aesthetic concepts retained from the nineteenth century was that "musically dependent" nations should assert independence, throwing off the dominance of the more mature cultures of Germany, France, and Italy. The United States was one of these dependent nations, securely in the German sphere despite the resisting efforts of some native composers. In 1895, though, a new call for native expression was inspired by Dvořák's advice to American composers to build a national style on the music of Negroes and Indians.[84] In addition to Dvořák's own example in nationalistic Czech music and the possibilities suggested for Americans in his "New World" Symphony (1893), the use of peasant tunes by the Russian nationalist composers was a frequently cited precedent:

> A Russian folk-song was no less scorned in the court of Catherine the Great than a ragtime song in our studios today. Yet Russian folk-song became the basis of some of the most vigorous art-music of the past century.[85]

Whether the American Negro should be considered the equivalent of a peasant (or whether he should even be considered American) and whether his music had the capacity of being developed into "high art" were issues that occupied many in the following years. As Krehbiel summarized in his study on racial and national music:

> There has been anything but a dearth of newspaper and platform talk about songs which the negroes sang in America when they were slaves, but most of it has revolved around the questions whether or not the songs were original creations of these native blacks, whether or not they were entitled to be called American and whether or not they were worthy of consideration as foundation elements for a school of American composition.
>
> The greater part of what has been written was the result of an agitation which followed Dr. Antonin Dvořák's efforts to direct the attention of American composers to the beauty and efficiency of the material which these melodies contain for treatment in the higher artistic forms. . . .
>
> It was thus that the question of a possible folk-song basis for a school of composition which the world would recognize as distinctive, even national, was brought upon the carpet.[86]

Rupert Hughes perceived ragtime's potential for being developed into something more serious and even prophesied that the day would come when it would achieve the doubtful status of a dry academic form comparable to the canon and fugue.[87] But it was not until the second decade of the century that the idea of an American classical music emerging from ragtime became topical. A heading in *Musical America*, "Works of American Composers Reveal Relation of Ragtime to Art-Song,"[88] reflects this train of thought, though the article fails to live up to the title's promise.

The attitude is expressed more concretely in James Weldon Johnson's novel in which the concept of a great American music emerging from ragtime is one of the focal points:

> My millionaire planned, in the midst of the discussion on music, to have me play the "new American music" and astonish everyone present. The result was that I was more astonished than anyone else. I went to the piano and played the most intricate rag-time piece I knew. Before there was time for anybody to express an opinion on what I had done, a big bespectacled, bushy-headed man rushed over, and, shoving me out of the chair, exclaimed: "Get up! Get up!" He seated himself at the piano, and, taking the theme of my rag-time, played it through first in straight chords; then varied and developed it through every known musical form. I sat amazed. I had been turning classic music into rag-time, a comparatively easy task; and this man had taken rag-time and made it classic. The thought came across me like a flash—It can be done, why can't I do it? From that moment my mind was made up. I clearly saw the way of carrying out the ambition I had formed when a boy.[89]

But it was again in the London *Times* article that the idea of ragtime providing the very basis for an American school of composition was most prominently put forth, bringing into the open a controversy which continued for the rest of the decade:

> Here, perhaps, then, for those who have ears to hear are the seeds from which a national art may ultimately spring. . . . We look to the future for the American composer, not, indeed, to the Parkers and MacDowells of the present who are taking over a foreign art and are imitating it with more or less success and with a complete absence of vital force, but to someone as yet unknown, perhaps unborn, who will sing the songs of his own nation, his own time, his own character.[90]

This article's impact, the number of written responses it induced, has already been alluded to (Chapter One, note 7, above). The national debate on ragtime had taken on intensified dimensions (characteristically, receiving a major impetus from Europe). Among the many comments that followed, either for or against the proposition, there were some which included discussions of "reputable music" that already reflected the influence of ragtime.[91] There were also comments from such "Americanist" composers as Charles Wakefield Cadman (1881–1943), whose musical nationalism was expressed through the use of Indian materials. Despite some reservations about the mass-produced quality of ragtime, he found that it contained the folk element, and especially the syncopation aspect of folk music, that he perceived in much of the best art music. He wrote that, along with Indian, Negro, and Creole music, ragtime contained the "germ of a national expression," and "needs but intelligent guidance to lead it to fruition and development." He warned against using literal or idealized folk tunes or syncopation in every composition, but was convinced that composers could find ways of capturing the dynamics of these elements. Most important, in "idealized and dignified forms of syncopation, coupled with a proper sense of balance and sanity," he found "the beginnings of a healthy, red-corpuscled American music. . . . The restless energy and indomitable will of America is somehow symbolized in terms of an intelligent syncopation."[92]

Moderwell's praise of ragtime also included the provision that it be used by American art composers:

> But here and nowhere else are the beginnings of American music, if American music is to be anything but a pleasing reflection of Europe. Here is the only original and characteristic music America has produced this far. Whether it can be made the basis for a national school of composition as great as the Russian I do not know. But I do know that there will be no great American music so long as American musicians despise our ragtime.[93]

Opposition to the proposal of founding a national school on ragtime rested on three arguments: (1) ragtime is musically unsuitable; (2) ragtime expresses only a small, and inferior, part of the American character; and (3) the very concept of musical nationalism is fallacious.

Mason, with his general aversion to ragtime, voiced the first two arguments, and hinted at the third. As a composer he actively confronted the issue of folk sources in art music; in 1919, shortly after writing the essay quoted from below, he wrote a *Quartet on Negro Themes*. But the black music that attracted him was that of the "old South." He found more dignity in the slave "shouts" than in the emancipated ragtime:

> We seem to discover such a richer vein in the songs of the negroes—not the debased forms found in rag-time and the "coon songs" of the minstrel shows, but the genuine old plantation tunes, the "spirituals" and "shouts" of the slaves.[94]

Somewhat inconsistently—for in later years he was to call for a music to express the "American temper," an attitude that he defined as the Anglo-Saxon reserve and sobriety of New England and the "old South"[95]—he questioned the concept of expressing nationality in music:

> It [the nationalistic aesthetic] often assumes that characteristic turns of idiom, such as certain modal intervals or rhythmic figures, are of intrinsic value in making music "distinctive." You can make a tune "American" by "ragging" its rhythm, as you make a story American by inserting "I guess" or "I reckon" at frequent intervals.[96]

Ultimately, the use or nonuse of ragtime was to be determined by composers rather than by theorizing critics. It is now clear that the adoption of this resource was sporadic and of limited success. A question that was not raised in the magazine debates, but which must have occurred to at least some composers who experimented in this direction, is whether ragtime could be transferred to a "higher form" without, in the process, losing its singular spirit.

## Notes

1. "Questions and Answers," *Etude* 16 (October 1898): 285.

2. "'Coon Songs' on the Wane," *American Musician and Art Journal* 22 (12 June 1906): 26a.

3. "Scores of Popular Songs Coming Out," *American Musician and Art Journal* 23 (14 March 1907): 26.

4. Ibid.

5. This last item differs considerably from the glorified sexuality of early jazz and rock lyrics, although the opposition to these later styles is voiced in language strikingly similar to the attacks on ragtime. For studies on the reactions to jazz and rock lyrics, see: Jonathan Kamin, "Parallels in the Social Reactions to Jazz and Rock," *Journal of Jazz Studies* 2 (December 1974): 95–125, and reprinted in *Black Perspective in Music* 3 (Fall 1975): 278–98; Morroe Berger, "Jazz: Resistance to the Diffusion of a Culture Pattern," *Journal of Negro History* 33 (October 1947): 461–94, and reprinted in Charles Nanry, ed., *American Music: Storyville to Woodstock* (New Brunswick, N.J.: Transaction Books, 1972), pp. 11–43; Neil Leonard, *Jazz and the White Americans* (Chicago: University of Chicago Press, 1960); David A. Cayer, "Black and Blue and Black Again: Three Stages of Racial Imagery in Jazz Lyrics," *Journal of Jazz Studies* 1 (June 1974): 38–71.

6. Charles E. Trevathan, *May Irwin's "Bully" Song* (New York: White-Smith Music Publishing, 1896); reprinted in Stanley Appelbaum, ed., *Show Songs from "The Black Crook" to "The Red Mill": Original Sheet Music for 60 Songs from 50 Shows, 1866–1906* (New York: Dover, 1974), p. 77. James Weldon Johnson wrote that prior to its publication this song had been a roustabout folk-song frequently heard along the Mississippi River; see Johnson, "Preface to the First Edition," *The Book of American Negro Poetry*, (rev. ed., New York: Harcourt, Brace and World, 1931), p. 31. The same observation was made by blues composer W. C. Handy: see W. C. Handy, *The Father of the Blues: An Auto-*

biography (New York: Macmillan, 1941), p. 118.

7. W. T. Jefferson, My Coal Black Lady. Symphony de Ethiopia (New York: M. Witmark, 1896).

8. Ben Harney, Mister Johnson Turn Me Loose (New York: Frank Harding, 1896). In the same year, the music was transferred to M. Witmark of New York, who published it in a new version, reprinted in Appelbaum, Show Songs, p. 98. Still another version of this song, as composed by Haering and Green and arranged by Gus Guentzel, was published by G. W. Warren, Evansville, Indiana, 1896, prior to Harney's first publication. Concerned about conflicting claims of authorship to this and other Harney pieces, including You've Been a Good Old Wagon and the Ragtime Instructor, publisher Isidore Witmark traveled to Louisville, Kentucky, and Evansville, Indiana, to determine who the true composer was. After interviewing individuals in the musical life of these cities, he was convinced of the validity Harney's claim. See Isidore Witmark and Isaac Goldberg, The Story of the House of Witmark: From Ragtime to Swingtime (New York: Lee Furman, 1939), p. 153.

9. Theodore A. Metz, Do Your Honey Do (Supplement to the Philadelphia Press, 14 November 1897). Additional samples of lyrics are presented in Isaac Goldberg, Tin Pan Alley: A Chronicle of The American Popular Music Racket (New York: John Day, 1930), pp. 155–63. For an interesting study of these lyrics, see W. K. McNeil, "Syncopated Slander: The 'Coon Song,' 1890–1900," Keystone Folklore Quarterly 17 (Summer 1972): 63–82.

10. Rupert Hughes, "A Eulogy of Ragtime," Musical Record, no. 447 (1 April 1899): 159.

11. Eugene Levy, James Weldon Johnson: Black Leader, Black Voice (Chicago: University of Chicago Press, 1973), p. 87.

12. Tom Fletcher, The Tom Fletcher Story: 100 Years of the Negro in Show

Business (New York: Burdge and Co., 1954), p. 141. See also Ann Charters, Nobody: The Story of Bert Williams (New York: Macmillan, 1970), p. 50.

13. Fletcher, Tom Fletcher Story, p. 138; Charters, Nobody, p. 49. In addition, publisher Isidore Witmark was responsible for much of the final version, composing the music for the verse and some of the words for the second verse; see Witmark and Goldberg, House of Witmark, pp. 195–96.

14. "Theatrical Comment," New York Age, 3 April 1913, p. 6.

15. By Lewis F. Muir and L. Wolfe Gilbert (New York: F. A. Mills, 1912); © Alfred Publishing Co., Inc. Used by permission of the publisher.

16. "Rag-Time," Times (London), 8 February 1913, p. 11.

17. Hiram K. Moderwell, "Ragtime," New Republic 4 (16 October 1915): 285.

18. Hiram K. Moderwell, "A Modest Proposal," Seven Arts 2 (July 1917): 373.

19. Ibid., p. 369.

20. James Weldon Johnson (words), Bob Cole and J. Rosamond Johnson (music), Under the Bamboo Tree (New York: Joseph W. Stern, 1902); reprinted in Robert A. Fremont, ed., Favorite Songs of the Nineties (New York: Dover, 1973), p. 330. The chorus of this song is a variant of the Negro spiritual Nobody Knows the Trouble I've Seen; see Edward Bennet Marks, They All Sang: From Tony Pastor to Rudy Vallée (New York: Viking Press, 1934), p. 97, and Eileen Southern, The Music of Black Americans: A History (New York: W. W. Norton, 1971), p. 304.

21. Levy, James Weldon Johnson, p. 89.

22. T. S. Eliot, "Fragment of an Agon," Criterion 4 (January 1927): 74–80; reprinted in T. S. Eliot, The Complete Poems and Plays: 1909–1950 (New York: Harcourt, Brace, 1952), p. 81.

23. Written by Dave Stamper, Gene Buck, and Herman Ruby. © Edward

B. Marks Music Corporation. Used by Permission.

24. T. S. Eliot, *The Waste Land* (New York: Boni and Liveright, 1922); reprinted in Eliot, *Complete Poems and Plays*, p. 41. See also R. B. Elderry, "Eliot's Shakespeherian Rag," *American Quarterly* (Summer 1957): 185–86.

25. Respectively: Arthur Weld, "The Invasion of Vulgarity in Music," *Etude* 17 (February 1899): 52; "The Ragtime Rage," *Musical Courier* 40 (23 May 1900): 20; "Our Musical Condition," *Negro Music Journal* 1 (March 1903): 138.

26. "The Popular Song Bugaboo," *Musical America* 16 (6 July 1912): 2; "The Popular Song Bugaboo: No. 2" (27 July 1912): 2; "Apaches, Mollycoddles and Highbrows" (17 August 1912): 2; "Where Professors and Socialists Fail to Understand Music" (31 August 1912): 26–27. See also summaries and discussions of Farwell's articles: "Ethics of Ragtime," *Jacobs' Orchestra Monthly* 3 (August 1912): 27–29; "Ethics of Ragtime," *Literary Digest* (10 August 1912): 225; Rudolph Bismark von Liebich, "The Benighted Lover of Ragtime as a Musical 'Man with the Hoe,'" and Alexander S. Thompson, "A Critical Answer to the Theory of 'Apaches, Mollycoddles and Highbrows,'" both in *Musical America* 16 (31 August 1912): 26; and Herbert Sachs-Hirsch, "Dangers That Lie in Ragtime," *Musical America* 16 (21 September 1912): 8.

27. Farwell, "Apaches, Mollycoddles and Highbrows."

28. Ibid.

29. Farwell, "The Popular Song Bugaboo: No. 2."

30. Farwell, "The Popular Song Bugaboo."

31. Karl Muck, "The Music of Democracy," *Craftsman* 29 (December 1915): 277.

32. Daniel Gregory Mason, "Prefers Demonstration to Cheers," *New Republic* 5 (4 December 1915): 122.

33. Leonard Liebling, "The Crime of Ragtime," *Musical Courier* 72 (20 January 1916): 21.

34. Harry Farjeon, "Rag-Time," *Musical Times* 65 (1 September 1924): 796.

35. See, for example, W. H. Amstead, "'Rag-Time': The Music of the Hour," *Metronome* 15 (May 1899): 4.

36. Respectively: "Musical Impurity," *Etude* 18 (January 1900): 16; "Passing of the Coon and Degrading Dance," *Gazette and Land Bulletin* (Waycross, Ga.), 27 January 1900, p. 2; "Rag-Time," *Musician* 5 (March 1900): 83; "War on Rag-Time," *American Musician* 5 (July 1901): 4; "Rag-Time Loses Favor," *American Musician and Art Journal* 28 (27 July 1912): 11; Harold Hubbs, "What Is Ragtime?" *Outlook* 118 (27 February 1918): 345.

37. "War on Rag-Time." See also "Origin of Rag Time," *Musician* 6 (September 1901): 277.

38. "Music for Piers and Parks," *New York Times*, 29 May 1902, p. 8.

39. "Must Avoid Ragtime," *Musical Courier* 69 (12 August 1914): 10.

40. Respectively: "What 'The Concert-Goer' Says of 'The Negro Music Journal,'" *Negro Music Journal* 1 (October 1902): 28; Leo Oehmler, "'Ragtime': A Pernicious Evil and Enemy of True Art," *Musical Observer* 11 (September 1914): 15.

41. As quoted in "Ethics of Ragtime," *Literary Digest* (10 August 1912): 225.

42. "To Replace Rag-Time," *Literary Digest* (22 March 1913): 641; see also Philip Gordon, "Ragtime, the Folk Song and the Music Teacher," *Musical Observer* 6 (November 1912): 724–25.

43. Respectively: W. F. Gates, "Ethiopian Syncopation—The Decline of Rag-Time," *Musician* 7 (October 1902): 341; Hubbs, "What is Ragtime?"

44. Respectively: Weld, "The Invasion of Vulgarity"; Paul G. Carr, "Abuses of Music," *Musician* 6 (October 1901): 299.

45. Walter Winston Kenilworth, "Demoralizing Rag Time Music," *Music Courier* 66 (28 May 1913): 22–23.

46. Oehmler, "'Ragtime,'" pp. 14–15.

47. Respectively: "Musical Impurity"; "Our Musical Condition"; Oehmler, "'Ragtime,'" p. 15; Edward Baxter Perry, "Ragging Good Music," *Etude* 36 (June 1918): 372. Perry (1855–1924) was a blind pianist who gained renown by presenting hundreds of lecture-recitals.

48. See "Questions and Answers," *Etude* 17 (August 1899): 245, and Gordon, "Ragtime, the Folk Song and the Music Teacher," p. 724.

49. Francis Toye, "Ragtime: The New Tarantism," *English Review* 13 (March 1913): 655–58; see also "Music in America," *New York Times*, 9 October 1911, p. 10; "American Music" and "Not a Ragtime Band This Nation of Ours," on pages 9 and 12, respectively, of *American Musician and Art Journal* 27 (28 October 1911).

50. "Rag-Time," *Times* (London), 8 February 1913, p. 11.

51. Moderwell, "Ragtime," p. 284.

52. Olin Downes, "An American Composer," *Musical Quarterly* 4 (January 1918): 28.

53. James Cloyd Bowman, "Anti-Ragtime," *New Republic* 5 (6 November 1915): 19; Mason, "Prefers Demonstration to Cheers."

54. "Rag Time and Royalty," *New York Times*, 10 October 1903, p. 6; see also "American Music and Ragtime," *Music Trade Review* 37 (3 October 1903): 8.

55. James Weldon Johnson, *The Autobiography of an Ex-Colored Man* (Boston: Sherman, French, 1912), chap. 5.

56. Natalie Curtis, "The Negro's Contribution to the Music of America," *Craftsman* 23 (15 March 1913): 660.

57. Moderwell, "A Modest Proposal," p. 369.

58. "Great American Composer— Will He Speak in the Accent of Broadway?" *Current Opinion* 63 (November 1917): 317.

59. Stanley C. Wise, "'American Music Is True Art,' Says Stravinsky," *New York Tribune*, 16 January 1916, sec. 5, p. 3; see also Liebling, "The Crime of Ragtime," pp. 21–22.

60. Respectively: "Questions and Answers," *Etude* 16 (October 1898): 285; "Martin Ballmann's Rag-Time Philosophy," *American Musician and Art Journal* 28 (28 September 1912): 5; Kenilworth, "Demoralizing Rag Time Music," p. 22; Moderwell, "Ragtime," p. 285; Gustav Kühl, "Rag Time," *Die Musik* 1 (August 1902): 1973, as translated by Gustav Saenger, "The Musical Possibilities of Rag-Time," *Metronome* 19 (March 1903): 11.

61. "Rag-Time," *Musician* 5 (March 1900): 83.

62. A. J. Goodrich, "Syncopated Rhythm vs. 'Rag-Time,'" *Musician* 6 (November 1901): 336. Goodrich (1847–1920), an eminent academician and theorist, apparently had a predilection toward denying originality to composers. In 1902, testifying on behalf of the *Musical Courier*, which was being sued for accusing Victor Herbert of plagiarism, he tried to demonstrate Herbert's "thefts" from Beethoven and Fauré. Herbert was ultimately awarded damages of $5,000. See Goldberg, *Tin Pan Alley*, pp. 222–24.

63. C. Crozat Converse, "Rag-Time Music," *Etude* 17 (June 1899): 185; (August 1899): 256.

64. Respectively: Hughes, "A Eulogy of Rag-Time," p. 158; John N. Burk, "Ragtime and Its Possibilities," *Harvard Musical Review* 2 (January 1914): 12.

65. Frederick James Smith, "Irving Berlin and Modern Ragtime," *New York Dramatic Mirror*, 14 January 1914, p. 38.

66. Moderwell, "Ragtime," p. 285.

67. Ibid.

68. "Dance Puzzle Stirs Teachers to Action," *New York Times*, 20 April 1914, p. 9.

69. "Rag-Time," *Times* (London).

70. Burk, "Ragtime and Its Possibilities," p. 12.

71. Daniel Gregory Mason, "Concerning Ragtime," *New Music Review and Church Music Review* 17 (March 1918): 114–15.

72. Charles Ives, *Essays before a Sonata* (New York: Knickerbocker, 1920); reprinted in *Essays before a Sonata and Other Writings*, ed. Howard Boatwright (New York: W. W. Norton, 1961), p. 94.

73. "American Music and Ragtime," p. 8.

74. "What Is American Music?" *Musical America* 3 (24 February 1906): 8.

75. Respectively: Johnson, *Ex-Colored Man*, chap. 5; "Rag-Time," *Times* (London); Curtis, "The Negro's Contribution," p. 660.

76. Moderwell, "Ragtime," p. 286.

77. Daniel Gregory Mason, "Folk-Song and American Music (A Plea For the Unpopular Point of View)," *Musical Quarterly* 4 (July 1918): 324–25.

78. *Opera Magazine* 3 (February 1916): 17–19; *Seven Arts* 2 (July 1917): 376–83. The second article, which is a reworking of the first, expressing essentially the same views, is paired with Moderwell's "A Modest Proposal," both being covered by the blanket title "Two Views of Ragtime." Seven years later Buchanan again repeated these arguments, in an updated form: "The National Music Fallacy: Is American Music to Rest on a Foundation of Ragtime and Jazz?" *Arts and Decoration* 20 (February 1924): 26.

79. Buchanan, "Ragtime and American Music," *Opera Magazine*, p. 17.

80. Charles L. Buchanan, "The Prodigal Popular Composer," *Opera Magazine* 2 (July 1915): 15.

81. Buchanan, "Ragtime and American Music," *Opera Magazine*, pp. 17, 19.

82. "Ragtime in the Trenches," reprinted in *Literary Digest* (8 April 1916): 997.

83. "Great American Composer," p. 316.

84. Antonin Dvořák, "Music in America," *Harper's New Monthly Magazine* (February 1895): 432. See also Gilbert Chase, *America's Music*, (2d ed., New York: McGraw-Hill, 1966), pp. 385–402; and H. Wiley Hitchcock, *Music in the United States* (2d ed., Englewood Cliffs, N.J.: Prentice-Hall, 1974), pp. 135–38, 143–44.

85. Moderwell, "Ragtime," p. 284.

86. Henry Edward Krehbiel, *Afro-American Folksongs: A Study in Racial and National Music* (New York: G. Schirmer, 1914), pp. vi–vii.

87. Hughes, "A Eulogy of Rag-Time," p. 159.

88. Arthur L. Judson in *Musical America* 15 (2 December 1911): 29.

89. Johnson, *Ex-Colored Man*, chap. 9.

90. "Rag-Time," *Times* (London).

91. Burk, "Ragtime and Its Possibilities," p. 13.

92. Charles Wakefield Cadman, "Cadman on 'Rag-Time,'" *Musical Courier* 69 (12 August 1914): 31.

93. Moderwell, "A Modest Proposal," pp. 375–76.

94. Mason, "Folk-Song and American Music," p. 326.

95. Daniel Gregory Mason, *Tune in America: A Study of Our Coming Musical Independence* (New York: Alfred A. Knopf, 1931), pp. 158–59.

96. Mason, "Folk-Song and American Music," p. 323.

# Part Two
# Piano Ragtime

In popular music it is only the rare instrumental work that commands the attention or following generated by songs. Instrumental music, more abstract than music with words, presents greater difficulties of portrayal to most commentators. It is not surprising, then, that piano ragtime received less press and magazine coverage than vocal ragtime.

This relative lack of attention by journalists should not be mistaken for an absence of appreciation on the part of a substantial portion of the musical public. The thousands of ragtime publications for piano testify to a strongly supportive public. There is also indication from a few writers of an awareness of the distinct qualities of piano ragtime. One such writer, in proposing that ragtime be used to awaken and stimulate "higher" musical interests in piano students, suggested that true ragtime was piano music, and that it was only a superficial view that packaged all of popular music into the single category of ragtime.[1]

This writer's perception of ragtime coincides with the modern view whereby the term, rather than being a coverall for popular music, refers primarily to a restricted body of piano music. It is evident, viewing the style historically, that despite the ties existing between vocal and piano strains of ragtime, a split occurred; vocal ragtime merged with the mainstream of popular music, while piano ragtime inclined toward what became known as jazz.

Against the background established in Part One, in which ragtime is considered in its most inclusive and multifaceted sense, it is now possible to focus more restrictively on ragtime for piano and appreciate more fully how it developed within this musical and cultural context.

## Note

1. Zarh Myron Bickford, "Ragtime as an Introduction and Aid to Better Music," *Melody* 2 (January 1918): 7.

Chapter IV

# The Varieties of Piano Ragtime

Piano ragtime is separated into at least three distinct sub-
groups: piano renditions of ragtime songs; "ragged" versions of preexisting unsyncopated music; and original, dance-
oriented ragtime compositions. Of these, the last is best known
today, having been best preserved in music publications and recordings. Our knowledge of the other two is far less complete;
improvisatory in nature, they were more varied and short-lived.
They were, however, integral to the life and development of ragtime, and must therefore be considered.

## Piano Renditions of Ragtime Songs

Ben Harney's reputation as the originator of piano ragtime
was based on his playing—and singing—of ragtime songs and, as
discussed below, his ragging of existing music. All of his known
compositions are songs,[1] and the publication of his *Cake-Walk in
the Sky* (1899) in both song and piano versions (see Plate VI–4) is
just one illustration of the practice of rendering songs on the
piano.
    The ubiquitous piano—available in homes, hotels, theaters,
and meeting-places—was a natural medium for the performance
of ragtime songs. References to this transfer are abundant:

> You will also find the "coon" songs on your friend's piano when
> you go to his house, and the chances are that he will insist upon
> "rendering" a few of them for your edification.[2]

This practice of playing coon songs at the piano was further nur-
tured by the publication of coon songs in syncopated piano med-

leys like Max Hoffmann's *Rag Medley* (1897; Example V–10),
*Ragtown Rags* (1898), and *A Night in Coontown* (1899); Ben
Jerome's *A Bunch of Rags* (1898); Adolphe Schroeder's *Rag-Time
Medley No. 1* (1899) and *Rag-Time Medley No. 2* (1899); and
"Blind" Boone's *Rag Medley No. 1* (1908, Example VIII–11a) and
*Rag Medley No. II* (1909, Example VIII–13).

A few coon songs were published with both regular (unsyncopated) piano accompaniments and with alternative ragtime
(syncopated) piano arrangements (Example IV–1). The Max
Hoffmann rag accompaniments of 1896 may be the earliest
piano music specifically labeled as ragtime:

It was Max Hoffman who became famous as the first white man
to make successfully the first rag arrangements. The work was
begun in Chicago, which still echoed with the joyousness of the

EXAMPLE IV-1. (a) Ernest Hogan, *All Coons Look Alike to Me* (New York:
M. Witmark and Sons, 1896), chorus 1–4, standard version;* (b) optional
rag chorus 1–4; (c) W. T. Jefferson, *My Coal Black Lady. Symphony de
Ethiopia* (New York: M. Witmark and Sons, 1896), chorus 1–5, standard
version; (d) optional rag chorus 1–5; (e) Ned Wayburn and Stanley Whiting, *Syncopated Sandy* (New York: Broder and Schlam, 1897), verse 1–4.

*The opening octave F in the bass is an obvious error; it should be G.

(a)

(b)

(c)

**CHORUS.** *Not too fast.*

This coal black la - dy, She is my ba - by, You can-not blame me, No! no!

*p*—*2nd*—*f*

(d)

**Rag accompaniment to Chorus "Coal Black Lady."**

Arr. by Max Hoffman.

*Moderato.*

My coal black la - dy, She is my ba - by, You cannot blame me no, no,

(e)

There's a high - tone col - ored gent, A coon with-out a cent, His
On a night way late last Fall, The coons they hired a hall, And

RAG TIME.

World's Fair of 1893. Additional refrains in the Frank Witmark style provided with rag accompaniments as developed by Hoffman, created a nationwide stir. . . .

They [the Witmarks] published the first rag arrangement he ever made, that of *All Coons Look Alike to Me*.[3]

This close link between coon songs and piano ragtime survived the coon-song phase of vocal ragtime, for later songs were equally amenable to piano performance. The hit song *Alexander's Rag-time Band* (1911) was also issued as a piano solo, and several publishers issued annual "dance folios," these being the year's song hits arranged for piano in ragtime and other dance styles.

### Ragging Unsyncopated Music

Rag accompaniments for coon songs probably originated as improvisations. Through this method the ragtime style was applied to virtually all kinds of existing musical material, from popular songs to classics. Improvised syncopation of marches was a favored practice among early ragtime pianists (see page 99–100 below), as was ragging popular songs.

I first heard ragtime in New Orleans about 1895. . . . It was in a cafe, and there was a little negro at the piano. He would play one of the standard songs of the day, such as "Mary and John," and then he would announce: "Here's the new music, the way us plays it," and he would break into ragtime.

In 1902, when I was eight, we moved to Jersey City and there I first heard early ragtime. . . .

What they played wasn't ragtime as we know it now. It was popular songs with a strong rhythm and with syncopated vamps, not a whole composition or arrangement.[4]

Patriotic and folk tunes were also ragged, and were sometimes interpolated into pieces contrapuntally, in quodlibet fashion. As pianist James P. Johnson (1894–1955) reported:

In my *Imitator's Rag* the last strain had *Dixie* in the right hand and *The Star Spangled Banner* in the left. . . . Another version had *Home, Sweet Home* in the left hand and *Dixie* in the right.[5]

This quodlibet technique is reflected, though without syncopation, in several published ragtime compositions. In the piano version of Irving Berlin's *Alexander's Ragtime Band* (1911), following the section which (in the song version) poses the question of hearing "Swanee River" in ragtime, there is a simultaneous rendering of Stephen Foster's *Old Folks at Home* ("Swanee River") and *Dixie*; in Jay Roberts's *Entertainer's Rag*, *Dixie* and *Yankee Doodle* are juxtaposed (Example IV–2).[6]

EXAMPLE IV-2. Jay Roberts, *Entertainer's Rag* (Oakland, Ca.: Pacific Music Co., 1910), vamp and D 1–8.

"Ragging the classics" was an especially popular exercise, and dates back to the beginning of the ragtime era. Discussing Ben Harney's exhibitions from around 1899, Witmark reported:

> His performances included the "ragging" of such popular classics as Mendelssohn's *Spring Song*, Rubinstein's *Melody in F*, and the *Intermezzo* from Mascagni's "Cavalleria Rusticana," which he would first play in their orthodox form. The effect was startling.[7]

James P. Johnson described having a similar repertoire during the early part of the century's second decade:

> Once I used Liszt's *Rigoletto Concert Paraphrase* as an introduction to a stomp . . .
> I did my variations on *William Tell Overture*, Grieg's *Peer Gynt Suite* and even a *Russian Rag* based on Rachmaninoff's *Prelude in C Sharp Minor*, which was getting popular then.[8]

Jelly Roll Morton, too, described how he "swung into the *Miserery* [sic] and combined it with the *Anvil Chorus*,"[9] and, as of this writing, nonagenarian Eubie Blake still thrills audiences with his ragged version of the *Tannhäuser Overture*.

The interest in ragtime improvisation prompted the issuance of ragtime manuals (instruction books designed to teach the art of "ragging"). The first was *Ben Harney's Rag Time Instructor* (1897), which presented ragtime versions of hymns, folksongs, and popular songs (Example IV–3). Another kind of manual is represented by Scott Joplin's *School of Ragtime* (1908). This instruction booklet offers exercises illustrating and analytically dissecting typical ragtime rhythms and figurations, but contains no complete pieces.

EXAMPLE IV-3. *Ben Harney's Rag Time Instructor*, arranged by Theodore H. Northrup (Chicago: Sol Bloom, 1897), exercise No. 2.*

*There is a proliferation of "arrangers" in ragtime publications, and the term assumes a variety of meanings. In some cases the arrangers did just what the term implies. Frequently, though, they were called upon simply to notate the music as performed by an illiterate musician; this may be the situation with the *Rag Time Instructor*, for it is known that Harney had John Biller notate *You've Been a Good Old Wagon* (see Witmark and Goldberg, *House of Witmark*, p. 153). In other instances, a famous musician might lend his name as "arranger" in order to help the sales of a piece by an unknown composer; this was true for Joplin's "collaboration" on Joe Lamb's *Sensation Rag* (see Blesh and Janis, *They All Played Ragtime*, p. 236). In a few cases, such as Joplin's *Original Rags* (1899), which gives credit to Charles N. Daniels, the reason for an "arranger" is not known.

Both approaches—the presentation of rhythmic exercises, and sample syncopated arrangements of well-known pieces—are used in the pedagogical writings of Axel Christensen and Edward R. Winn. Christensen directed a chain of ragtime schools around the country—as of December 1914 he had fifty schools—and published a monthly magazine, the *Ragtime Review*,[10] and a variety of instructional booklets. His first manual was *Christensen's Rag-Time Instruction Book for Piano* (1904; revised 1906, 1907, 1908, 1909, 1915). The success of this volume prompted the publication of similar manuals: *Christensen's Instruction Books for Vaudeville Piano Playing* (1912), *Picture Show Collection for Piano* (n.d.), *Axel Christensen's New Instruction Book for Rag and Jazz Piano Playing* (1920), *Saxophone Rag Jazz Instructor* (1922), *Axel Christensen's Instruction Book for Jazz and Novelty Playing* (1927), and *Axel Christensen's Instruction Book for Modern Swing Music* (1936).

Edward R. Winn in 1915 published an instruction manual, *How To Play Ragtime (Uneven Rhythm)*, and in later years wrote booklets on jazz and blues. In addition, he designed an extensive monthly course, "Ragtime Piano Playing," which began appearing in magazines in 1915.[11] The ultimate goal of these "methods" is articulated in the introduction to Winn's monthly course:

> Aside from the technic required, ragtime presents two unusual problems to the pianist, namely, the ability to harmonize offhand or enlarge upon and make adaptations to the harmony given, and then to syncopate (rag) the tones thus produced. To play a composition as arranged and written for piano is one thing; to convert a melody and accompaniment into effective ragtime is quite another.[12]

Illustrating the aim to be achieved by students, Winn wrote out sample "improvisations," ragged versions of such pieces as *Marching through Georgia*, *My Old Kentucky Home*, *Old Black Joe*, Rubinstein's *Melody in F*, and Mendelssohn's *Spring Song*. (Copyright restrictions probably accounted for the use of unprotected materials.) To complement these arrangements Winn had a monthly column in the magazine *Melody*—"'Ragging' the Popular Song Hits"—in which he discussed and presented syncopated versions of more recent songs.[13]

These various trends and procedures—ragged versions of well-known popular, folk, patriotic, and classical melodies—were also found in regular sheet-music publications. Ned Wayburn's *Ragtime Jimmie's Jamboree* (1899) contains syncopated versions of the *Star Spangled Banner*, Mendelssohn's *Wedding March*, and Paul Dresser's popular song *On the Banks of the Wabash*. A number of patriotic tunes appear in Edward Claypoole's *American Jubilee* (1916); bugle calls are used in Eubie Blake and Carey Morgan's *Bugle Call Rag* (1916) and Val Marconi's *The Bugle Calls in Ragtime* (1921). Franz Lehar's operetta *The Merry Widow*, first produced in Vienna in 1905, was a hit in New York by 1908 and consequently attracted the attention of several rag-

time composers, resulting in Edward Laska and Charles Eliott's
*Coontown's Merry Widow*, Clinton Keithley's *Merry Widow Rag*,
and Victor Maurice's *Merry Widow Glad Rags*. Of all classical
composers, Mendelssohn, the darling of turn-of-the-century
piano teachers, was the most frequent target for ragtime parody;
versions of the *Wedding March* are innumerable, and *Spring Song*
is a close second, as in Egbert Van Alstyne's *Darkie's Spring Song*
(1901) and the opening of Julius Lenzberg's *Operatic Rag* (1914).
Liszt is the model for Lenzberg's *Hungarian Rag* (1913) and
Rachmaninoff for George L. Cobb's *Russian Rag* (1918); operatic
themes from various composers are used in Felix Arndt's *An
Operatic Nightmare (Desecration No. 2)* (Example IV–4).

EXAMPLE IV–4. Felix Arndt, An *Operatic Nightmare (Desecration No. 2)*.
*Fox Trot. A Rag Classic* (Cleveland: Sam Fox, 1916), measures 50–53.

Copyright © 1916 and 1944, Sam Fox Publishing Co., Inc., New York,
N.Y. Used by permission.

"Ragging the classics," a musical abuse of the "great masters," was a way for ragtimers to strike back at their academic
critics. This intention is clear in Arndt's title for his "desecration"
of opera, the classical medium most valued by musical snobs.
Some of the critics reacted predictably, publicly denouncing the
practice:

> We have musical unions in many of our cities, and one of the
> first rules they should pass is that any member found guilty of what
> is called "ragging" a classic should be dismissed from the organiza-
> tion in disgrace, and never again permitted to appear in any repu-
> table organization.[14]

Even Rupert Hughes, amidst his general praise of ragtime, expressed reservations about indiscriminate ragging:

> The latest phase of the rag-time mania is the publication of such
> tunes as "The Star Spangled Banner," Mendelssohn's "Wedding
> March," and even the trovatore "Miserere," arranged in rag-time.
> Their bad taste will serve at least this use: that it will display the
> elasticity and energy and the captivation of rag-time.[15]

But "ragging the classics" could also make a favorable impression; James Weldon Johnson, for one, has his fictional ragtime pianist claim the credit for originating this practice:

> It was I who first made rag-time transcriptions of familiar classic selections. I used to play Mendelssohn's "Wedding March" in a manner that never failed to arouse enthusiasm among the patrons of the "Club."[16]

The procedure used to rag a classic was, of course, no different from that used to rag any other melodic material, and was of no greater consequence musically. Nor was the adaptation of patriotic and classical tunes for dance purposes even innovative, for it had long been a practice in 19th-century America to create dance medleys from such sources. *The Home Circle*, for instance, a large collection of dance music from 1859, contains such arrangements as the *Papageno Polka* (based on whimsical themes from Mozart's *The Magic Flute*), *Operatic Cotillon* ("Introducing Airs from 'Martha,' 'Fille du Regiment,' 'Fra Diavolo,' . . . "), *Jullien's American Quadrille* ("Introducing . . . 'Hail to the Chief,' 'Yankee Doodle'"), and the like.[17] Thus, despite the outrage generated by the practice, "ragging the classics" was simply a continuation of an established musical game.

## Original Ragtime Compositions for Piano

Piano arrangements of ragtime songs and syncopated versions of familiar melodies comprise only a small proportion — probably less than 5 percent — of ragtime publications for piano. The bulk of the printed output is in the form of dance music on original themes, the music that James P. Johnson referred to as "real ragtime,"[18] and the music which is today most generally regarded as ragtime.

As a body of musical literature, this kind of ragtime is especially amenable to systematic study. It is set apart stylistically from other types of ragtime by its link to dance conventions, and is distinguished from other dance music by its adherence to a relatively narrow, but characteristic, range of rhythmic traits; it has discernible roots in earlier styles and its changes take place in gradual and recognizable patterns. Within the genre there is both a consistent language, lending itself to general imitation, and sufficient differentiation for the individual stylist. Finally, the music was produced in substantial quantities, indicating widespread interest.

Precisely how much ragtime was produced is difficult—

perhaps impossible—to determine. One collector is reported to
own "over 10,000 sheets of rag music,"[19] while another more
modestly estimates the full output at about 3,500, his own collection consisting of 1,500 pieces.[20] A major difficulty in reconciling
these divergent figures is that there is little agreement on what
constitutes a rag—on whether one should include ragtime songs,
novelty piano of the 1920s, cakewalks of the late 1890s, and so on.
Whatever the disagreements on specifics, there is general concurrence that the number of publications was substantial.

Objective, "official" publication figures are nonexistent.
Since there is no accurate count of the legions of small music-
publishers who emerged only briefly, there is insufficient data to
estimate the number of rag (or any other) publications issued.
Copyright listings are of little help—virtually every published rag
bears a copyright designation on its title page, but many of these
are feigned, as publishers and composers did not always bother to
apply for protection. Among those piano rags with legitimate
copyrights more than half, judging by the present survey, are
without generic identification either in title or in registration description. One would therefore have to examine tens of
thousands of published piano pieces to determine which ones are
rags.

The present stylistic study focuses upon the dance-oriented
piano ragtime published between 1897 and 1920. Some consideration is given to earlier pieces exhibiting ragtime characteristics
and to post-1919 rags and "novelty piano," but the detailed examination is concerned with music that can most reasonably be
viewed as ragtime: music that is labeled "rag" or "ragtime" in
title, subtitle, descriptive legend, or tempo indication (such as
"tempo di rag"), and music that corresponds stylistically to most
of the works with "ragtime" labels.

Using these criteria, 1,035 rags have been examined in detail
and included in various statistical tabulations.[21] This figure represents the total number of rags available to me at the time of writing, pieces found in published anthologies (see Appendix), at the
Lincoln Center research branch of the New York Public Library
(a collection of over 600 rags), and in various private collections.
The holdings at Lincoln Center are a "random selection," com-
prised of donations from many sources and including, in addition
to New York and Chicago publications (the two main publishing-
centers of popular music), works from such diverse locations as
San Francisco, Nashville, Cincinnati, and Omaha. Published

anthologies, by virtue of being selected by a compiler, are not at all random; they overrepresent the best-known composers—Scott Joplin, James Scott, and Joe Lamb. In a smaller sampling such overrepresentation would distort the findings, slanting impressions in favor of the stylistic traits of these three composers. In the present sampling, though, the many hundreds of more randomly selected pieces outweigh the former, clearly revealing how atypical are the works of Joplin and his circle. It is evident in the stylistic proportions cited below, imperfect though they may be from a strictly scientific point of view, that the truly "typical" rag  was a highly stereotyped, mediocre product. These findings, in reflecting the real world of ragtime, serve as a background for understanding and appraising the more original creations of the genre.

The years selected for study, described as "the ragtime era," were determined by the dates of greatest publishing activity in ragtime. The first instrumental rags date from 1897 (one year after vocal rags appeared in print), and the genre extends, roughly, through 1919, by which time it is clearly dying out. The number of rags examined for each year is as follows:

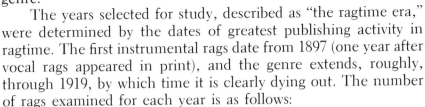

| 1897 | 10 | 1903 | 73 | 1909 | 73 | 1915 | 43 |
|------|----|------|----|------|----|------|----|
| 1898 | 29 | 1904 | 32 | 1910 | 84 | 1916 | 33 |
| 1899 | 124 | 1905 | 30 | 1911 | 66 | 1917 | 16 |
| 1900 | 37 | 1906 | 38 | 1912 | 48 | 1918 | 16 |
| 1901 | 31 | 1907 | 47 | 1913 | 50 | 1919 | 7 |
| 1902 | 42 | 1908 | 52 | 1914 | 54 | | |

In general, these figures are in accordance with what is known of ragtime publishing from other sources. In 1897 the term "rag" was introduced to published instrumental music and was a novelty used tenuously by publishers; *Metronome*, a favorite magazine for dance-music advertising, did not begin to carry ragtime advertisements until January 1898. The response to the increased production of 1898 must have been encouraging, for 1899 witnessed a virtual flood of ragtime compositions, an obvious exploitation of a successful fad. Following the overproduction of rags in 1899, a leveling-off occurred, accompanied by more or less steady production for the next nine years. Another peak was reached during 1909–1911, followed again by a plateau and then a gradual decline. By 1917 "jazz" was becoming the motto of popular music, and the decrease in pieces designated as "rags" was correspondingly steep.[22]

Despite the abundance of ragtime publications for piano, few composers seem to have acquired the wide recognition enjoyed by many songwriters of the period. Piano composers and specific pieces are referred to in articles, but the same names rarely recur. For the most part, composers or works praised by one writer were ignored by others. In all of the literature surveyed, only two names stand out: Kerry Mills and Scott Joplin. Mills is mentioned mostly in connection with his 1897 cakewalk *At a Georgia Campmeeting*, which is usually discussed as though it were purely band music; there is not a single reference to this work as a piano piece, nor a single piano recording made of this piece during the ragtime era, even though in band versions it was one of the most frequently recorded works.[23]

Scott Joplin's music was also played by bands, but he was clearly regarded as a composer for the piano. Joplin unquestionably enjoyed a special reputation and was referred to with more praise and respect than was any other composer of piano ragtime. Yet this acclaim did not delude him into thinking that his work was sufficiently acknowledged by the public. As his wife recounted:

> I used to wonder sometimes whether Scott would ever receive recognition during my lifetime. You know, he would often say that he'd never be appreciated until after he was dead.[24]

A probable reason for his dissatisfaction was that, while ragtime musicians often knew several of his pieces, his fame with the general public rested upon a single work, the *Maple Leaf Rag*. James P. Johnson, in discussing his repertory from 1912, recalled playing only two other Joplin rags—*Sunflower Slow Drag* (1901) and *Euphonic Sounds* (1909). To his reference to *Maple Leaf Rag* he appended the comment: "Everybody knew that by then."[25]

Apparently everyone did know *Maple Leaf Rag*. One critic, decrying the coon-song type of popular music, contrasted it with "the 'rag' dance [which] is always a fairly welcome addition to modern music—such as the 'Maple Leaf Rag.'"[26] Another, discussing the positive aspects of ragtime, cited "the once famous 'Maple Leaf Rag.'"[27] The ragtime pedagogues Axel Christensen and Edward R. Winn both held Joplin in high regard. Christensen, in writing about ragtime publisher John Stark (1841–1927), praised him primarily for bringing Joplin before the public:

> It was he who discovered Scott Joplin, who put on paper for the first time that wonderful composer of classic ragtime. It was he

who gave to the public the famous and never dying "Maple Leaf Rag," the "Cascades Rag," and the like, numbers that will outlive many generations.[28]

Winn, in an advertisement for his ragtime manual, introduced an endorsement from Joplin with the following description:

> Scott Joplin, the world's greatest composer of Ragtime, who wrote the celebrated "Maple Leaf Rag," "Mint Leaf Rag," "Treemonisha," opera in ragtime, and many other famous ragtime compositions.[29]

Even Jelly Roll Morton, who was inclined to minimize the accomplishments of others, referred to Joplin as "the greatest ragtime writer who ever lived and the composer of *Maple Leaf Rag.*"[30]

But the *Maple Leaf Rag* was a singular case. No other piano rag, by Joplin or anyone else, repeated its unique success. This was the observation of ragtime-Dixieland pianist J. Russel Robinson (1892–1963), and the evidence supports his view:

> One of the tunes I played a lot while touring the South [circa 1908] was Scott Joplin's "Maple Leaf Rag." . . . I think it is one of the finest tunes ever written, . . . the King of Rags, and in my way of thinking, nothing that Joplin or any other rag writers wrote ever came close to it.[31]

Perhaps the experience of Walter Harding (c. 1883–1973) most accurately reflects the state of public recognition of Joplin and of ragtime composers in general. During his active days as a ragtime pianist he did not know of Joe Lamb or James Scott, the two composers linked with Joplin by present-day writers; after singling out the *Maple Leaf Rag*, he ranked other Joplin rags below unnamed pieces by more "popular" composers:

> I don't recall hearing any rags by Lamb or Scott in those days and of Joplin, aside from the Maple Leaf Rag there were few that attained popularity. I played his Pineapple, Cascades and a few others, but for the most part it was rags by Wenrich, Bernard, Snyder, and similar composers.[32]

That there was only one spectacular success in the piano ragtime canon seems remarkable. Certainly the publication of thousands of piano pieces must have been supported and encouraged by substantial sales, but there is a dearth of printed commentary about this music. At a time when the public was going wild over ragtime songs, there is no indication of a similar wide-spread infatuation with any piano rag other than *Maple Leaf Rag*. With this additional evidence of the subservient position of piano rags to vocal rags the puzzle is not so much why more piano pieces did not capture the popular imagination as it is how and why this feat was accomplished by the *Maple Leaf Rag*.

## The Score versus Performance

There is little doubt that much ragtime piano music heard in performance was never captured in notated form. James Weldon Johnson's depiction of a ragtime improvisation, for one, "sounds" far more involved and free-wheeling than samples preserved in published versions:

> The barbaric harmonies, the audacious resolutions, often consist-ing of an abrupt jump from one key to another, the intricate rhythms in which the accents fell in the most unexpected places, but in which the beat was never lost, produced a most curious effect. And, too, the player—the dexterity of his left hand in mak-ing rapid octave runs and jumps was little short of marvelous; and with his right hand he frequently swept half the keyboard with clean-cut chromatics.[33]

While the probable poetic license of this passage may justify some skepticism, the description is not without parallels in accounts of actual ragtime performances. Hughie Woolford, in his employ-ment of fast passage-work in both hands, has been likened to later jazz virtuoso Art Tatum,[34] and James P. Johnson, judging by his own reports of his improvisational style, similarly went far beyond the limits of printed ragtime:

> I played rags very accurately and brilliantly—running chromatic octaves and glissandos up and down with both hands. It made a terrific effect.
> I did double glissandos straight and backhand, glissandos in sixths and double tremolos.[35]

The extent to which the sheet music represents the com-poser's true intent is in some cases also open to question. Eubie Blake has testified that composers were urged by publishers to simplify difficult passages that might discourage sales,[36] and Luckey Roberts's *Junk Man Rag* (1913) even bears the label "Simplified."

While much of the music-buying public probably did play the music as written (or at least made an attempt to do so), it is unlikely that professional ragtime musicians, accustomed by training and inclination to ragging all kinds of musical material, would slavishly adhere to a printed score. The lone exception found to this assumption, underlining the validity of the generalization, is in J. Russel Robinson's comment that he was one of the few pianists who played the *Maple Leaf Rag* as written, since most were incapable of reading the music.[37] James P. Johnson has also referred to the casual way Joplin's music was played:

> Scott Joplin's pieces were popular. They got around the country, but the ticklers I knew just played sections of them that they heard someplace. I never knew they were Joplin until later.[38]

Others, too, spoke of players' lack of faithfulness to the score. Brun Campbell (1884–1953), who studied with Joplin in 1898, told an interviewer: "None of the original pianists played ragtime the way it was written, they played their own style."[39]

The practice of improvising on a rag composition is probably well illustrated by Jelly Roll Morton's two recordings of *Maple Leaf Rag*, made at the Library of Congress in 1938.[40] Though Morton's historical accuracy may be suspect, and though his performances may have been influenced by later jazz developments, these renditions do appear as plausible samples of the improvisatory art of the competent ragtime pianist.

With some ragtimers there seems to have been at least an intent to have their own written scores respected. Early Saint Louis ragtimer Tom Turpin (1873–1922) is reported to have played his rags exactly as written,[41] and Artie Matthews (1888–1959) wrote at the head of several of his *Pastime Rags*, "Don't Fake."[42] Scott Joplin, in his *School of Ragtime*, warned against imprecise performance and summarized in the last exercise:

> We wish to say here, that the "Joplin ragtime" is destroyed by careless or imperfect rendering, and very often good players lose the effect entirely by playing too fast. They are harmonized with the supposition that each note will be played as it is written.[43]

Joe Lamb played his own pieces as written[44] and assured a researcher that Joplin, with whom he was acquainted, did the same:

> Personally, I don't think there was any difference between Joplin of 1914 and Joplin of 1908. . . . I don't think he would add any notes in 1914 to any piece he wrote in, say, 1908. To my recollection he played his rags the way he wrote them. That's the way I always did.[45]

Other witnesses recalled that Joplin might make some slight changes in his playing, but nothing of substance:

> Joe [Jordan] never heard him [Joplin] play any rags other than his own, and he played them almost exactly like the sheet music. . . .
>
> I asked Joe how Joplin rags sounded when they were played in the old days. He assured me that all one would have to do to get the sound would be to read and play them as written in the indicated tempos.
>
> He [Joplin] didn't appear to add any notes [to the *Maple Leaf Rag*] outside of what was in the music, except that he added an introduction and a fill at the end.[46]

The piano rolls made by Joplin, as recorded on Biograph BLP-1006Q, reveal alterations greater than those suggested by the above quotations, although they are still of a minor nature, consisting mostly of chord arpeggiations and passing- and neighbor-note embellishments. Trebor Tichenor, one of the producers of the Biograph recording, analyzed the rolls and, finding some altered passages physically impossible to perform, has concluded that the rolls were edited.[47] Most of the embellishments, though, make no extraordinary demands on a competent performer, thus leaving open the question of the extent of any editing.

The issues of performance practice—of the degree of adherence to the score, of stylistic trends in improvisation—will probably remain obscure, although some enlightenment undoubtedly could be derived from systematic studies of piano rolls and recordings of the period.

To be sure, the notated music is of at least equal importance for an understanding of the period, for it was as sheet music that millions became familiar with the style. Amateurs played the music essentially as written, professionals used it as a common starting-point for a variety of improvisatory styles, and composers—whether depicting rough guidelines or precise, formal intent—provided models on which others worked, contributing to, or further developing, the syncopated language. More clearly than any other source, the published sheet-music chronicles the evolution of tastes and ideas in piano ragtime.

## Notes

1. See the list in Rudi Blesh and Harriet Janis, *They All Played Ragtime* (4th ed., rev., New York: Oak Publications, 1971), p. 286.

2. Arthur Weld, "The Invasion of Vulgarity in Music," *Etude* 17 (February 1899): 52. See also "The Ragtime Rage," *Musical Courier* 40 (23 May

1900): 20; "'Coon Songs' on the Wane," *American Musician and Art Journal* 22 (12 June 1906): 26a.

3. Isidore Witmark and Isaac Goldberg, *The Story of the House of Witmark* (New York: Lee Furman, 1939), pp. 169–70. Ned Wayburn contended that his *Syncopated Sandy* (1897) was the first rag arrangement—see "Who Was Sponsor?" *Melody* 2 (December 1918): 4—but the publication dates support the Witmark/Hoffmann claim.

4. Respectively: "The Origin of Ragtime," *New York Times*, 23 March 1924, sec. 9, p. 2; Tom Davin, "Conversations with James P. Johnson" [Part 1], *Jazz Review* 2 (June 1959): 16.

5. Tom Davin, "Conversations with James P. Johnson" [Part 2], *Jazz Review* 2 (July 1959): 13.

6. Roberts's *Entertainer's Rag* and hundreds of other piano rags are reprinted in various anthologies. For a listing of the contents of selected anthologies, see the Appendix.

7. Witmark and Goldberg, *House of Witmark*, p. 155.

8. Davin, "Conversations with James P. Johnson" [Part 2], pp. 12–13.

9. Alan Lomax, *Mister Jelly Roll: The Fortunes of Jelly Roll Morton, New Orleans Creole and "Inventor of Jazz"* (2d ed., Berkeley, Ca.: University of California Press, 1973), p. 149.

10. Also titled *Christensen's Ragtime Review*; published December 1914 to January 1918; merged with *Melody* in April 1918.

11. *Cadenza* 21–23 (March 1915–October 1916), and *Tuneful Yankee/Melody* 1–2 (January 1917–June 1918).

12. Edward R. Winn, "Ragtime Piano Playing: A Practical Course of Instruction for Pianists," *Tuneful Yankee* 1 (January 1917): 42–43.

13. *Melody* 2 (January–September 1918), passim.

14. Edward Baxter Perry, "Ragging Good Music," *Etude* 36 (June 1918): 372; see also Sherwood K. Boblitz, "Where Movie Playing Needs Reform," *Musician* 25 (June 1920): 8; "Editorials," *New Music Review and Church Music Review* 22 (October 1924): 464.

15. Rupert Hughes, "A Eulogy of Rag-Time," *Musical Record*, no. 447 (1 April 1899): 159.

16. James Weldon Johnson, *The Autobiography of an Ex-Colored Man* (Boston: Sherman, French, 1912), chap. 8.

17. *The Home Circle: A Collection of Piano-Forte Music, Consisting of the Most Favorite Marches, Waltzes, Polkas, Redowas, Schottisches, Galops, Mazurkas, Quadrilles, Dances, &c. . . .* , vol. 1 (Boston: Oliver Ditson, 1859).

18. Davin, "Conversations with James P. Johnson" [Part 1], p. 17.

19. "Bob Darch Unearths Treasures," *Ragtimer* (September/October 1970): 8.

20. David Jasen, personal communication, 23 June 1975.

21. There is no significance to this number other than as a large sampling.

22. The frequent statement that ragtime was declining in numbers by 1910 apparently derives from Winthrop Sargeant's assertion of a qualitative decline in effect by that time. See Sargeant, *Jazz: Hot and Hybrid* (3d ed., enl., New York: Da Capo Press, 1975), p. 141, and cf. Gilbert Chase, *America's Music from the Pilgrims to the Present* (2d ed., rev., New York: McGraw-Hill, 1966), p. 447.

23. David Jasen, *Recorded Ragtime, 1897–1958* (Hamden, Conn.: Archon Books, Shoe String Press, 1973), s.v. *At a Georgia Campmeeting*, pp. 16–17.

24. Kay C. Thompson, "Lottie Joplin," *Record Changer* 9 (October 1950): 18.

25. Davin, "Conversations with James P. Johnson" [Part 2], p. 11.

26. "Scores of Popular Songs Coming Out," *American Musician and Art Journal* 23 (14 March 1907): 26.

27. John N. Burk, "Ragtime and Its Possibilities," *Harvard Musical Review* 2 (January 1914): 12.

28. Axel Christensen, "Chicago Syncopations: John Stark, Pioneer Pub-

lisher," *Melody* 2 (October 1918): 8.

29. Edward R. Winn, undated advertisement, reprinted in *Rag Times* 7 (January 1974): 8. The reference to a "Mint Leaf Rag" is intriguing, as this piece is otherwise unknown.

30. Lomax, *Mister Jelly Roll*, p. 149.

31. J. Russel Robinson, "Dixieland Piano," *Record Changer* (August 1947): 7.

32. Walter N. H. Harding, untitled letter, *Ragtime Society* 3 (April 1964): 25. Harding played ragtime professionally from 1909 to 1914, and was personally acquainted with several of the celebrated composer-performers of the day—Mike Bernard (Barnett, 1881–1936), Percy Wenrich (1880–1952), and Joe Jordan (1882–1971). Harding later amassed a collection of sheet music and antiquarian books and music dating back to the seventeenth century which, upon his death at the age of ninety as a "penniless recluse" in a ramshackle Chicago apartment, was valued at an estimated one to three million dollars. His entire estate went to the Bodleian Library of Oxford University. See "Organist Dies at 90, Leaving Fortune in Rare Sheet Music," *New York Times*, 14 December 1973, p. 34; "'Penniless' Ragtime Pianist Leaves Fortune in Books," *Ragtimer* (January/February 1975): 13; Jean Geil, "American Music in the Walter N. H. Harding Collection at the Bodleian Library, Oxford University," *Notes* 34 (June 1978): 805–813.

33. Johnson, *Ex-Colored Man*, chap. 6.

34. Tom Fletcher, *The Tom Fletcher Story: 100 Years of the Negro in Show Business* (New York: Burdge and Co., 1954), p. 164.

35. Davin, "Conversations with James P. Johnson" [Part 2], p. 12.

36. Max Morath, "A Personal Observation," *Max Morath's Giants of Ragtime* (New York: Edward B. Marks, 1971), p. 6.

37. Robinson, "Dixieland Piano," p. 7.

38. Davin, "Conversations with James P. Johnson" [Part 1], p. 16.

39. Quoted by Paul E. Affeldt, liner notes to *The Professors*, vol. 2 (Euphonic ESR-1202); see also Harding, untitled letter, p. 24; and Percy Franks, untitled letter, *Ragtimer* (January/February 1971): 12.

40. Re-released on *They All Played the Maple Leaf Rag* (Herwin 401).

41. Trebor J. Tichenor, "'The Real Thing' as Recalled by Charles Thompson," *Ragtime Review* 2 (April 1963): 5. Thompson (1891–1964) was a St. Louis ragtime pianist and composer.

42. Numbers 1 (1913), 2 (1913), and 4 (1920).

43. Scott Joplin, *School of Ragtime* (New York: Scott Joplin, 1908), Exercise No. 6.

44. Cf. recording of Lamb playing, *Joe Lamb: A Study in Classic Ragtime* (Folkways FG-3562).

45. Michael Montgomery and Trebor Tichenor, liner notes to *Scott Joplin—1916* (Biograph BLP-1006Q).

46. Respectively: Dick Zimmerman, "Joe Jordan and Scott Joplin," *Rag Times* 2 (November 1968): 5; Dick Zimmerman, "Ragtime Recollections: An Interview with Dai Vernon," *Rag Times* 2 (May 1968): 7.

47. Montgomery and Tichenor, liner notes.

CHAPTER V

# Early Piano Ragtime

### *Early Rags*

Many of the identifying traits of ragtime are already present in samples from its earliest years of publication, and most of the basic conventions were well established by 1901.[1] There were, however, stylistic features emphasized in early ragtime that were discarded in later compositions. Because of this unmistakable evolutionary trend in ragtime, the earlier rags are discussed as a separate subcategory.

There is no distinct break, no single year separating "early rags" from later types, but, based on the statistical analyses of various trends (specified below), this category is here designated as works published before 1901. Two additional qualifications are required for the "early rag" classification. First, the piece must be primarily for piano. This qualification excludes coon songs, but includes works that have a single vocal chorus along with several piano sections. Second, the piece must in some way be identified as a rag. Some of the means of identification—use of the term "rag" on the sheet music and stylistic correspondence to most pieces with "rag" labels—have already been outlined. Another identification should be recognized, that of contemporaneous acceptance of a piece as a rag. This final guideline allows some interesting findings. For one, it establishes that contemporaries applied the term to piano pieces published before 1897, the year the term first appeared in piano titles. The popular-song writer R. M. Stults, for example, referred to Kerry Mills's *Rastus on Parade* (1895) and *Happy Days in Dixie* (1896) as rags:

And who will venture to say that the author of this widely-known piece [*At a Georgia Campmeeting* (1897)] is not a genius in his line. It was this same composer who also created "Rastus on Parade," "Happy Days in Dixie," and "Whistling Rufus" [1899] —four consecutive "rag-time" hits.[2]

The first ragtime anthology, *Brainard's Ragtime Collection* (1899), presents an even earlier work, E. A. Phelps's *The Darkies' Patrol* (1892), as a rag. This collection, to be sure, includes several compositions that totally lack any semblance to ragtime and must be rejected as rags. *Darkies' Patrol*, however, in addition to having been identified as a rag by the publisher, exhibits the rhythmic traits of ragtime (see discussion below and Example V–7); it thereby qualifies as one of the earliest, if not *the* earliest, published rag.

### Ragtime Syncopation

It has been demonstrated that almost all writers of the period thought of ragtime as syncopated music. These impressions notwithstanding, there are early pieces, accepted by contemporaries as rags, that are unsyncopated, and many with syncopation in only one (frequently the first) of the three or four 16-measure strains; the unsyncopated strains are essentially marches (Example V–1). Syncopation, though, is clearly the dominating and distinctive element in the evolution of ragtime. It is most often present in the treble melody, against a metrically accented march-accompaniment bass (such as the bass in Example V–1). The rhythmic divisions of these syncopations are of a few characteristic types, with the shorter durations being one-eighth of a measure, or, to put it another way, one-half of the duration of a bass note. Thus, bass motion in eighth notes accompanies treble syn-

EXAMPLE V–1. Kerry Mills, *Whistling Rufus* (New York: F. A. Mills, 1899). B′ 1–16.

copations in sixteenths, and a bass in quarter notes supports treble syncopations in eighths (Examples V–2 and V–3).

In early ragtime, two types of rag syncopations emerge as
most important, the foundation for most variants and later developments: *untied syncopations*, restricted to separate halves of a
measure (Example V–2),[3] and *tied syncopations*, connecting the
halves of a measure (Example V–3a, b). Although a tie across the
bar line (Example V–3c) would appear to be a small and logical
development, it is rare in the early period.

EXAMPLE V–2. Untied syncopations.

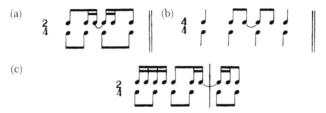

EXAMPLE V–3. Tied syncopations.

A third kind of rhythm is prominent, which—although the
syncopation does cross the middle of the measure—appears to be
related more closely to the untied syncopation than to the tied,
perhaps as a higher level or augmentation. This *augmented syncopation* is different from the others: the bass and treble rhythms
have a one-to-one relationship, the basic unit of motion being
one-quarter of a measure. Therefore the syncopated portions of
the rhythm, instead of falling *between* the left-hand articulations,
coincide with them, producing a syncopated effect that is relatively weak (Example V–4). This rhythm is common in early rags,

EXAMPLE V–4. Augmented syncopations.

especially in second and third themes (Example V–5), but is not characteristic of later rags. Since ragtime composers showed only a temporary interest in augmented syncopation, in this study it is excluded from the blanket term of *ragtime syncopation*.

EXAMPLE V-5. (a) W. H. Krell, *Mississippi Rag* (New York: S. Brainard's Sons, 1897), B 1–7; (b) G. M. Blandford, *The Black Venus* (Boston: Vivian Music Publishing Co., 1899), C 1–6.

(a)

(b)

UNTIED SYNCOPATION RAGS

Rags using *untied syncopation* exclusively, without a single appearance of *tied syncopations*, constitute the majority of early rags.

An early piece such as Mills's *Rastus on Parade* has little ragtime syncopation at all (as opposed to augmented syncopation); it appears only in the introduction and in measure 13 of the opening strain (Example V–6).

In contrast, the earlier *Darkies' Patrol* makes extensive use of untied syncopation (Example V–7; note that

♫ ♪ ♪♫ = ♫♪♫ )

With the introduction of the term "rag" in piano titles, the incidence of syncopations, of both the untied and the tied varieties, increases markedly. Untied syncopation, however, still constitutes the commonest understanding of ragtime. *Ben Harney's Rag Time Instructor*, the first work to present formally the principles of ragtime, has arrangements entirely devoid of tied syncopation

EXAMPLE V-6. K. Mills, *Rastus on Parade* (Detroit, Mich.: F. A. Mills, 1895), Introduction, A 1–16.

EXAMPLE V-7. E. A. Phelps, *The Darkies' Patrol* (New York: S. Brainard's Sons, 1892), A 7–12.

(Example IV–3). Similarly, in some of the most prominent pieces
of the period, such as Mills's *At a Georgia Campmeeting*,
Holzmann's *Smoky Mokes* (1898), and Howard and Emerson's
song *Hello! Ma Baby*—which is syncopated only in the section
using the word "ragtime"—untied syncopation is the exclusive
type of ragtime syncopation (Example V–8).

## TIED SYNCOPATION RAGS

Whereas the category of *untied syncopation* rags is defined
partially by the complete absence of tied syncopations, the category of *tied syncopation* rags includes both types of rhythm, for
tied syncopations usually occur in conjunction with those that
are untied.

EXAMPLE V–8. (a) K. Mills, *At a Georgia Campmeeting* (New York: F. A.
Mills, 1897), Introduction, A 1–16; (b) [Joseph] Howard and [Ida] Emerson, *Hello! Ma Baby* (New York: T. B. Harms and Co., 1899), chorus
1–5.

(b)

Despite the greater prominence in early ragtime of untied syncopations, both rhythms are present in pieces from the beginning of the period. The songs from 1896 that are appended with ragtime accompaniments use tied syncopation (see *My Coal Black Lady*, Example IV–1d), as does Harney's *You've Been a Good Old Wagon* (Example V–9a). Tied syncopation is absent in a section without lyrics labeled "dance" (Example V–9b), but it is possible that measures 2–3 contain a typographical error: the slur curve connecting A to the second B may have been intended as a tie connecting the two Bs. The present configuration seems awkward and atypical, and when this passage was adapted by Max Hoffmann the following year for his *Rag Medley*, the Bs were, in fact, tied (Example V–10). If the typographical error is assumed, or, more simply, if the Hoffmann adaptation is considered, two kinds of tied syncopation are evident. The first, represented in Example V–9a, ties together syncopated and unsyncopated halves of the measure: ; an extension of this type, the tying together of two syncopated halves– –is possible but less frequent. The second kind of tied syncopation, illustrated in Example V–10, creates its effect by joining together two unsyncopated halves: . This second kind is actually similar to untied syncopation, but with an important metrical accent shift: .[4]

EXAMPLE V-9. Ben Harney and [John] Biller, *You've Been a Good Old Wagon but You've Done Broke Down* (New York: M. Witmark and Sons, 1896): (a) vamp 4, verse 1–4; (b) dance 1–4.

(a)
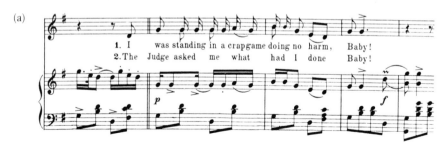

(b)

The preeminence of untied syncopation in early ragtime is evident from the following supporting statistics. Of the 200 early pieces surveyed, 59 percent use untied rhythms as the exclusive rag syncopation; only 17 percent use tied, or tied in conjunction with untied. The balance consists of pieces called rags that are totally unsyncopated or use only the augmented rhythm (19 percent), and those pieces that emphasize dotted rhythms (5 percent).

EXAMPLE V-10. Max Hoffmann, *Rag Medley* (New York: M. Witmark and Sons, 1897), measures 1–4.

## Ragtime Melodies

Ragtime melodies do not bear any distinctive traits except in regard to rhythm; if the syncopations were smoothed out the melodies would be indistinguishable from those of other dances of the time. One modern writer has endeavored to demonstrate the existence in "classic ragtime" (a term discussed in Chapter Ten) of traditional black musical characteristics in the form of pentatonic melodies,[5] but the thesis, relying on such arguments as a diatonic melody being a "filled-in" pentatonic structure, is unconvincing. Occasional suggestions of pentatonic melodies can be found in early (non-"classic") ragtime (see the first strain of Kerry Mills's *Whistling Rufus*, 1899), but there is no significant pentatonic presence in the melodies of either black or white composers. Of greater importance are the early rags which affect a folksy quality by opening in a minor key: 18 percent of the early rags fall into this category. (In comparison, for the years 1901–1904 the proportion of minor-key openings decreases to 4 percent, and thereafter minor keys remain unimportant in ragtime.) It must be concluded that in ragtime, aside from the rhythmic patterns, composers wrote within the safe, recognizable confines of conventional popular melody.

## Form

### BASIC DESIGN

The principle of form, one of the most consistent features of ragtime composition, was seldom, if ever, remarked upon by its contemporaries. No doubt this omission was because ragtime has no unique form, but inherits its design from earlier dance music, most notably the march. Following the formal principle established by the march, ragtime composition is almost invariably constructed according to an additive process in which several complete, independent 16-measure sections (each referred to as a "theme" or "strain") are joined without transitional connection. The number of themes may vary from two to ten, but rags composed of three or four themes are in the overwhelming majority, accounting for 89 percent (60 percent with three themes, 29 percent with four) of all the early rags surveyed. (These proportions change little in following years. Three-theme rags comprise 57 percent of the total in the entire period, and four-theme rags 35 percent.)

These 16-measure themes are arranged in various patterns, resulting in compositions with from three to ten distinct sections (excluding introductions, breaks or interludes, and immediate repeats). Thirty-one different patterns (ABAC, ABACD, ABACDA, and the like) have been noted. Despite this great variety, a few general types account for the majority (80 percent) of rags. The most frequently used pattern opens with two themes in the tonic key, forming two or three sections: A B, or A B A. This opening is

I I    I I I

followed by a "trio" consisting of one or two themes in the subdominant: C, or C D. Typical patterns for complete rags are

IV    IV IV

A B A C or A B C D; 30 percent of the early rags fit this pattern.

I I I IV    I I IV IV

A second, closely related type, comprising 20 percent of the sample, has a tonic da capo ending, either A, A B, or A B A; thus, for example, A B C D A B.

I I IV IV I I

A third type (15 percent of the total) is characterized by a transposed repeat. This group consists almost entirely of pieces in which the B theme is repeated, without the A theme, as part of the trio. A typical configuration is A B A C B.

I I I IV IV

A fourth important type (18 percent of the total) consists of rags with minor-key openings. Almost invariably the B theme is in the relative major; in almost two-thirds of the cases the trio (C) is also in this key, and in over one-third the trio is in the subdominant of the relative major.[6] Examples of patterns for minor keys are: A B A C A, A B C A.

i III i III i    i I IV i

III

The remaining rags (17 percent) include many that are one-of-a-kind, and they range from conventional structures with atypical tonal plans to unpatterned successions of up to ten different strains.

In almost all rags, whether they fit the four major categories or not, there is a system of immediate repeats, usually indicated by repeat bars. Including this consideration, common patterns are:

||:  A  :||:  B  :||  A  ||:  C  :||  C′  ||
    I        I     I    IV    IV

||:  A  :||:  B  :||  A  ||:  C  :||:  B  :||
    I        I     I    IV    IV

||:  A  :||:  B  :||:  C  :||  A  ||
    i    III    III    i

It is natural for those accustomed to the convention of tonic endings to question whether, in fact, da capo repeats of the opening tonic material are implied even when not explicitly stated. The evidence, however, makes it clear that nontonic endings were intended. In much of the sheet music, da capo repeats are specifically ruled out by the "Fine" designation. Early recordings and piano rolls also confirm the practice of nontonic endings. In this, as in other aspects of structure, the rag was simply following the patterns established in the contemporary march, in which subdominant endings are common.

## INTRODUCTIONS AND BREAKS

Introductions and breaks affect the larger concepts of ragtime structure. Introductions, almost always consisting of 4 measures, occur in 88 percent of the sample. Most frequently, they are thematically unrelated to the rest of the piece (64 percent); those related to one of the main themes are usually based upon either the opening phrase or the final phrase of the A theme. Slightly more than half of all the introductions have at least two measures of unharmonized, octave passages (see introductions in Examples V–6 and V–8a).

Breaks (called *interludes* by some writers) are linking passages which occasionally occur between strains.[7] Breaks appear in 47 percent of the early rags examined, with 43 percent of the breaks falling within the trio after the C theme. (Breaks preceding the C theme become prominent a little later, and are discussed in Chapter Seven.) While the pattern ". . . C-break-D" is not uncommon, ". . . C-break-C" is much more frequent. (The second C is often varied slightly by fuller chords or octave reinforcement.)

Breaks are usually recognized by their shorter or irregular lengths of 4, 8, 10 or 12 measures, but 16-measure breaks are also possible. A frequent characteristic of the shorter break is a prolonged dominant harmony, often with neighbor- and grace-note embellishments of the dominant tone against dominant and diminished chords (Example V–11). An extension of this "dominant break" is the "vi-V break," wherein the dominant prolongation is preceded by two, four, or more measures sustaining the submediant (Example V–12a-b). A further development has applied dominants preceding each harmonic area, with the dominant prolongation being longer than the submediant (Example V–12c-d). In both of these formats, the "vi-V break" is retained through the entire ragtime period, and beyond into later styles.

EXAMPLE V–11. "Dominant breaks." (a) Bernard Franklin, *Blackville Society* (Boston: G. W. Setchell, 1899); (b) James W. Casey, *Little Alligator Bait* (New York: M. Witmark and Sons, 1900); (c) K. Mills, *At a Georgia Campmeeting*; (d) A. Holzmann, *Bunch o' Blackberries* (New York: Leo Feist, 1899).

EXAMPLE V–12. "vi-V breaks." (a) E. E. Huston, *At an Alabama Corn Shuckin'* (Birmingham, Al.: Southern Music Co., 1900); (b) R. J. Hamilton, *Alabama Hoe Down* (New York: S. Brainard's Sons Co., 1899); (c) A. Pryor, *A Coon Band Contest*; (d) W. H. Tyers, *Barn Yard Shuffle* (New York: Jos. W. Stern and Co., 1899).

## THE 16-MEASURE STRAIN

Each of the main sections of a rag follows the same basic organization, and each is complete and independent. With some notable exceptions, the various themes of a piece are not related, and motivic resemblances (to whatever extent they exist) are usually insignificant and reflect overuse of some characteristic cliché rather than a conscious attempt at organic unity.

The internal structure of each strain is usually an even division into four 4-measure phrases, forming a symmetrical double period. These double periods are completely traditional, falling into a variety of evenly balanced, antecedent-consequent patterns, with the second phrase closing on a dominant semi-cadence, and the final phrase ending with a masculine, authentic—frequently perfect authentic—cadence. (Examples V–8a and V–13 at A′).

A major exception to the dominant semi-cadence of the second phrase occurs when the first phrase starts on a nontonic chord and is paralleled by the same opening in the third phrase. The most prevalent nontonic opening chord is the V4/3, which appears in at least one section in 30 percent of the rags surveyed (Examples V–14 and V–15a). As it is the B section which most often opens with the V4/3 chord, one might mistakenly conclude

EXAMPLE V-13. G. Blandford, *The Black Venus*, A 14–16, A' 1–16.

that the B strain is an organic continuation of the A, suggestive of the binary structure of a Baroque dance. But the lack of thematic connection—as well as the occasional use of this opening chord in other strains—mitigates against such an assumption.

In general, harmonic motion tends to be slow, with a single harmony frequently spanning two measures, and at times extending over a complete 4-measure phrase and even beyond (Example V-13 at A', measures 1–7). A notable exception to this slow harmonic motion is the final phrase, which is occasionally marked by increased harmonic activity, strongly directed progressions rich in applied dominants, and other contrasting chromaticisms (see measures 13–16 of Examples V-14 and V-15).

Measure 13, which opens the final phrase, is favored with special treatment. It is here that augmented sixth chords and flat-VI chords most frequently appear (Example V-16).[8] More common than these chromatic approaches is a device that produces an opposite, but still notable, effect: the sudden replacement of the prevailing harmonic texture with bare octaves (Examples V-6, V-8a, V-13.

These climactic final phrases do not occur in every rag, and they rarely occur more than once in a single rag; they are more than isolated phenomena, however, and the consistent choice of measure 13 for emphasis qualifies these events as characteristic features.

EXAMPLE V-14. Scott Joplin, *Maple Leaf Rag* (Sedalia, Mo.: John Stark and Son, 1899), B 1–16.

EXAMPLE V-15. (a) Fred S. Stone, *The Bos'n Rag* (Detroit: Whitney-Warner Publishing Co., 1899), B 1–16; (b) *Bos'n Rag*, A 13–16; (c) Ben Harney, *The Cake Walk in the Sky* (New York: M. Witmark, 1899), F 12–16.

(a)

(b)

(c)

EXAMPLE V-16. (a) A. Holzmann, *Smoky Mokes*, C 13–16; (b) Paul Cohn, *Honolulu Rag Time Patrol* (Chicago: Sol Bloom, 1899), D 12–16.

(a)

(b)

Because of the highly stereotyped nature of "early ragtime," it is possible to construct a generalized model of the typical early rag. This model is characterized primarily by two types of *ragtime syncopation:* (1) *untied syncopation,* which is restricted to each half of a measure, and (2) *tied syncopation,* which is tied across the center of a measure. Of the two, untied syncopation is far more common in early ragtime. Syncopation need not occur in each of the three or four 16-measure themes of a rag, but it typically appears at least in the first theme. Preceded by a 4-measure introduction, the first two themes (called A and B) are in the tonic key, and there may be a reprise of the first theme after the second (A B A). The third and, if there is one, the fourth themes are in the subdominant key. Should there be no fourth theme, the third may be repeated after a break of 4, 8, 10, 12, or 16 measures characterized by either a sustained dominant harmony (dominant break), or a dominant prolongation preceded by a submediant area (vi-V break). The main 16-measure themes are evenly divided into four-phrase double periods. The fourth phrase of a theme may be more prominent than the others due to some special harmonic treatment such as an increased harmonic rhythm, the use of an augmented sixth chord or some other chromatic harmony, or, in contrast, due to the complete absence of harmonic texture in favor of unsupported octaves.

By 1901 many of these conventions of piano ragtime were firmly established. Structural features (with a few exceptions, discussed in Chapters Six and Seven) remained fairly constant, deviating little from the proportions cited. The stylistic changes characterizing ragtime's later evolution were shifts in emphasis rather than radical departures, and were built upon the basic principles found in early ragtime.

## Notes

1. As this study now concentrates on piano music, the term "ragtime," unless specified to the contrary, is to be understood as meaning "piano ragtime composition."

2. R. M. Stults, "Something about the Popular Music of Today," *Etude* 18 (March 1900): 97.

3. Some literature refers to this rhythm as a "cakewalk figure," but as cakewalk music is frequently unsyncopated, this association will be avoided. See Winthrop Sargeant, *Jazz: Hot and Hybrid* (3rd ed., enl., New York: Da Capo Press, 1975), pp. 120, 131–32, 138; and *Die Musik in Geschichte und Gegenwart*, s.v. "Gesellschaftstanz," cols. 29–30.

4. Composer Aaron Copland has described this figure as a polyrhythm:

See Copland, "Jazz Structure and Influence on Modern Music," *Modern Music* 4 (January/February 1927): 10–11.

5. A. R. Danberg Charters, "Negro Folk Elements in Classic Ragtime," *Ethnomusicology* 5 (September 1961): 174–83.

6. The term "subdominant of the relative major" might appear to be an awkward designation of a key that could be described simply as VI. With the strong preference for subdominant trios, though, "IV of III" is more faithful to the conception of key relationships.

7. The term "break" should be understood here not in its jazz sense (a 2- to 4-measure solo against a concurrent suspension of explicit metric reinforcement), but according to the common usage of march-band musicians —an interlude between main thematic sections. Breaks that develop contrapuntally (cf. Example V–12d) are sometimes called "dogfights."

8. The term "flat VI chord" refers to the major triad built on the lowered sixth degree of a major scale. It functions like an augmented sixth chord in that it usually moves to a dominant chord.

# CHAPTER VI

# Musical Sources of Early Ragtime

Contemporary speculations about the origins of ragtime often treated the subject as if it were a completely new, unprecedented phenomenon; when sources were suggested, they were usually highly improbable, ranging from Hungarian folk-music to Beethoven. Ragtime, though, rather than appearing spontaneously, had precedents in published American music in the late 1880s and early 1890s. These publications may be of limited value in tracing the ultimate sources—some of which probably existed only in an unwritten tradition—but they do clarify the immediate musical lineage of ragtime. They are the real materials from which the style emerged.

## The March

As was already mentioned, the march is one of the major sources of ragtime composition. The most explicit connection is found in cover descriptions, titles, and subtitles (such as *Honolulu Rag Time Patrol. March and Two-Step; The Cake Walk in the Sky*, "March à la Ragtime," and the like), and tempo indications ("Tempo di Marcia") appearing on about 30 percent of the publications. Further confirmation of this relationship between the march and ragtime is found in testimony of contemporary witnesses. Eubie Blake and James P. Johnson have both referred to early ragtimers as "march kings,"[1] and Blake has related how "One-Leg" Willie Joseph would "bring the house down with *The Stars and Stripes Forever* in march time, ragtime, and 'sixteen' [boogie-woogie]."[2] Ragging marches, and in particular Sousa

marches, was apparently common. The poet Paul Laurence
Dunbar has already been quoted, and Louis Chauvin (1881–
1908), one of the Saint Louis ragtimers associated with Joplin, is
reported to have played Sousa regularly: "When he would sit
down he always played the same Sousa march to limber up his
fingers, but it was his own arrangement."[3]

Sousa, although not a composer of ragtime, was an advocate,
praising it and programming it at his concerts. (The Sousa Band
recorded many ragtime numbers, but without Sousa's participa-
tion.)[4] His name was also often attached to advertisements for
rags ("The latest Cake-Walk, as played by Sousa's Band," "As
played by John Philip Sousa," and so on),[5] publishers obviously
seeing an advantage in claiming association with him.

In terms of function, the march and the rag shared common
ground in providing music for the two-step, a dance with
sufficient flexibility to permit both syncopated and unsyncopated
accompaniment. In the quotation below Sousa uses the terms
"march" and "two-step" synonymously; in fact, his *Washington
Post March* (1889) is credited with having launched the two-step,
and for a while the dance was even referred to as the "Washington Two-Step."[6]

The most conclusive substantiation must be in the music itself, and in this respect the evidence is abundant. When early
rags are compared with marches of the same and immediately
preceding years, the parallels are so close that significant distinctions can be found in only two areas: meter and rhythm. Marches
were written in meters of C, ₵, 2/4, and 6/8; rags were written in
all of these except 6/8. The normal rhythm of marches excludes
the tied and untied syncopations of ragtime; if these syncopations
are used, the march becomes a rag.

In other respects, even in most details, each characteristic of
ragtime composition has its counterpart in the march. The conception of form and tonal design is identical, and an explanation
by Sousa of the nontonic ending to a march casts further light on
the acceptance of this convention in ragtime:

> In reply to your question, "Is it proper that a two-step ending in a
> trio should end in a key foreign to the one it begins in," permit me
> to say this:
> In the accepted form of compositions of march order it was al-
> ways customary to make the third part go to the subdominant, the
> most usual, and the dominant, the most unusual form. In my
> childhood in Washington I noticed that the bands parading with

the regiments in nearly every instance, although the composition called for a da capo, would finish playing on the last strain of the march; therefore, if it was done practically in the use of the march I could not understand why it should not be done theoretically in the writing of the march. Accordingly, in composing my marches I ignored the old established rule and wrote with the idea of making the last strain of the march the musical climax, regardless of the tonality.[7]

By the time rags were being published, subdominant endings were an accepted part of the musical language both in performance practice and in composition.

March introductions are frequently of 8 measures rather than the 4 measures of rags. In other respects, though, the introductions are similar, including extensive use of unharmonized octaves (Example VI-1).

Breaks, also a regular feature of marches, frequently occur within the trio between repeats of the C strain, and fall into the "dominant" and "vi-V" categories (Example VI-2).

As with the rag, the normal march theme is 16 measures long forming a 4-phrase double period. Sousa wrote a number of A

EXAMPLE VI-1. (a) John Philip Sousa, *Semper Fidelis* (New York: Carl Fischer, 1888), Introduction and A 1-2; (b) George Rosey, *The Chinatown March* (New York: Jos. W. Stern and Co., 1896), Introduction.

EXAMPLE VI-2. (a) "Dominant break." J. P. Sousa, *The Washington Post* (Philadelphia: Harry Coleman, 1889); (b) "vi-V break." J. P. Sousa, *The Stars and Stripes Forever* (Cincinnati: John Church Co., 1897).

C'

con't.

EXAMPLE VI-3. (a) Harry C. Smith, *Admiral Dewey's March* (Boston: Oliver Ditson Co., 1898), A 15–16, B 1–4; (b) J. P. Sousa, *The Washington Post*, B 13–16; (c) J. P. Sousa, *The High School Cadets* (Philadelphia: Harry P. Coleman, 1890), B 13–16; (d) J. P. Sousa, *Semper Fidelis*, A 13–16.

(a)

(b)

(c)

(d)

themes that modulate and end in the dominant key (the B theme being back in the tonic), but this practice of modulation was not especially prevalent among other march composers. Other details, such as the V4/3 opening (Examples VI–1a and VI–3a), the appearance at measure 13 of flat VI or augmented sixth chords (Example VI–3b-c), and unharmonized octaves (Example VI–3d) are as prominent in marches as in rags.

It is clear that all of the structural and harmonic practices of ragtime stem from the march. The rhythmic character of the rag, too, except for the one defining factor of syncopation, has its precedents in the march.

## The Cakewalk

The cakewalk, a grand-promenade type of dance of plantation origins in which the slave couple performing the most attractive steps and motions would "take the cake," enjoyed a dramatic revival shortly before the establishment of ragtime.[8] Spurred by exhibitions and contests in the early 1890s, interest in the cakewalk eventually brought this plantation dance to the ballrooms of the United States and Europe, where it retained a following into the first decade of the twentieth century.[9] The basic music for the cakewalk was the march. One might like to think that the marches were syncopated in performance, but evidence on this point is slight. On at least one occasion—at an early cakewalk jubilee held at Madison Square Garden—the music was provided by a white band (led by a black conductor). An unsympathetic report describes the cakewalk as "a series of dreary marches" and the music as "wretched"; there is no indication that the music was syncopated.[10]

The growing popularity of this dance naturally led to the publication of music written specifically as cakewalk marches (Plate VI–1). Musically these pieces are distinguished from other marches of the period by several ethnic-identifying conventions: opening strains are frequently in a minor mode (Example VI–4a); strain B or C may be slightly syncopated with the augmented syncopation figure (Example VI–4b); and the final strain may include, or be replaced by, a coon-song chorus. All three of these traits are found in varying degrees in early ragtime, but were short-lived and died out in the early twentieth century as ragtime lost its ethnic flavor.

Once ragtime and the term identifying it gained currency, the distinction between cakewalk and rag was by no means clear.

PLATE VI-1. A cakewalk march from 1896.

EXAMPLE VI-4. Jacob Henry Ellis, *Remus Takes the Cake* (New York: (Willis Woodward & Co., 1896): (a) A 1–4; (b) B 1–4.

As Stults's reference to Mills's cakewalks as "ragtime hits" indicates, for contemporaries there was no real differentiation between the two. Indeed, as cakewalks adopted the smaller rhythmic divisions of ragtime syncopation, syncopated cakewalks, syncopated two-steps, and ragtime became one and the same. Certainly the titles, subtitles, and cover descriptions say as much—*Cake Walk in the Sky. Ethiopian Two-Step*, "March à la Ragtime"; *The Bos'n Rag. Cake Walk*, "A Rag Two Step with Catchy Singing Chorus"; *Southern Hospitality. Rag-time Cake-Walk*—as does the music.

## Black Character Pieces and Patrols

As detractors of ragtime were wont to point out, the rhythmic configurations constituting ragtime syncopation were not new; such rhythms had long been part of the language of Western music. What was significant, though, was that these rhythms were used with sufficient consistency to define the ragtime idiom, and that the intent of such rhythms, an intent made abundantly clear from the sheet-music covers and titles, was to reproduce the character of "quaint" black music.

The reasons for the black identification of these rhythms can be found in earlier Afro-American music and in minstrelsy, as described in various modern publications.[11] As the ragtime era approached, the identifying rhythmic conventions were well established and could be found in "character pieces" depicting blacks, or, by extension, the South. As composer R. Nathaniel Dett specifically noted: "The rhythmic figure,

. . . is of most frequent occurrence in the music of the ante-bellum [black] folk-dances, and its marked individuality has caused it to be much misused for purposes of caricature."[12]

A most pertinent caricature, important because of ragtime's links with the march, was in the minstrel patrol. (A "patrol" is a march with a crescendo-decrescendo dynamic contour.) From the time of the Civil War, when blacks enlisted in the Union army, comic portrayals of supposedly inept black soldiers were a staple of the minstrel stage.[13] By the 1880s (if not earlier) the music for these skits sometimes assumed a Negro character by being syncopated. *Patrol Comique* (1886), which has a cover drawing of banjo-playing and dancing, uniformed blacks (Plate VI–2), and *The Hottentots: Patrol Characteristic* (1889) are typi-cal. Both make occasional use of untied syncopation and other ethnic-suggesting features such as pentatonic and minor modes (Example VI–5). As syncopated marches, these pieces already contain the most important traits of ragtime.

EXAMPLE VI-5. (a) Thomas Hindley, *Patrol Comique* (New York: New-York Publishing Co., 1886), A 13–18, B 1–4; (b) Fred Neddermeyer, *The Hottentots. Patrol Characteristic* (New York: J. Schott, 1889), A 2–4.

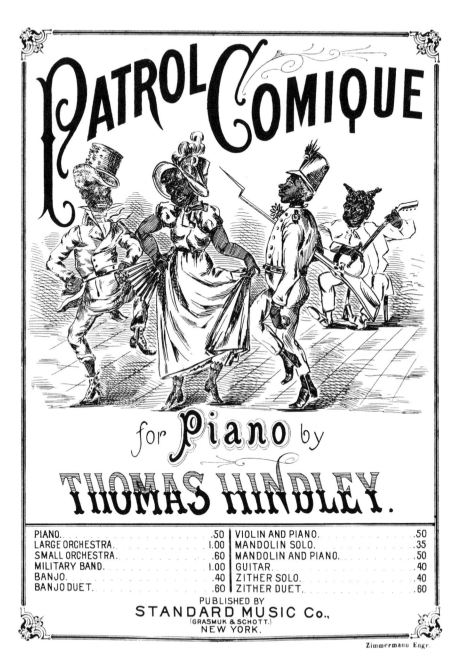

PLATE VI-2. Cover for a "black" patrol.

These developments were not unique to the patrol. *The Darkie's Dream* (1891), a "parlor" piece, has untied syncopations along with dotted rhythms (Example VI–6), and *Aunt Dinah's Wedding Dance. An Ethiopian Melange* (1895) exhibits several ragtime traits. The latter is constructed from a succession of seven 8-measure dance themes (and one vocal chorus), supposedly representing dances typically found at Negro weddings.

EXAMPLE VI-6. G. L. Lansing, *The Darkie's Dream* (New York: Hitchcock and McCargo Publishing Co., 1891), B 1–4.

Some of the dances bear labels: "Break down," "Wing dance," and "Cake walk." Musically, most sections are indistinguishable from a march, the exceptions being the two "Break down" strains; the first features untied syncopations, while the second uses the occasional ragtime figuration of "stop time" (Example VI–7a-b). The break (Example VI–7c), with its octave and grace-note embellishments of the dominant tone against dominant and di-

EXAMPLE VI-7. Dan Emerson, *Aunt Dinah's Wedding Dance* (New York: T. B. Harms, 1895); (a) C 1–6; (b) H 1–4; (c) break.

minished harmonies, has direct parallels with the "dominant breaks" of ragtime.

After the advent of ragtime, the continued existence of the black character piece was brief. Unavoidably, it resembled ragtime, but in vying for the more respectable parlor side of the popular-music market the disreputable label of "ragtime" was avoided.

In two pieces typical of this genre, *An African Reverie* (1900) and *African Dreamland. Intermezzo* (1903), the racial evocation, the syncopated treble rhythm against the metrically regular bass, and the basic phraseology are suggestive of ragtime (Example VI-8). Equally noteworthy, though, are the obvious genteel pre-

EXAMPLE VI-8. (a) H. B. Newton, *An African Reverie* (New York: F. A. Mills, 1900), A 1–10; (b) George Atwater, *African Dreamland* (New Haven, Cn.: Chas H. Loomis, 1903), A 8–18.

tensions. Each piece is prefaced with a poetic quotation: "'Play, music, then.' Shakespeare" (*African Reverie*); "Music, which gentler on the spirit lies/Than tired eyelids on the tired eyes" (*African Dreamland*). The titles, too, seek to associate with the relatively respectable position of the black African rather than with the lowly status of the black American. As an additional gesture toward refined musical culture, *African Dreamland* makes extensive use of precious expressive indications: *zeffiroso, ben cantando, dolce, risoluto, furioso*. Musically, too, there are reflections of the parlor tradition rather than that of ragtime. In *African Reverie* the romantic feminine cadence at measure 4 is uncharacteristic of ragtime, as is the fussiness of the rhythmic distinctions between untied syncopation and triplets in measures 5–7. In *African Dreamland* the pauses in the rhythmic momentum at measures 15–17 are more suggestive of the refined drawing-room than the ragtime dance-floor. Unable to avoid the pervasive influence of ragtime completely, music of this kind assumed an air of dignity by grafting some gestures of gentility onto the structure of the "less cultured" popular idiom.

## Coon Songs

While many coon-songs are unsyncopated, the genre as a whole—as was shown in the first three chapters—was perceived as one of the major manifestations of ragtime. Some notable coon-songs are the first publications to carry the label "ragtime." At the same time, they made the link with syncopations explicit (Examples IV–1a-c, V–9).

In its later phase the coon song became a contemporary of piano ragtime, and while each developed along individual lines, the two genres often merged. This intermixing is evident in the multiple publications of pieces in song and instrumental arrangements, the piano versions often being available in both ragtime and schottische styles. This is true for such prominent songs as Howard and Emerson's *Hello! Ma Baby*, Harney's *Cake Walk in the Sky*, and Hogan's *All Coons Look Alike to Me* (Plates VI–3, 4, 5). Similarly, the merger is complemented by coon songs which have dance sections (such as *You've Been a Good Old Wagon*: Example V–9b) and instrumental pieces that include coon-song choruses. Finally, the ragtime medleys, such as those by Max Hoffmann, piano arrangements of the year's coon-song hits, also reflect the kinship of the two genres.

PLATE VI-3. A cover listing editions available in different styles and mediums.

PLATE VI-4. The addition of a "march à la ragtime" banner across the top adapted this coon-song cover for an instrumental edition.

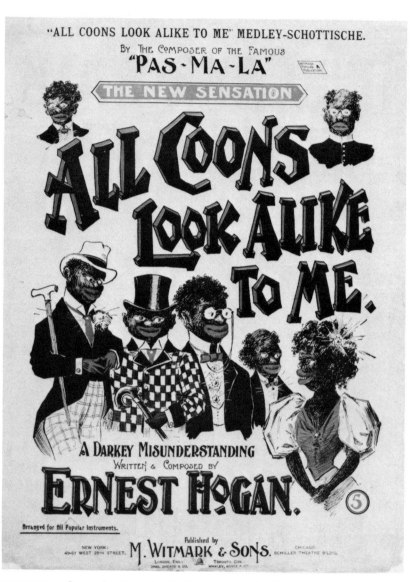

PLATE VI-5. Cover for the schottische version of a famous coon song.

## Caribbean Dance Rhythms

Another possible source of ragtime rhythm is dance music of the Caribbean or South America, from pieces variously referred to as danzas, habaneras, and tangos. Characterized by bass figurations of either ♫ ♫ or ♪. ♫ ♫, the treble melodic rhythms are often identical to untied and tied rag syncopations.

In the danza context these rhythms predate written ragtime, a notable use being by mid-nineteenth century composer Louis Moreau Gottschalk (Example VI–9). It is inviting to speculate that Gottschalk was invoking the sounds of the slave-inhabited plantations of his native Louisiana, that he was influenced by an embryonic ragtime of black origins. His specific references, though, fail to support this idea; these syncopations appear most frequently in his characterizations of the Caribbean rather than the southern United States. Racially, too, the music fails to match the ragtime hypothesis. His *Souvenir de Porto Rico*, for example, is subtitled *Marche des gibaros*, referring to the white peasantry of that island. Gottschalk's danza pieces are apparently derived from a nonnotated folk music, but it does not seem likely that this music is the direct ancestor of ragtime.

EXAMPLE VI-9. Louis Moreau Gottschalk, *Souvenir de Porto Rico* (1857), measures 173–177.

Yet during the ragtime era no less a figure than Ben Harney declared ragtime's debt to Latin American music: "RAG TIME (or Negro Dance time) originally takes its initiative steps from Spanish music, or rather from Mexico, where it is known under the head and names of Habanara, Danza, Seguidilla."[14] While Harney's opinion found much support, especially among those more willing to grant an innovative role to Spanish culture than to Afro-American, others such as Rupert Hughes and John Burk specifically denied that there were significant musical resemblances between Spanish music and ragtime, despite notational similarities (see page 47 above).

The danza rhythms do appear in later instructional writings on ragtime (perhaps reflecting a performance practice),[15] but their use in published piano rags is infrequent except for an occasional one or two measures (Example VI–10). The more extensive appearance of these rhythms in the Joplin-Chauvin *Heliotrope Bouquet* (1907) and Artie Matthews' *Pastime Rags* Numbers 3 and 5 (1916 and 1918) are clearly exceptions not representative of ragtime publications in general (Example VI–11).

EXAMPLE VI-10. Henri Klickman, *Smiles and Chuckles* (Chicago: Frank K. Root, 1917), A 12–16.

EXAMPLE VI-11. (a) Scott Joplin and Louis Chauvin, *Heliotrope Bouquet. A Slow Drag Two Step* (New York: Stark Music Co., 1907), A 1–4; (b) Artie Matthews, *Pastime Rag No. 5* (St. Louis, Mo.: Stark Music Co., 1918), A 3–6.

Actually, composers working in both styles seem to have permitted ragtime to influence their Caribbean dance compositions, rather than vice versa. Latin American dances are almost invariably presented within the structural and harmonic framework of the two-step (Example VI–12) and at times are indistinguishable, except in name, from rags or other non-Latin dances. *The Tango: Two-Step* by Joe Jordan, an accomplished and knowledgeable musician, is not unusual in the way it bridges both styles. The music, reflecting the title's vacillation, includes sections in both tango and rag styles (Example VI–13). Other pieces exploited the tango fad of the 1910s by using the word in a title, but without providing the musical characteristics of the dance. E. Lorenz Barber's *My Tango Queen (Tango—One Step—Two Step or Trot)*, for instance, while also trading upon the many earlier "ragtime queen" titles, claims to fit almost every dance category, but fails to fulfill its main title designation (Example VI–14).

Thus, ragtime and Latin American dance music do touch upon one another and have brief moments of convergence and blending, but the two seem to be distinct strains with essentially separate developments.

EXAMPLE VI–12. Neil Moret [Charles N. Daniels], *Cubanola (Cuban Danza)* (St. Louis, Mo.: Daniels, Russell and Boone, 1902),* C 1–5.

*This piece was subsequently reissued under a different name by the Whitney-Warner Publishing Co., Detroit. As the latter firm had already published a piece with a similar title—H. B. Blanke's *Cubanola (A Spanish Serenade)*—Daniel's work was retitled *Dolores*.

EXAMPLE VI–13. Joe Jordan, *Tango: Two-Step* (Chicago: Will Rossiter, 1913): (a) C 5–8; (b) B 1–5.

(a)

(b)

Copyright © Estate of Joe Jordan. Used by permission.

EXAMPLE VI-14. E. Lorenz Barber, *My Tango Queen* (New York: John T. Hall Publishing Co., 1914), A 1–8.

## Other Source Attributions

Other music proposed as sources for ragtime are such contemporary dances as cotillions (or cotillons), quadrilles, polkas, and schottisches. Most often these attributions are made in a general way, without any effort to illustrate the supposed derivations. In one rare instance in which there is an attempt to trace the influence of these dances on rags, the procedure is defective.[16]

It is true that all of these dances share with the rag a common sectional format, an additive structure joining complete musical units. But as these dances do not, in this respect, add to the rag anything that was not obtained from the more direct source of the march, any indebtedness must be regarded as slight.

It is possible that certain melodies were transferred from one dance to another, especially in the improvised ragging of an existing piece. Jelly Roll Morton has claimed to have evolved *Tiger Rag* from a quadrille,[17] and James P. Johnson has referred to similar ragtime transformations during the first decade of the twentieth century: "Most East Coast [ragtime] playing was based on cotillion dance tunes, stomps, drags and set dances."[18] But even if a rag should be based on a borrowed cotillion melody, this is a shallow reason to attribute "influence"—one might just as well cite Mendelssohn as a ragtime influence by way of his *Spring Song*.

Examination of other aspects of the cotillion—or of the similar quadrille—reveals even less justification for considering it, as a genre, a significant source of ragtime. Both the cotillion and quadrille are sets of dances in five musical sections. Each section, in either a 2/4 or 6/8 meter, is built from smaller segments of 8 measures, the total number of measures being designed to match prescribed dance steps. The rhythms have no distinguishing characteristics other than a march-like evenness. (There are also hybrids with more pronounced rhythmic traits, such as waltz, polka, and redowa quadrilles.) Usually, each section is in a different key, but there is no consistent tonal design paralleling the tonic-subdominant relationship of the march and the rag. The melodies may be original, but are often borrowed from various popular, folk, or operatic sources. Under these circumstances, it is difficult to justify naming either of these dances as an important source for ragtime.[19]

The claims proposing the polka as a source for ragtime are equally without basis. It is true that in the 1890s the polka was occasionally listed on two-step dance music, along with other dances: *Impecunious Davis. Characteristic Two-Step March, Polka, & Cake-Walk* (1899); *Happy Mose. Cake Walk, Two Step or Polka* (1899); *At a Georgia Campmeeting*, "A Characteristic March which can be used effectively as a Two-Step, Polka or Cake Walk" (1897); *Ash-Cake Shuffle. A Characteristic March and Two Step*, "Can also be used as a Polka or Rag-Time Cake Walk" (1899). But this inclusion of the polka simply reflects the apparent loss or disregard of earlier rhythmic conventions associated with the polka, such as figurations of fast triplets and pairs of sixteenth notes followed by an eighth note. As the rag did not draw upon these traditional polka rhythms it would seem that the rag had a greater effect on the contemporary polka than the other way around.

Finally, a consideration of the schottische also fails to reveal any derivative relationship with ragtime. As schottische versions of coon songs were sometimes offered as alternatives to ragtime versions (see Plates VI–3 and VI–5), one might mistakenly assume that the two dances are related, but it is the differences between the schottische and the rag that made dual publication practical. Schottisches, unlike rags, are characterized by dotted rhythms, and it is therefore the dotted sections of coon songs that are featured in schottische editions (Example VI–15).

EXAMPLE VI–15. (a) Representative schottische. J. A. Hardy, *Banjo. Schottische Characteristic* (New York: Howley, Haviland and Co., 1896), A 1–3; (b) and (c) Schottisches based on coon songs: E. Hogan, *All Coons Look Alike to Me. Schottische*, arranged by F. W. Meacham (New York: M. Witmark and Sons, 1897), A 1–3; J. Howard and I. Emerson, *Hello! Ma Baby*, arranged by Max Dreyfus (New York: T. B. Harms and Co., 1899), A 1–3.

One suspects that theories attributing significant influence to the dances discussed above have been developed on insufficient data, perhaps on nothing more than an offhand remark by a ragtimer. There has been no adequate demonstration of a derivative role, and the evidence examined suggests that none exists.

### Notes

1. Rudi Blesh, "Scott Joplin: Black-American Classicist," Introduction to *The Collected Works of Scott Joplin*, ed. Vera Brodsky Lawrence (New York: New York Public Library, 1971), p. xvi; Tom Davin, "Conversations with James P. Johnson" [Part II], *Jazz Review* 2 (July 1959): 12.

2. Blesh, "Scott Joplin," p. xvi. Blake, keeping the tradition alive today, still "brings the house down" with his own version of this Sousa march.

3. Rudi Blesh and Harriet Janis, *They All Played Ragtime* (4th ed., rev., New York: Oak Publications, 1971), p. 57.

4. James R. Smart. *The Sousa Band: A Discography* (Washington, D.C.: Library of Congress, 1970), pp. 2–3.

5. Respectively: advertisement for *Honey in the Cornfield*, appearing on p. 3 of G. M. Blandford, *Black Venus* (1899); cover banner for John Rastus Topp, *The Shuffling Coon* (1897).

6. "Decadence of the Waltz: Sousa's Marches Held Responsible by Dancing Masters for the Reign of the Two-Step," *New York Times*, 10 September 1899, p. 16; Paul E. Bierly, *John Philip Sousa: American Phenomenon* (New York: Appleton-Century-Crofts, 1973), pp. 7, 48.

7. John Philip Sousa, "A Letter from Sousa," *Etude* 16 (August 1898): 231. Twenty years later Sousa was still referring to this topic, but had developed a more whimsical presentation: "The old method ended the march in the tonality of the original key. . . . Speaking gastronomically, when they got to the ice cream, they went back to the roast beef. And the beef had no new sauce on it, no new flavor" (*Boston Post*, 10 March 1918, as quoted in Bierly, *John Philip Sousa*, p. 124).

8. For background on the cakewalk, see: Marshall Stearns and Jean Stearns, *Jazz Dance* (New York: Macmillan, 1968), pp. 22–23, 117–24; Blesh and Janis, *They All Played Ragtime*, pp. 96–100; and Tom Fletcher, *The Tom Fletcher Story: 100 Years of the Negro in Show Business* (New York: Burdge and Co., 1954), pp. 103–116. According to Fletcher, the cakewalk was also known as the "chalkline-walk" and the "walk-around" (p. 103).

9. Some brief items in the *New York Times* present a sketchy but nonetheless revealing running chronology of contemporary reactions to the growing popularity of this dance: "The Cake Walk," 28 February 1892, p. 4; "The Cake Walk a 'Fake' Walk," 28 February 1892, p. 5; "Theatrical Gossip," 26 April 1892, p. 8; "An Old-Time Cake Walk," 2 March 1895, p. 6; "The Farrells Took the Cake," 3 March 1895, p. 5; "Fun at the Cake Walk," 4 May 1895, p. 6; "'Black America' at the Garden," 17 September 1895, p. 10; "Walking for the Cake," 7 February 1897, p. 2; "Cake Walk Broken Up," 13 February 1898, p. 2; "Cakewalk Trust the Latest," 26 November 1900, p. 3; "The Cake Walk in Vienna," 1 February 1903, p. 5. For a sample of the German dismay over the continental acceptance of this dance, see "Der Cake Walk," *Illustrierte Zeitung* (Leipzig) (5 February 1903): 202–203.

10. "The Cake Walk a 'Fake' Walk."

11. Eileen Southern, *The Music of Black Americans: A History* (New York: W. W. Norton, 1971), pp. 185, 206–208, 313–14; Gilbert Chase, *America's Music from the Pilgrims to the Present* (2d ed., rev., New York: McGraw-Hill, 1966), pp. 255–57, 307–311, 429–36; H. Wiley Hitchcock, *Music in the United States: A Historical Introduction* (2d ed., Englewood Cliffs, N.J.: Prentice-Hall, 1974), pp. 107–108, 119–22; Hans Nathan, *Dan Emmett and the Rise of Early Negro Minstrelsy* (Norman, Okla.: University of Oklahoma Press, 1962), pp. 189–213.

12. R. Nathaniel Dett, Introduction to *In the Bottoms: Characteristic Suite* (Chicago: Clayton F. Summy, 1913).

13. Robert C. Toll, *Blacking Up* (New York: Oxford University Press, 1974), pp. 120–24, 263.

14. "Preface," *Ben Harney's Rag Time Instructor* (Chicago: Sol Bloom, 1897).

15. Edward R. Winn, *How To Play Ragtime (Uneven Rhythm)*, (n.p., 1915), p. 25; Winn, "Ragtime Piano Playing: A Practical Course of Instruction for Pianists," *Melody* 2 (April 1918): 23; Scott Joplin, *School of Ragtime* (New York: Scott Joplin, 1908), Exercises, 2, 3, and 6.

16. William J. Schafer and Johannes Riedel, *The Art of Ragtime: Form and Meaning of an Original Black American Art* (Baton Rouge, La.: Louisiana State University Press, 1973), pp. 63–64, 87. For a specific criticism of the authors' efforts in this

regard, see the present writer's review in *Black Perspective in Music* 3 (Spring 1975): 105–107.

17. The claim was made on Morton's Library of Congress recordings (1938); see Blesh and Janis, *They All Played Ragtime*, p. 176. Morton's veracity in this regard has been disputed; see Ian Whitcomb, "Shelton Brooks Is Alive & Strutting," *Jazz Report* 7, no. 2 [ca. 1970]: no pagination.

18. Davin, "Conversations with James P. Johnson" [Part II], p. 17.

19. In addition, the term "cotillion" was used simply to designate a formal ball.

CHAPTER VII

# A Cohesive Style Develops

M any of the conventions established during the early years of ragtime remained virtually unchanged as the style matured. There were, though, some important shifts in emphasis and new elements that affected the character of the music, kept it viable and growing, and prevented its immediate waning as the prophesied "passing fad." The present chapter examines the elements that were most characteristic of ragtime during the first two decades of the twentieth century.

## Loss of Ethnic Identity

Public acceptance of ragtime, as shown by the enormous increase in commercial publications in 1899, was coupled with the gradual absorption of its name and style into the mainstream of American popular music. Ragtime as an exoticism, as a quaint music from the fringes of society, was replaced by ragtime the white American popular music. Through 1902 the vast majority of rag publications still made obvious reference to the music's black origins, usually by the title or cover picture (Plates VII–1 and VII–2), and sometimes with the inclusion of a coon-song chorus. In 1903 there was a substantial reduction in the percentage of ethnic depictions, to about 50 percent, and by 1904 reference to blackness in ragtime appeared in only a minority of publications, about 20 percent, the proportions growing smaller in the following years (Plates VII–3 and VII–4). Probably as a result of the same trend, there was a sharp decrease in modal, "folksy," minor-key openings, falling from a proportion of 18 percent in the period from 1897 to 1901 to less than 5 percent in any year after 1904.

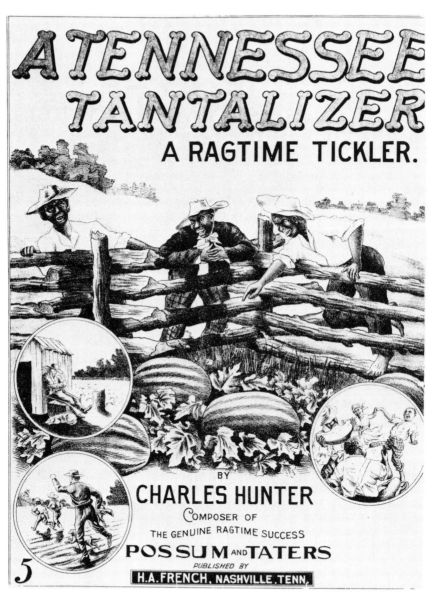

PLATE VII-1. A cover from 1900 depicting various racial stereotypes, such as thievery, dancing, and a love for watermelon.

PLATE VII-2. The cakewalking "belle," as pictured on this 1903 cover, was soon to be displaced as the typical representative of ragtime.

PLATE VII-3. The new image of ragtime: 1905.

PLATE VII-4. Ragtime reaches the salon: cover from 1912.

Paralleling the decrease in black references in titles and cover depictions was the fading popularity of the cakewalk, the plantation-derived dance with obvious racial implications. Although one-third of the early rags made some reference to cakewalks, either in the title or subtitle, use of this term greatly decreased by 1903 and was practically nonexistent, except as a conscious anachronism, after 1904.

## Rhythmic Changes

The concept of ragtime rhythm underwent a marked shift in the first decade of the twentieth century, and the distinction between early and later stages of ragtime history is based largely on this shift. The main alteration was the sudden decrease in the use of untied syncopation as compared with tied syncopation. Whereas through 1900 59 percent of the rags used untied syncopation as the exclusive type of ragtime syncopation and only 17 percent were based on tied syncopation, the proportions shifted dramatically in the first decade of the twentieth century. The ratio between untied- and tied-syncopation rags in 1900 is about 3:1; the following year the proportion shifted to 1:2 in favor of tied-syncopation rags. A sampling of the next few years reveals the irreversible trend away from untied syncopation: in 1902, 1:3; in 1905, 1:7; in 1908, 1:20. After 1906 untied syncopation was rarely used as the exclusive type, and although it was retained to some degree in the majority of rags, it often appeared in only three or four measures.

An important trait strongly, but not exclusively, linked with tied syncopation is the textural emphasis of a syncopation, an increased density that highlights the agogic accents of a figuration.[1] The untied syncopation most often has an undifferentiated texture (such as all single notes), while tied syncopation tends to feature a more complex mixture of simultaneous intervallic densities, with the heavier—and thereby louder—sonorities underlining the syncopated effect. Example VII–1a-c illustrates the distinctions, the final excerpt presenting both approaches.

It must be emphasized that this trait is a tendency, not an ironclad rule; tied syncopation did occur in single-note textures (Example VII–2a), and mixed textures could be used effectively with untied syncopation (Example VII–2b). The heavier density was also used to support a nonagogic, tonic (pitch) accent on a weak beat, thereby giving it a syncopated effect (Example VII–3).

EXAMPLE VII-1. (a) Nellie Brooks Ransom, *The Climax* (Toledo, Oh.: McCormick Music Co., 1900), A 5–8; (b) Harry C. Thompson, *A Black Bawl* (Chicago: W. C. Polla and Co., 1905), A 1–7; (c) Charles Hunter, *Why We Smile* (Nashville: Frank G. Fite, 1903), A 5–7.

(a) Undifferentiated texture—all single notes

(b) Intervallic support of tied syncopations

(c)

As a general rule, though, textural emphasis accompanied tied syncopation, and as this rhythm attained favor in the first decade of the century, a corresponding and most significant development in textural variety took place, a development that affected the entire flavor of ragtime. (More will be said later on the subject of textural variety.)

EXAMPLE VII-2. (a) Floyd Willis, *The Queen Rag* (Cincinnati: Joseph Krolage Music Co., 1911), A 1–3; (b) Arthur Marshall, *The Pippin* (New York: Stark Music Co., 1908), C 9–12.

EXAMPLE VII-3. Percy Wenrich, *The Smiler* (Chicago: Arnett-Delonais Co., 1907), A 1–2.

Equally striking in its conclusiveness was the reduced use of the augmented syncopation figure. Through 1899 this figure dominated at least one strain of almost every rag published. In 1900 its use was drastically diminished; it appeared in only about one-third of the pieces, and rarely in more than a single section of a work. After 1903 its use as the dominating rhythm of a section of a rag became relatively rare.

## Secondary Ragtime

Along with the reversed emphasis in established rhythms came the prominence of a new rhythm, labeled by a writer in 1925 as "secondary ragtime":

A Negro guitar-player once asked me, "You know the difference between primary rag and secondary rag?"

His primary rag was syncopation; his secondary rag was the

superimposition of *one*, two, three upon the basic one, two, three, four.

Graphically it may be expressed thus:

Winthrop Sargeant further described this rhythm as

the superimposition of a rhythm of different phrase-lengths, but of identical units, upon the prevailing rhythm of the music. Usually the superimposed rhythm falls into phrases of three eighth-note units which are set against a background of the normal four-quarter rhythm of jazz.

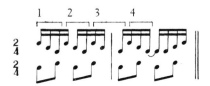

It can be noted that this rhythmic pattern usually repeats the same three notes in either an ascending or a descending line, and that the pattern is most often produced four times (Example VII–4). This is not syncopation, for there is no displacement of the normal metric accents. Within the repeating three-note motif, however, the accent continually shifts; when the motif is presented four times, each presentation is in a new metric context:

If, for example, we consider the changing context of the first note of each three-note group, it will be observed that it occurs: (1) on the primary strong beat; (2) before the secondary strong beat; (3) on a weak beat; (4) before a weak beat. Should the pattern be heard a fifth time, as in Northup's *Cannon Ball* (Example VII–5), the first note on the secondary strong beat (measure 6, second beat) is strongly reminiscent of the opening of the pattern, which probably accounts for the preference for shorter groupings.

The ragtime composer's attraction to the secondary rag idea is apparent in the frequency of its use and the number of variant forms in which it was cast. The three-note grouping, for example, could be extended beyond three pitches without losing the

EXAMPLE VII-4. George Botsford, *Black and White Rag* (Detroit: Whitney-Warner Publishing Co., 1908), A 1–4.

EXAMPLE VII-5. Joseph Northup, *The Cannon Ball* (Chicago: Harold Rossiter Co., 1905), A 5–6.

polyrhythmic effect (Example VII–6a), or the secondary rag pattern could be presented without accompaniment, the normal pulse being sufficiently strong to stand temporarily without explicit bass reinforcement (Example VII–6b-c).

One important variant reduces the three-note group to two notes while retaining the three-unit rhythmic pattern:

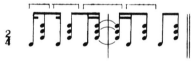

As in Example VII–7 (measures 5–8), the characteristic of a repeating group of three rhythmic units—here, sixteenths—is retained, creating the same essential effect as the main form of secondary ragtime.

Invariably in this type of formation, harmonic sonorities alternate with single notes. Occasionally, as in Example VII–8a, the harmonic effect is enhanced by juxtaposing an "inverted pedal" (the repeated notes in the top voice) against a moving inner voice. It is also possible, although less frequent, to have some melodic motion in both outer and inner parts (Example VII–8b).

EXAMPLE VII-6. (a) George Botsford, *Black and White Rag*, B 1–3; (b) 12–16; (c) Paul Pratt, *Hot House Rag* (St. Louis, Mo.: John Stark and Son, 1914), A 1–2.

(a)

(b)

(c)

EXAMPLE VII-7. C. Hunter, *Why We Smile*, B 1–8.

EXAMPLE VII-8. (a) S. Joplin, *Gladiolus Rag* (New York: Jos. W. Stern and Co., 1907), D 1–4. (b) S. Joplin, *Pine Apple Rag* (New York: Seminary Music Co., 1908), B 3–6.

(a)

(b)

Sargeant suggests that secondary rag began with Northup's *Cannon Ball* in 1905 (see Example VII–5) and gained popularity in the years immediately following.[4] The latter contention is supported by our findings; the procedure seems to have been rare until 1907, at which time it began to appear in about one piece out of six. But secondary ragtime was known prior to 1905, the date of origin designated by Sargeant. In its three-note form it is found in Charles Mullen's *Levee Rag* (1902), and in the two-note form it appears in Joplin's *Original Rags* (1899) (Example VII–9).[5] Once introduced, the secondary ragtime figure extended through the entire period under investigation and beyond, becoming an important element of the "novelty piano" style of the 1920s.

## Form

The shift in rhythmic impulses is the most definitive change distinguishing the second phase of piano ragtime. Alterations in other areas are less immediate and striking, although they still have an effect on the style.

The conception of outer form, the arrangement of three or four 16-measure themes in tonic-subdominant relationship—with

EXAMPLE VII-9. (a) Charles E. Mullen, *Levee Rag* (Chicago: Will Rossiter, 1902), B 1–8; (b) S. Joplin, *Original Rags*, arranged by Charles N. Daniels (Kansas City, Mo.: Carl Hoffman, 1899), E 1–4.

three-theme rags having a greater frequency than those with four themes—remained essentially as it had been established in the earlier years. The only structural change of any significance was the increased use of a break before the trio (such as A B break C). Up to 1901, almost all breaks occurred within the trio (such as A B C break C); after that date the number of trio-introducing breaks—and they are, in fact, introductions[6]—increased gradually. By 1906 the practice stabilized; thereafter, trio-introducing breaks occur in about 21 percent of the rags, approximately equaling the number of inner-trio breaks. Unlike the latter, though, introductory breaks generally do not exceed four measures in length, and do not present the vi-V harmonic design; instead, they follow the patterns set by the regular introductions. In addition, while they fall between strains in different keys—tonic and subdominant—they usually are not modulatory, but simply begin in the latter key.

### Unifying Relationships

The relationship between themes within a piece is not a major concern in ragtime, but the increasing sophistication of some composers makes this a factor of some interest.

Occasionally, several themes of a work may have a common cadence pattern (Example VII–10), but the significance of this device should not be exaggerated. It occurs in compositions of no particular merit and is of no more consequence than similar or identical cadential formulas in various movements of a baroque suite.

EXAMPLE VII-10. Leo Berliner, *Africana. A Rag-Time Classic* (New York: Jos. W. Stern and Co., 1903): (a) A 13–16; (b) B 13–16.

(a)

(b)

There are instances, revealing a little more skill, in which a single motive is used to generate thematic material for several strains. In Joplin's *Original Rags*, for example, melodic identity obviously links the introduction and the B strain (Example VII–11); less apparent is the motivic connection, by virtue of the appoggiatura ♯2–3 (A♯–B) motion, with the E strain (Example VII–9b).

A sense of continuity joining adjacent strains is also present in other Joplin pieces. In his *Pine Apple Rag*, for instance, the two-note secondary-rag formula ending the A section leads directly into the B section, where it becomes the dominating motive (Example VII–12).

While such devices as melodic inversion are not really part of the ragtime language, they do appear sporadically. In Irene Giblin's *Chicken Chowder* (1905), ascending and descending chro-

EXAMPLE VII–11. S. Joplin, *Original Rags:* (a) Introduction 1–4; (b) B 1–4.

(a)

(b)

EXAMPLE VII–12. S. Joplin, *Pine Apple Rag*, A 13–B 2.

Copyright © 1908 by Mills Music, Inc. Copyright renewed. Used with permission. All rights reserved.

matic scales are used to simulate inversion, thereby tying together the A and C strains (Example VII–13).

The inversion relationship between the B and C strains of Joplin's *The Nonpareil* (1907) is far more subtle; it may even have been unintentional. The two strains are noticeably similar in their atypical openings: sixteenths in the bass and quarter notes in the treble. That the melodic G to E♭ at the beginning of theme B is mirrored by the E♭ to G in the first measure of theme C is easily perceived, suggesting that the two strains may be linked by inversion. This relationship is expanded on another level in that the

EXAMPLE VII-13. Irene Giblin, *Chicken Chowder* (New York: Jerome H. Remick and Co., 1905); (a) A 1–8; (b) C 1–8.

(a)

(b)

melodic outline (i.e., the basic melodic shape, excluding the embellishing tones) of C 1–4 corresponds to the inversion of the melodic contour of B 1–2 (Example VII–14). If one accepts this analysis as plausible, the parallel between the sustained D in B 2 and the prolongation of its inversion (A♭) in C 2–3 is an intriguing reinforcement of the hypothesis. Unfortunately, there is nothing else in this piece to give more definitive support.

George Botsford achieves a unification of all sections in his *Black and White Rag*. This rare sense of continuity is effected by tying all strains together with a common rhythmic formula—a secondary-rag pattern plus a single type of tied syncopation (Example VII–15). The A strain opens with four measures of a repeated three-note secondary-rag pattern, followed by two measures of tied syncopation in a lower neighbor-note arrangement.

EXAMPLE VII-14. S. Joplin, *The Nonpareil* (St. Louis, Mo.: Stark Music Co., 1907): (a) B 1–2; (b) C 1–4, with melodic analysis.

EXAMPLE VII-15. G. Botsford, *Black and White Rag*: (a) A 1–6; (b) B 1–4; (c) C 1–8.

(c)

Strain B begins with the same rhythms, but in a varied manner: two measures of secondary rag with changing pitches, followed by two measures of tied syncopation, the first being in the lower neighbor-note arrangement. The C strain reverses the order; the tied-syncopation, lower neighbor-note arrangement is in the first four measures and the repeated-note, secondary-rag pattern in the next four. In each strain the same basic material is used, but is shifted and changed sufficiently to create variety; the result is an unusually convincing integration.

Interesting as is this example of Botsford's, it is atypical; the organic connection of ragtime strains is a feature that occurs only occasionally.

### Development of "Measure 13" Conventions

The increasing sophistication in harmonic usage in ragtime is particularly noticeable around the final, climactic phrase of each strain. One result of this trend is that unaccompanied octaves, while remaining as a typical feature of introductions, are either discarded or modified for use at measure 13. One approach retains the bare sound—most often as single notes rather than as octaves—but adds interest either through secondary-ragtime rhythm or the outline of a diminished seventh chord (Examples VII–6b and VII–18b). A new dimension may also be added by harmonizing the octaves; the resulting "parallel octaves" should be viewed here not necessarily as untutored or careless musicianship, but as the enrichment of an older convention (Example VII–16).

EXAMPLE VII-16. Joe Jordan, *Double Fudge* (St. Louis, Mo.: Joseph F. Hunleth Music Co., 1902), C 13–16.

Another development of this convention, one particularly favored by Joplin, replaces the octaves with harmonically richer parallel sixths or tenths (Example VII–17a-b). In *Fig Leaf Rag* (strain B) he went one step further and varied the idea of parallel tenths by concluding each figuration in contrary motion.

EXAMPLE VII-17. S. Joplin: (a) *The Easy Winners* (St. Louis, Mo.: Scott Joplin, 1901), B 13–16; (b) *The Sycamore* (New York: Will Rossiter, 1904), C 13–16.

(a)

(b)

The practice of chromatic enrichment at the opening of the final phrase increased, especially with the use of diminished seventh chords and, as earlier, flat VI and augmented sixth chords of all types. The diminished seventh chords appear in measure 13 in about 10 percent of the post-1901 rags, and are used both in block formations (Example VII–18a) and in chord outlines (Example VII–18b-c). Flat VI and augmented sixth chords also appear at measure 13, or sometimes at measure 14, in 10 percent of the rags surveyed (Example VII–19). The "incorrect" spellings in the Johnson and Wiley examples —(a) and (c) — are typical of rag publications. In contrast, Joplin's careful nota-

EXAMPLE VII-18. (a) Harry C. Thompson, *A Black Bawl*, C 11-16; (b) Harry J. Lincoln, *Beeswax Rag* (Williamsport, Pa.: Vandersloot Music, 1911, B 13-16; (c) S. Joplin, *Sugar Cane* (New York: Seminary Music Co., 1908), C 13-16.

(a)

(b)

(c)

EXAMPLE VII-19. (a) Charles L. Johnson, *Cum Bac Rag* (New York: Jerome H. Remick and Co., 1911), B 12–16; (b) Tom Turpin, *St. Louis Rag* (New York: Sol Bloom, 1903), A 12–16; (c) Clarence Wiley, *Car-Barlick-Acid* (Oskaloosa, Iowa: Clarence C. Wiley, 1903), A 13–16; (d) S. Joplin, *Gladiolus Rag*, D 13–16.

(a)

(b)

(c)

(d)

tion of the flat VI of D♭ as a B♭♭ triad is characteristic of his
meticulous workmanship and his concern with chords of this
type. His habitual use of flat VI and augmented sixth chords goes
back to his pre-rag marches (see, for example, his *Combination
March*, 1896, E 13) and extends throughout his career. One could
even surmise that his *Breeze from Alabama* (1902) is a unique ex-
periment in expanding the flat-VI idea to the tonal organization
of an entire piece. After a conventional opening with two themes
in the tonic key (C major), the trio opens not in the anticipated
subdominant but in the key of the flat VI (A♭ major). In this
section (theme C) there then occurs what is probably the most
startling modulation in ragtime literature—a sudden shift to F♭
major (notated as E major)—the flat VI of the flat VI (C–A♭–F♭).
This new key extends from measures 9 to 13 of theme C (measures 45–48 of the entire 92-measure piece—the exact center of
the work!), at which point the tonic E-major triad once again
functions as a more conventional flat-VI chord going to the cadential I6/4 in A (Example VII–20). The traditional subdominant

EXAMPLE VII-20. S. Joplin, *A Breeze from Alabama* (St. Louis, Mo.: John
Stark and Son, 1902), C 5–16, break 1.

key is used for the second trio theme, and the piece ends with a reprise of the B theme in the original tonic key of C major, which may now be interpreted as D♭♭, the flat VI of F♭, or the flat VI of the flat VI of the flat VI (C–A♭–F♭[E]–D♭♭[C]: Example VII–21). In addition, the piece is virtually saturated with flat VI and augmented sixth chords, occurring not only in theme C but also at B 7, D 13, and twice in the first break.

EXAMPLE VII-21. S. Joplin, A Breeze from Alabama: tonal outline.

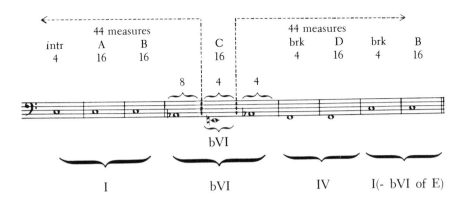

There is no indication that Joplin ever returned to the thought processes that produced this work, nor is there evidence that anyone recognized the significance of this novel tonal plan. Although unusual key relationships sometimes occur in rags, they appear to be the result of sloppy pastiches; from what is known of Joplin and what we can deduce from his music, he was too conscientious for such a haphazard procedure. The most logical conclusion is that this piece represents a structural extension of an attractive ragtime convention.

Compared with the hypothetical model of the early rag suggested at the end of Chapter Five, the model of the mature rag presents both similarities and significant changes. A sociological distinction is that ragtime lost much of its ethnic identification; instead of being thought of solely as black music, it became accepted as the music of all Americans. Accompanying this shift was a great reduction in the use of "folksy" minor keys.

The most dramatic musical changes were rhythmic: the manner of syncopation was reversed, with tied syncopation becoming more important than untied; secondary-ragtime patterns became widely used; augmented syncopation, once a regular feature, virtually disappeared as a prominent figure. There was also heightened awareness of the possibilities of texture, resulting in several enriching features: contrasts in density to emphasize syncopated accents; occasional use of inner voices; abandonment of unharmonized octaves at measure 13 and replacement by parallel sixths and tenths. The concept of form remained essentially as it had been in the 1890s, with one exception: in addition to "inner-trio" breaks, "trio-introducing" breaks were increasingly used.

Ragtime from the first—and part of the second—decade of the twentieth century was based on the conventions established for the genre in the 1890s. But these conventions were not accepted intact; they were modified, altering the character of the music and making it responsive to changes in society and to aesthetic demands.

## Notes

1. This feature was recognized by at least one commentator during the ragtime era. See John N. Burk, "Ragtime and Its Possibilities," *Harvard Musical Review* 2 (January 1914): 12.

2. Don Knowlton, "The Anatomy of Jazz," *Harper's Magazine*, (April 1926): 581. See also Olly Wilson, "The Significance of the Relationship between Afro-American Music and West African Music," *Black Perspective in Music* 2 (Spring 1974): 7–9.

3. Winthrop Sargeant, *Jazz: Hot and Hybrid* (3rd ed., enl., New York: Da Capo Press, 1975), pp. 58–59. The concept of secondary ragtime is generally recognized among ragtime enthusiasts today, but the term has not been accepted. Instead, many writers refer to "three over two." Although it is understandable why this descriptive terminology has been chosen and ac-

cepted, it is musically inaccurate, suggesting a totally unrelated figuration:

4. Sargeant, *Jazz*, p. 135.

5. Hans Nathan traces the two-note variant back to some mid-nineteenth-century minstrel pieces, but the evidence is inconclusive. See Hans Nathan, *Dan Emmett and the Rise of Early Negro Minstrelsy* (Norman, Okla.: University of Oklahoma Press, 1962), pp. 209–220, Ex. 88.

6. In a recorded interview, ragtime composer Joe Lamb used the expression "introduction to the trio"; cf. his discussion of *The Ragtime Nightingale* on *A Study in Classic Ragtime* (Folkways FG-3562).

# CHAPTER VIII

# The Erosion of a Distinctive Style

M any of the earlier ragtime conventions continued in force during the second decade of the century, but there were also significant incursions—primarily rhythmic—of traits that had previously been outside the genre's sphere. The familiar and almost exclusively used patterns of tied and untied syncopations and secondary ragtime gradually lost their dominance as other figures became prominent. However justifiable and necessary this broadening of the ragtime concept may have been on evolutionary and aesthetic grounds, an inevitable result was weakened identity and erosion of the style's most distinctive qualities.

### Dotted Rhythms

The most noticeable shift in ragtime of the 1910s is in the increased use of dotted rhythms, such as

During the first decade of the century this figure was rarely more than incidental, appearing in less than 6 percent of published piano rags. Beginning in 1911, however, there was a sudden and dramatic upsurge in the use of this rhythm, the number of prominent occurrences almost doubling for each of the next few years: 1911, 12 percent; 1912, 23 percent; 1913, 46 percent. A high level of use continued to the end of the ragtime period, going as high as 58 percent in 1916.

Dotted figures and ragtime syncopations commonly occur in the same passages, but the dotted figures themselves are usually unsyncopated: ♫ ♩ ♫♩ (Example VIII–1). In some instances, syncopated and dotted segments are connected by a tie: ♫ ♩♩♩♩ (Example VIII–2); least frequent are passages in which dotted notes are syncopated: ♩♩♩♩♩♩ (Example VIII–3). The apparent reluctance to fully adapt the traditional ragtime rhythms (untied and tied syncopation) to the new trend favoring dotted rhythms did not apply to secondary ragtime, which seems to have been transformed more completely (Example VIII–4; also, compare VIII–5b and d).

The rhythmic animation inherent in dotted figures evidently reduced the need for syncopation in ragtime. As a result, there was a corresponding, though not quite so steep, rise in the number of dotted but substantially unsyncopated rags (see, for example, Harry Belding, *Good Gravy Rag*, 1913; Eugene Platzmann and Ted Eastwood, *Kee-to-Kee*, 1918; Edward B. Claypoole, *Ragging the Scale*, 1915).

EXAMPLE VIII-1. George P. Howard, *Sam Fox Trot. Rag Two-Step* (Cleveland: Sam Fox Publishing Co., 1915), D 1–4.

EXAMPLE VIII–2. Joseph F. Lamb, *Cleopatra Rag* (St. Louis, Mo.: Stark Music, 1915), A 1–4.

EXAMPLE VIII-3. James Scott, *Dixie Dimples* (Kansas City: Will L. Livernash, 1918), A 6–7.

EXAMPLE VIII-4. Wilbur C. Sweatman, *Down Home Rag* (Chicago: Will Rossiter, 1911), A 1–4.

One can only speculate on the reasons for the new prominence of dotted rhythms. It is possible that the shift in notation was merely a reflection of prevailing performance practices, although a sampling of piano rolls on recently released recordings argues against this theory. (Undoubtedly, a thorough study of performance practices as represented on piano rolls and early recordings could shed some much-needed light on this issue.) It is also plausible that ragtime composers were seeking new rhythmic combinations in reaction to the conventional patterns, which by 1911 may have appeared hackneyed and stereotyped. A third hypothesis links the shift to a merging of rags with the new dances that appeared soon after 1910, the fox trot and the turkey trot. One article from 1916 does make this connection, referring to "Some of the latest ragtime numbers in fox trot rhythm."[1] The significance of these dances is that, syncopated or not, trots were usually dotted. There are also a few published pieces that explicitly illustrate the transformation from standard rag to fox trot. Euday Bowman's *12th Street Rag* was originally published in 1914 as an undotted rag; in 1919 it was reissued in a dotted version, labeled "Fox Trot Arrangement" (Example VIII–5). In another piece, Clarence Woods's *Sleepy Hollow Rag* (1918), a footnote explains that the designated dance character, a "slow drag" rag, can be altered to accommodate other dances by dotting the rhythms (Example VIII–6).

Whatever the initial impulse, the success of a few dotted rags in 1911 probably encouraged imitations, and in this regard one must consider the effect of Irving Berlin's spectacularly popular song, *Alexander's Ragtime Band* (1911). Although heavily dotted and virtually unsyncopated, this song was almost universally accepted, however mistakenly, as an archetype for ragtime. (That

EXAMPLE VIII-5. (a) Euday Bowman, *12th Street Rag* (Ft. Worth, Tx.:
Euday L. Bowman, 1914), Introduction 1–5; (b) A 1–4; (c) *12th Street
Rag*, arranged by C. E. Wheeler (Kansas City, Mo.: J. W. Jenkins'
Sons, 1919), Introduction 1–5; (d) A 1–4.

(a)

(b)

(c)

(d)

Copyright MCMXIV by Euday L. Bowman. Copyright MCMXIX by J. W.
Jenkins' Sons Music Co. Copyright MCMXLII by Shapiro, Bernstein and
Co., Inc. Copyright renewed MCXMLI by Euday L. Bowman and assigned
to Shapiro, Bernstein and Co., Inc. Copyright renewed MCMXLVII by
James S. Sumner and assigned to Jerry Vogel Music Co., Inc. Published by
consent of the copyright owners.

EXAMPLE VIII-6. Clarence Woods, *Sleepy Hollow Rag* (Kansas City, Mo.:
Will L. Livernash, 1918): (a) A 1–4; (b) footnote.

(a)

(b)

\* *This number can be played for anything except a waltz by slightly
altering the style and tempo as illustration. This illustration also
gives an example of a simplified movement for measurues containing
tremolo effect.*

*etc.*

the piano version is notated without dots would seem to indicate
that at the time of publication this rhythmic shift was still not
fully acceptable for piano rags; compare the rhythms of the song
and piano versions in Example VIII–7.)[2] It is likely that the unprecedented success of this song played an important part in
changing attitudes, in gaining acceptance for dotted notes and
unsyncopated rhythms in ragtime. Similarly, the success of other
1911 rags featuring dotted rhythms can be cited. *Down Home Rag*
(Example VIII–4), for instance, had three printings between 1911
and 1913[3] and therefore can be assumed to have exercised some
influence. With the precedents established by successful dotted
rags in 1911, the exclusive rights held by earlier ragtime conventions were broken.

Despite the wide acceptance of dotted notes in ragtime at
that time, there was some resistance to this trend. A critic in 1913
protested the incorporation of unsyncopated rhythms in the ragtime category, and ragtime pedagogue Edward Winn, writing as
late as 1918, managed to ignore dotted rhythms in his copious
surveys of ragtime techniques.[4] James Scott and Joe Lamb, two

EXAMPLE VIII-7. *Alexander's Ragtime Band:* (a) Rhythms of song version (note values halved for comparison); (b) Rhythms of piano version.

composers who continued writing rags after—in the case of Lamb, long after—it ceased to be fashionable, experimented briefly with dotted rhythms (see Examples VIII–3 and VIII–2), but then returned to the earlier conventions. This return is especially noticeable in the later works of Lamb, works that were first published in 1964.[5] More directly, composer-performer Mose Gumble explicitly denied dotted notes to ragtime: "Dotted notes and rests do not constitute rag. On the other hand, the tying of notes over the subsequent bars does."[6]

This demonstrated opposition notwithstanding, the incursion of dotted rhythms was accomplished. More than any other single factor, dotted notes changed the character of ragtime.

## Other Expansions of the Ragtime Language

Perhaps as a side effect to the acceptance of unsyncopated, dotted passages, the spectrum of musical gestures going under the ragtime label became broader and more inclusive. In the rhythmic sphere, this tendency is observable in an increased proportion of complete strains without a single—or, sometimes, just one—syncopation, and in a wider use of triplets (Example VIII–8).

EXAMPLE VIII-8. Edward B. Claypoole, *Ragging the Scale* (New York: Broadway Music Corp., 1915), B 1–4.

Textural divergences also appeared: a greater prominence of various alternating hand patterns, often combined with chord arpeggiations (Example VIII–9), and an increased use of left-hand tenths, which occasionally replaced the more conventional octaves (Example VIII–10; see also Example VIII–6). The rarity of

EXAMPLE VIII-9. E. J. Stark, *Billikin Rag* (St. Louis, Mo.: Stark Music
Co., 1913), A 1–7; (b) Robert Hampton, *Cataract Rag* (St. Louis, Mo.:
Stark Music Co., 1914), D 1–3.

(a)

(b)

EXAMPLE VIII-10. Thomas Pitts, *Meadow Lark Rag* (San Francisco: Chas.
N. Daniels, 1916), C 5–7.

tenths in early ragtime publications was undoubtedly a conces-
sion made by composers to the real or assumed limitations of the
music-buying public. As indicated in Chapter Four, at least some
pieces were deliberately simplified to encourage sales. Undoubtedly, some composers did utilize tenths regularly in performance
without reflecting this practice in publications. Luckey Roberts's
published rags in the middle 1910s make little use of tenths, although James P. Johnson has testified that they were a regular
feature of Roberts's performing style during those same years.[7]
Johnson has also placed the development of the use of tenths in

New York, reasoning that it was part of the more demanding technical standards required to compete with the superior, classically oriented musicians present in the metropolitan area:

> The other sections of the country never developed the piano as far as the New York boys. . . . The people in New York were used to hearing good piano played in concerts and cafés. The ragtime player had to live up to that standard. . . .
>
> New York developed the orchestral piano—full, round, big, widespread chords and tenths—a heavy bass moving against the right hand. The other boys from the South and West at that time played in smaller dimensions—like thirds played in unison. We wouldn't dare do that because the public was used to better playing.
>
> . . . In the rags, that full piano was played as early as 1910. Even Scott Joplin had octaves and chords, but he didn't attempt the big hand stretches.[8]

The evidence on the extent to which tenths were used in ragtime performance in Saint Louis during the first decade of the century is contradictory. Joe Jordan has said that it was "quite common,"[9] while Charles Thompson's remark about Louis Chauvin, who died in 1908, suggests that it was unusual: "He was stretching tenths way ahead of his time."[10]

There is no definitive answer to this issue as applied to performance; the evidence is clear, however, in regard to published ragtime. Left-hand tenths become more prevalent in the second decade of the century, but they were still not a major factor in the style.

### Bluesy Rags and Raggy Blues

It is natural that ragtime and blues, emerging from the same cultural and social milieu, should be related. In a few pieces this relationship is strikingly close; in some others it is more distant but nevertheless unmistakable. In the majority of cases, though, blues influence in published ragtime was slight until the second decade of the twentieth century. With the unveiling of blues in published form in 1912 that influence increased substantially, and blues became another important factor in the disintegration of ragtime as a distinctive genre.

The genesis of blues is obscure, but the style clearly existed as a recognizable type prior to its surfacing in print as popular music in 1912. Jelly Roll Morton, for one, referred to hearing some form of blues in New Orleans earlier than 1900,[11] and although *Jelly Roll Blues*, his first publication, was not issued until 1915, it is supposed to have been composed in 1905.[12]

All the rags used in this study have been analyzed for blues elements, which, for the most part, take the form of "blue notes,"[13] although occasionally other features are present. In two cases (to be discussed below) rags have been found with strains that may be the earliest published blues choruses.

The frequency with which blues elements appear in rags increases chronologically, indicating that even before 1912 awareness of the blues style was growing. In pre-1912 rags blue notes are found most often—but not exclusively—in rags by black composers. Joplin's first published rag, *Original Rags*, uses the characteristic blues motion of ♯2–3 (Examples VII–9b and VII–11), an inflection also present in a vocal chorus in Boone's *Rag Medley No. 1* (1908: Example VIII–11a).[14] Among some white composers, too, there was an awareness of the blues gesture, as evidenced by Charles Johnson in A *Black Smoke* (1902) and J. Russel Robinson in *Minstrel Man* (1911), to name two (Examples VIII–11b-c). A close approximation of the "blues break," which typically occurs in the second half of a blues phrase, is presented in several pieces—for example, Joplin's *Paragon Rag* (1909) and Scott's *Ragtime Oriole* (1911) (Example VIII–11d).

The most exceptional appearance of blues in ragtime from the early 1900s is in *One o' Them Things?* (1904). Subtitled "Rag Time Two-Step," it nevertheless departs from the usual 16-measure strain pattern and opens with a 12-bar blues chorus; in so doing, it may be the first true publication of a blues (Example VIII–12).[15] Although the first ending does not correspond exactly to what became the standard blues pattern, the second ending does. An additional feature typical of blues is the parallel melodic structure of the first two phrases (measures 1–4 and 5–8).

Another possible "first" is the "Alabama bound" chorus of Boone's *Rag Medley No. II* (1909), which may be the earliest publication of "boogie-woogie" (Example VIII–13).[16] The usual 12-measure structure of blues is here compressed to 8 measures, but such variants are not uncommon. More significant than this deviation are the piece's basic blues harmonic pattern, extensive use of blue notes, parallel melodic pattern between the first two phrases (measures 1–2 and 3–4), and boogie-woogie bass. (To retain perspective, it must be recognized that these passages are exceptions; generally, the blues influence in ragtime prior to 1912 was slight: about 3 percent of the rags of this period have been found to exhibit blues characteristics.)

EXAMPLE VIII-11. (a) "Blind" Boone, *Rag Medley No. 1* (Columbia, Mo.: Allen Music Co., 1908), Introduction, A 1–2; (b) C. Johnson, *A Black Smoke* (Kansas City, Mo.: Carl Hoffman, 1902), B 7–8; (c) J. Russel Robinson, *Minstrel Man* (St. Louis, Mo.: Stark Music Co., 1911), C 1–4; (d) S. Joplin, *Paragon Rag* (New York: Seminary Music Co., 1909), B 1–4.

(a)

(b)

(c)

(d)

EXAMPLE VIII-12. (a) James Chapman and Leroy Smith, *One o' Them Things?* (St. Louis, Mo.: Jos. Placht and Son, 1904), A 1–12; (b) Standard blues pattern.

(a)

(b)          Standard Blues Pattern

| I | I | I | I♭⁷ |
|---|---|---|---|
|   |   |   | (V⁷ of IV) |
| IV | IV | I | I |
| V | V | I | I |
|   | (or IV) |   | (or V⁷) |

EXAMPLE VIII-13. "Blind" Boone, *Rag Medley No. II* (Columbia, Mo.: Allen Music Co., 1909), "I'm Alabama bound."

    The emergence of blues from the musical subculture in 1912 and its formalization and dispersion through publication altered its relationship with ragtime. The public's growing awareness of blues made it part of the common language of popular music, and as there developed an almost indiscriminate mixing of blues and ragtime, distinctions between the two were frequently clouded.

    That W. C. Handy's *Memphis Blues* was accepted as ragtime (see above, pages 6–7, 48) may seem surprising today, but there was a basis for this perception; blues were considered to be rags, and the cover of the piano version of *Memphis Blues* designates the piece as "A Southern Rag."[17] This is not an isolated instance; other publications also indicate a blues-rag mixture in their titles, subtitles, and tempo descriptions: W. C. Handy's *Jogo Blues* (1913), marked "Tempo di Rag (a la Memphis Blues)"; Harry J. Lincoln's *Checkers Rag (Blues or Fox Trot)*, 1913; Charles L. Cooke's *Blame It on the Blues* (1914), marked "Tempo di Ragioso"; Theron Bennet's *Some Blues (For You All). A Southern Rag* (1916); and Henry Lodge's *Baltimore Blues. Fox Trot Rag* (1917).

    Musically, too, hybrids appeared. Handy, referring to the

genesis of his *St. Louis Blues* (1914), wrote: "My aim would be to combine ragtime syncopation with a real melody in the spiritual tradition."[18] Ragtime rhythms and other ragtime features are present in numerous other blues. The *Memphis Blues*, for instance, begins with the 12-bar pattern that is today recognized as standard for blues, but the immediate strophic variant typical of blues is absent; instead, the following section is an unrelated 16-measure strain closely resembling a ragtime strain: a V4/3 opening, frequent use of a march bass, tied syncopations, and secondary-ragtime figures (measures 9–12).[19] If there were a steadier rhythmic impulse delivered from the bass, this section would be indistinguishable from a rag. The third strain then returns to the 12-bar format, but reflects current dance practices, including ragtime, in its subdominant key.

Combinations of 12- and 16-bar strains are present in many other blues publications of the period. One such piece, H. Alf Kelly and J. Paul Wyer's *A Bunch of Blues. Fox Trot* (1915), has two strains in the 12-bar blues pattern and three in the 16-measure form of ragtime, the latter sections using blue notes and ragtime rhythms. The frequency with which pieces of this type occurred during the 1910s clearly demonstrates the influence that ragtime had on blues at that time.[20]

The growing popularity of blues undoubtedly led some composers and publishers to use the term simply as a sales device, with little or no musical justification. Charles L. Cooke's *Blame It on the Blues. A Weary Blue*, for instance, can claim the use of blue notes in the A strain, but nowhere else, and it is structurally and rhythmically ("Tempo di Ragioso") a typical rag. Other pieces, such as J. Bodewalt Lampe's *Harmony Blues* (1917), are totally devoid of any musical basis for the blues label.

On the ragtime side of this transaction, the blues influence, which was so slight before 1912, after that date increases markedly. The actual percentage of identifiable rags with strong blues influence rises to about 15 percent by 1915, and if the substantial number of hybrids going under a blues or fox-trot label were considered, the proportion would be much higher. As earlier, blue notes are the most common blues element found in rags. Occasionally other blues influences are also present. In Luckey Roberts's *Pork and Beans* (1913), the blues-suggesting flatted fifths in the D strain may have generated a misprint for, although it is a 16-measure strain, a double bar is placed after the twelfth measure, as it would be in a blues (Example VIII–14). The blues

EXAMPLE VIII-14. Luckey Roberts, *Pork and Beans* (New York: Jos. W. Stern, 1913), D 9–16.

Copyright © Edward B. Marks Music Corporation. Used by permission.

influence on the C theme of Joplin's *Magnetic Rag* (1914) is of more substance: in addition to blue notes, the appropriate harmonic-formal design is followed. The strain is of 24 measures—unusual for a rag—and is broken into uneven segments of 14 and 10 measures. The first 14 measures parallel the 12-measure form of the blues, with a 2-measure interpolation extending the subdominant area (Example VIII–15).[21]

As with the dotted fox trots, the mixture of blues and rags enriched the ragtime language, but in so doing detracted from its distinctiveness. Not that the mixture was universally applied to ragtime; to the end, some rags were written without a trace of blues. With the increase of blues and the fading of ragtime, though, there was also a growing proportion of hybrids, of pieces that fit both categories, of bluesy rags and raggy blues.

## Jazz

Jazz, in its broadest and most inclusive sense, replaced ragtime as the most prominent American popular music. The blurred distinctions between jazz and ragtime, so evident in articles from about 1917 on, were matched by an indiscriminate mixing of terminology in the published music, a single piece sometimes bearing the multiple labels of rag, fox trot, blues, and jazz; for example: *Kee-to-Kee (A Modulating Rag). Fox Trot*, marked "Moderato a la Jazz"; *Hide and Seek. Jazz Fox Trot*; and *Jazz Band Blues. Jazz Fox Trot*.

As presented in published form, jazz of this period is usually

EXAMPLE VIII-15. S. Joplin, *Magnetic Rag* (New York: Scott Joplin Publishing Co., 1914): (a) C 1–14, C' 1–2; (b) Analysis.

(a)

(b)                    Analysis of C 1–14

| | I | | I | | I | | I♭⁷ | | | | |
|---|---|---|---|---|---|---|---|---|---|---|---|
| | IV | | IV | | IV | | IV | | I | | I |
| | V | | V | | I | | V⁷ | | | | |

characterized by a dotted rhythm, either with or without syncopation, and is indistinguishable from fox trots and late, dotted versions of ragtime (Example VIII–16a, b). Not all samples are dotted, though. In some instances, even the most conventional rags may be placed in the jazz category. Henry Lodge's *Bounding Buck* (1918), an ordinary undotted, tied-syncopation rag, is subtitled both "A Rag Dance" and "Fox Trot," and is concluded with a 2-measure coda marked "Jazz Break" (Example VIII–16c).[22] In an extreme case, Arthur Pryor's *A Coon Band Contest* (1899), a typical early rag using untied syncopation, was reissued in 1918, unaltered except for a new, more fashionable descriptive designation: "Jazz Fox Trot."

It is clear that the piano sheet music bearing the label "jazz" does not reflect the musical phenomenon which was fascinating so much of the American and European public; it has neither the heightened rhythmic variety mentioned by the commentators of the time nor any suggestion of the improvised counterpoint that has come to be known as "Dixieland jazz." These publications have nothing to distinguish them from the various styles of ragtime being written at the same time, and this very fact of identity underlines the loss of ragtime's uniqueness.

## Novelty Piano

Few composers were still writing ragtime—in name and in style—in the 1920s. The 1920s were represented primarily by the new syncopated art of jazz and, to a lesser extent, the semi-virtuosic style of "novelty piano."

Some current writers refer to novelty piano as "novelty *ragtime*," suggesting that it falls within the province of ragtime.[23] But the term "novelty ragtime" is of recent origin, and was not used by composers of the style—neither by Zez Confrey (1895–1971), with whom the style is most closely associated, nor by his contemporaries. If anything, Confrey was allied with the popular conception of jazz rather than with ragtime. In his book *So This Is Jazz* (1926), Henry Osgood stated: "It was only when Zez Confrey came along with his ingenious 'Kitten on the Keys' that a genuinely pianistic idiom for jazz was established"; elsewhere in the book he headed a chapter "Piano Jazz: Those Kittenish Keys!"[24] Similarly, in 1927 Aaron Copland considered the jazz age to be typified by Confrey's *Stumbling* (1922) and *Kitten on the Keys* (1921), and Gilbert Seldes expressed the same opinion.[25]

It must be granted that novelty piano has its roots in ragtime.

EXAMPLE VIII-16. (a) James White, *Jazz Band Blues*. *Jazz Fox Trot* (Chicago: May Hill, 1918), B 1–8; (b) Eugene Platzmann and Ted Eastwood, *Kee-to-Kee (A Modulating Rag)*. *Fox Trot* (New York: Artmusic, 1918), B 5–8; (c) Henry Lodge, *The Bounding Buck* (New York: M. Witmark, 1918), B′ 12–16, coda.

a)

Copyright MCMXVIII by May Hill. Transferred to Roger Graham Music Publisher in 1919. Copyright renewed 1945.

b)

c)

Certainly, some of Confrey's earliest pieces closely correspond to both conventional and later rag styles. The B strain of his *Kitten on the Keys* follows the established patterns of tied-syncopation ragtime, and even the dotted figures of the A section fall within the later dotted-rag style, combining with the secondary-ragtime figure (Example VIII–17). *My Pet* also manifests secondary-ragtime traits, but here, instead of the accentual shift within the

EXAMPLE VIII-17. Zez Confrey, *Kitten on the Keys* (New York: Mills Music, 1921): (a) B 1-4; (b) vamp, A 1-4.

three-unit group—the general characteristic of secondary ragtime—the notated accents enforce the effect of a temporary change to triple meter (Example VIII–18a).[26] While other pieces suggest roots in the secondary-ragtime pattern, more significant was Confrey's inclination to expand and develop this device beyond its ragtime context (Example VIII–18b-d). His link with ragtime became even more tenuous as his pieces developed in new directions, foreign to ragtime (Example VIII–19).[27] In addition to the non-rag appearance of these works, the brilliant, high-speed performance demanded by Confrey's music is at odds with the spirit of the dance-oriented moderate tempo of ragtime.

Similarly, in the novelty-piano music of other composers, ragtime figurations were used occasionally in the early 1920s, but discarded as the style developed. It is clear also that a stylistic distinction was perceived by the music's contemporaries, for the term "ragtime" was used only rarely in the music publications.

EXAMPLE VIII-18. Z. Confrey: (a) *My Pet* (New York: Mills Music, 1921), A 6–10; (b) *Greenwich Witch* (New York: Mills Music, 1921), B 1–3; (c) *Stumbling: Paraphrase* (New York: Leo Feist, 1922), B 1–4; (d) *Stumbling*, B′ 1–4.

(a)

(b)

(c)

(d)

EXAMPLE VIII-19 Z. Confrey: (a) *Coaxing the Piano* (New York: Mills Music, 1922), A 1–4; (b) *Dizzy Fingers* (New York: Mills Music, 1923), vamp, A 1–8.

(a)

(b)

There is little justification, then, for applying the artificial, newly invented designation of "novelty ragtime"; to do so obscures the meanings of both ragtime and novelty piano.[28]

## Other Applications and Misapplications

The term "ragtime" has been applied inappropriately to other styles as well, most notably to stride piano (in this case, mislabeled "stride ragtime"), which shares with ragtime a left-hand pattern of deep bass notes alternating with closed-position chords in mid-piano. Figures commonly placed in this category are Fats Waller and James P. Johnson, and representative works include pieces they wrote in the 1930s and '40s.[29] In his early days Johnson did work within the sphere of the current ragtime fashions, and to this extent his personal manner was grounded in ragtime. But his musical language, expanding within the context of later jazz styles, outgrew the restricted conventions of ragtime. Placing all of his music in the "ragtime" category overlooks this stylistic development and inappropriately distends ragtime's coverage. Such overextensions of terminology lead to the type of misunderstanding evidenced in one textbook which includes jazz pianist Art Tatum in the category of ragtime.[30] The practice of forcing virtually every pre-bop jazz-piano style into the ragtime orbit misrepresents historical fact, serves no practical objective, and results only in confusion. Rather than invent new encumbrances for "ragtime," a term already heavily weighted with meanings, a more sensible and useful practice would be to restrict applications to the word's original connotations.

## Notes

1. Leonard Liebling, "The Crime of Ragtime," *Musical Courier* 72 (20 January 1916): 21.

2. Permission to quote music denied by the publisher.

3. Elliott Shapiro, "'Ragtime' USA," *Notes* 8 (June 1951): 460.

4. Edward R. Winn, *How to Play Ragtime (Uneven Rhythm)* (Edward R. Winn, 1915); "Ragtime Piano Playing," *Cadenza* 21–23 (March 1915–October 1916): passim; and "Ragtime Piano Playing: A Practical Course of Instruction for Pianists," *Tuneful Yankee/Melody* 1–2 (January 1917–June 1918): passim.

5. Joseph F. Lamb, *Ragtime Treasures*, Foreward by Rudi Blesh (Rockville Centre, N.Y.: Belwin Mills, 1964).

6. Monroe H. Rosenfeld, "'Ragtime'—A Musical Mystery: What It Is and Its Origin," *Tuneful Yankee* 1 (January 1917): 10.

7. Tom Davin, "Conversations with James P. Johnson" [Part 2], *Jazz Review* 2 (July 1959): 12.

8. Ibid. [Part 1] (June 1959): 17.

9. Dick Zimmerman, "A Visit with Joe Jordan," *Rag Times* 2 (September 1968): 6.

10. Trebor J. Tichenor, "'The Real Thing' as Recalled by Charles Thompson," *Ragtime Review* 2 (April 1963): 5–6.

11. Alan Lomax, *Mister Jelly Roll: The Fortunes of Jelly Roll Morton, New Orleans Creole and "Inventor of Jazz"* (2d ed., Berkeley, Ca.: University of California Press, 1973), pp. 6, 20–21. For other testimony and evidence, see: W. C. Handy, *Father of the Blues: An Autobiography*, ed. Arna Bontemps (New York: Macmillan, 1941), p. 99; Eileen Southern, *The Music of Black Americans: A History* (New York: W. W. Norton, 1971), pp. 332–33; Gilbert Chase, *America's Music from the Pilgrims to the Present* (2d ed., rev., New York: McGraw-Hill, 1966), p. 456; William Ferris, "Blues Roots and Development," *Black Perspective in Music* 2 (Fall 1974): 123.

12. Lomax, *Mister Jelly Roll*, p. 292.

13. Blue notes are certain chromatic alterations superimposed on the major scale. The most common scale-steps for these alterations are the sharped second (or flatted third), sharped fourth (or flatted fifth), and sharped sixth (or flatted seventh).

These tones are used primarily by the right hand and frequently form dissonant clashes with the unaltered scale-steps used in either right- or left-hand harmonies.

14. Blind from infancy, John W. Boone (1863–1927) reputedly had the ability to duplicate any piano performance he heard. He gave concerts widely for some thirty years, programming classics, folk-music arrangements, and ragtime.

15. This point is made by Trebor Tichenor, who includes the piece in his anthology. See *Ragtime Rarities: Complete Original Music for 63 Piano Rags*, comp. and with Introduction by Trebor Tichenor (New York: Dover, 1975), p. vii.

16. Boogie-woogie is a type of blues characterized by a broken-octave, "walking" bass.

17. The cover is reproduced on the back cover of *Ragtimer* (March/April 1969).

18. Handy, *Father of the Blues*, p. 120.

19. Permission to quote from *Memphis Blues* denied by publisher, Handy Bros. Music Co. The music is reprinted in W. C. Handy, ed., *Blues: An Anthology* (3rd ed., rev., ed. by Jerry Silverman, New York: Macmillan, Collier Books, 1972), pp. 69–73.

20. Those interested in pursuing this line of investigation are referred to W. C. Handy, ed., *Blues: An Anthology*. See Handy's *Memphis Blues*, *St. Louis Blues*, *Jogo Blues*, *Beale Street Blues*, and *Ole Miss* (pp. 70, 82, 78, 116, and 179); Will Nash's *Snakey Blues* (p. 108); Spencer Williams's *Tishomingo Blues* (p. 120); and Douglas Williams's *Hooking Cow Blues* (p. 123).

21. Joplin used blues form in an earlier work as well. In his opera *Treemonisha* (1911), measures 21–24 of "A Real Slow Drag" follow the pattern of the first eight measures of a blues.

22. This is apparently an example of what jazz clarinetist Garvin Bushell (b. 1902) has referred to as the earliest musical application of the term "jazz":

"We didn't call the music jazz when I was growing up . . . except for the final tag of a number. After the cadence was closed there'd be a one bar break and the second bar was the tag—5, 6, 5, 1. Sol, la, sol, do. Da da—da DUM! That was called the jazz." See Nat Hentoff, "Garvin Busell and New York Jazz in the 1920's," *Jazz Review* 2 (January 1959): 11.

23. The foremost promoter of the term "novelty ragtime" is David Jasen, whose views on the subject have been accepted by most writers on ragtime. See by Jasen: *Recorded Ragtime, 1897–1958* (Hamden, Conn.: Archon Books, Shoe String Press, 1973), p. 5; "Zez Confrey: Creator of the Novelty Rag," *Rag Times* 5 (September 1971): 4–5; liner notes on *Zez Confrey Played by John Jensen* (Genesis GS-1051); and with Trebor Jay Tichenor, *Rags and Ragtime: A Musical History* (The Seabury Press, 1978), pp. 214–39.

24. Henry O. Osgood, *So This Is Jazz* (Boston: Little, Brown, 1926), pp. 32, 76.

25. Aaron Copland, "Jazz Structure and Influence on Modern Music," *Modern Music* 4 (January/February 1927): 11–12; Gilbert Seldes, *The Seven Lively Arts* (New York: Harper and Bros., 1924; rev. ed., New York: Sagamore Press, 1957), pp. 89, 91.

26. Both *My Pet* and *Kitten on the Keys* bear copyright registrations of 11 March 1921, the earliest copyrights obtained by Confrey. David Jasen, however, reports possession of a piano roll of *My Pet* made by the composer in 1918; this suggests the possibility that *Kitten on the Keys* also dates from several years earlier than its copyright date, a hypothesis supported by the piece's adherence to ragtime figurations. One can speculate that if these works had been published in 1918 rather than 1921 they might have been called rags.

27. These particular pieces are cited because they are considered to be rags by some present-day writers and are listed in Jasen's *Recorded Ragtime*.

28. The interested reader is referred

to several currently available anthologies that contain novelty-piano music: *The Exciting Era of Zez Confrey* (New York: Mills Music, 1963); *Jazz Gallery* (New York: Sam Fox, 1961): *Dizzy Piano: Famous Novelty Solos from the Golden Age of Jazz* (New York: Sam Fox, 1960): *The Jazz Master* (London, England: Keith Prowse, 1972).

29. See, for instance, Rudi Blesh and Harriet Janis, *They All Played Ragtime* (4th ed., rev., New York: Oak Publications, 1971), pp. 288–89, 295–96, and Jasen and Tichenor, *Rags and Ragtime*, pp. 240–48.

30. Paul O. W. Tanner and Maurice Gerow, *A Study of Jazz* (2d ed., Dubuque, Iowa: Wm. C. Brown, 1973), p. 53.

# Part Three
# The Historical Perspective

The various ways in which ragtime has been perceived in the past eighty years are revealed in the literature about it. Part One surveyed the attitudes expressed about ragtime by its contemporaries and established that, for the public, this genre was represented primarily by the song. Part Three will examine how these attitudes have changed since the ragtime era: Chapter Nine traces the views as they evolved from 1930 to the present and Chapter Ten evaluates how modern writers have approached a major theoretical issue, that of the subdivision of piano ragtime into several stylistic categories.

CHAPTER IX

# The Historiography of Ragtime

*Vocal Ragtime versus Piano Ragtime*

Fewer ragtime articles were written in the 1930s than at any other time in the music's history. Of those writers who did concern themselves with this subject, most considered song to be ragtime's principal form. The chapter on ragtime in Goldberg's *Tin Pan Alley* (1930)[1] is concerned primarily with coon songs and show music; the discussion of piano ragtime is restricted to some brief references to Ben Harney, the "forgotten" Scott Joplin, and Kerry Mills.[2]

In Alain L. Locke's *The Negro and His Music* (1936) ragtime is specifically linked to the stage in a chapter entitled "Ragtime and Negro Musical Comedy: 1895–1925."[3] Ragtime is viewed foremost as vocal music and the piano phase is relegated to a secondary and mostly corrupt role:

> What passed for ragtime was not the full rhythmic and harmonic idiom of the genuine article as used, for example, by Will Marion Cook and the Negro musical comedy arrangers who had chorus and orchestra at their disposal, but the thin and rather superficial eccentric rhythm as it could be imitated on the piano or in the necessarily simplified "accompaniments" of popular sheet music of the day.[4]

Exceptions to the view of piano ragtime as a false form are made only for the music of Scott Joplin, Kerry Mills, and, inappropriately, Irving Berlin, whose song *Alexander's Ragtime Band* is depicted as the culmination of mature instrumental ragtime. Similarly, in Helen L. Kaufman's *From Jehovah to Jazz* (1937), Irving Berlin is considered the focal point of ragtime, with musical-comedy composer Jerome Kern (1885–1945) being one of the luminaries.[5]

The first significant shift in orientation from the vocal medium to the piano was in Winthrop Sargeant's thoroughly competent study of jazz, *Jazz: Hot and Hybrid* (1938).[6] Unquestionably, his conception of ragtime as a pianistic expression contrasts sharply with the published opinions of the time:

> Ragtime was essentially an instrumental art. Few of the best rags offered melodies that could be sung. None of the really good ones had vocal refrains or were encumbered with words. The song writers attempted for years to capitalize on the trend by writing vocal tunes in which texts extolling the virtues of the dance were accompanied by slightly "ragged" piano accompaniments. The results were usually feeble imitations. One need only examine the so-called ragtime songs of such writers as Irving Berlin and George M. Cohan to be struck with their unimaginativeness in comparison with the real rags of the period. The rags were written by instrumentalists who knew their instruments intimately and exploited their practical potentialities. Few of the big commercial names of Tin Pan Alley knew enough about music in the practical sense to turn out acceptable rags.
>
> The dominating instrument of the period was the piano, and the good rag composers were usually pianists.[7]

Placed alongside the writings of his contemporaries in the 1930s, Sargeant's views are extraordinary. His elevation of piano ragtime and scornful rejection of the Irving Berlin and Tin Pan Alley conception of vocal ragtime anticipated attitudes that have since become basic axioms for most ragtime enthusiasts. Moreover, his discussion of piano ragtime was not restricted to Scott Joplin and Kerry Mills. In his analyses of jazz rhythm he drew upon a broad spectrum of piano rags by a number of composers, highlighting tied and untied syncopations (although not using that terminology) and secondary ragtime.[8] In spite of the fact that ragtime was not Sargeant's major concern in this book, his observations of the music were far more perceptive than most analyses that have since been written.

Sargeant's interest in piano ragtime is probably attributable to his concern with true jazz, which is mainly an instrumental form, rather than with general popular music. It is not surprising, then, that subsequent writers on popular music failed to recognize the importance of Sargeant's views, and for the next few years discussion of vocal ragtime continued to dominate the literature.

In 1939 a major book on popular music appeared, *The Story of the House of Witmark: From Ragtime to Swingtime*, written by Isidore Witmark, one of the pioneering music publishers in the early days of ragtime, in collaboration with Isaac Goldberg.[9] Giving an insider's view of the popular music business, the volume offers a wealth of information, but in its views on ragtime the main focus is still on vocal music.

This persuasion carried into the early 1940s. An article from 1940, "Negro Producers of Ragtime," mentions Scott Joplin and Tom Turpin, but the emphasis is on the vocal idiom.[10] Finally, a master's thesis from 1942, "Ragtime," delineates the characteristics of ragtime as found in fifty coon-songs and the *Maple Leaf Rag*.[11]

## The Ragtime Revival

In the early 1940s, at the same time that a few New York musicians were formulating what was to become bebop, a San Francisco group was similarly rejecting what it considered the sterility of big band pop-swing. But rather than probe new means of expression as the bopsters did, this latter group—Lu Watter's Yerba Buena Jass Band—sought revitalization and aesthetic satisfaction in the "traditional jazz" of the 1920s. Their music met with an unexpectedly exuberant response among local jazz enthusiasts, a reception that was repeated in 1941–1942 as recordings brought them to an even larger audience. Almost incidental to this revival of the New Orleans–Chicago "Dixieland" styles was the resuscitation of ragtime, for among Yerba Buena's best-selling recordings were Joplin's *Maple Leaf Rag*, Mills's *At a Georgia Campmeeting*, and—their biggest success—George Botsford's *Black and White Rag*.

It is to Yerba Buena that we trace the beginnings of the "ragtime revival," although in some ways the designation "revival" is not quite accurate: only the piano literature of ragtime was brought back, and even this was filtered through the improvised freedom and embellishment of an ensemble jazz style of a later age. Nevertheless, Yerba Buena created a new audience for ragtime, an audience for an increasing number of performing groups (and piano soloists),[12] and an audience for the first historical and biographical sketches. From that day to the present, interest in ragtime has been continuous and active.

Complementing the performance phase of the ragtime revival was a new concern with ragtime as history. The pioneering figure in this area was Roy Carew (1884–1967). A lifelong devotee of piano ragtime, Carew played his first rag, Charles Hunter's *Tickled to Death* (1899), around the turn of the century, and soon afterward became an amateur composer of ragtime (professionally, he was a tax auditor for the Internal Revenue Service). His interest in ragtime was enhanced in 1904 when, upon moving to New Orleans, he became acquainted with pianist-composer Tony Jackson (1876–1921). His cultivation of friendships within the ragtime community found new significance in the 1930s with his eventful meeting and subsequent friendship with ragtime-jazz pianist Jelly Roll Morton (1885–1941). Finding Morton in financial difficulties, Carew formed the Tempo Music Publishing Company as a means of publishing and protecting the composer's music and assuring him of an income. After Morton's death, Carew became executor of his estate.

Carew began publishing historical articles in 1943 in *Record Changer*, an inauspicious pamphlet concerned with jazz discography. Beginning with reminiscences of Tony Jackson and Jelly Roll Morton, he then turned his attention to Scott Joplin, Brun Campbell, Shep Edmonds, and others. By the end of the decade he had brought out biographical and historical information never before available in print and had laid the foundation for ragtime studies.[13]

## MISTER JELLY ROLL AND THEY ALL PLAYED RAGTIME

Consummating the researches of the 1940s are two monumental books that appeared in 1950: Alan Lomax's *Mister Jelly Roll: The Fortunes of Jelly Roll Morton, New Orleans Creole and "Inventor of Jazz,"* and Rudi Blesh and Harriet Janis's *They All Played Ragtime*.[14] *Mister Jelly Roll* was an outgrowth of Morton's recording sessions at the Library of Congress in 1938, in which the pianist performed, sang, and related anecdotes.[15] As a biography of one of the most flamboyant and enterprising figures in ragtime-jazz history, the book goes beyond the range of ragtime considerations; based primarily on the words of Morton, whose boasting was as legendary as his musical talent, it must be read with caution.[16] Still, however one-sided, this book provides a unique and invaluable portrait of the times.

Using Scott Joplin and "classic ragtime" (a term to be explored in the next chapter) as a fulcrum, *They All Played Rag-*

*time* provides a broader view of ragtime history. The first book devoted entirely to this subject, it contains an impressive amount of historical information, joining the investigative efforts of the 1940s to extensive new researches and interviews with surviving ragtimers. In its main objective, the study of the personalities and interrelationships of the period, *They All Played Ragtime* is unmatched and has become a prime source for later works on the subject. In other respects, though, Blesh and Janis are less successful. Their comments on the music are of limited value because of their personal, intuitive, and nontechnical approach. Even more questionable is the confusing, frequently impenetrable entanglement of fact, speculation, and pure fiction. There are some overlays of fiction that are sufficiently obvious:

> He thought of the young Scott Hayden. . . . Joplin thought of Arthur Marshall . . . ; he thought of these two boys whom he had befriended, and some of the warmth he had given them came back to warm his chilled heart.[17]

Other passages, such as the following commentary on an important issue of performance practice, are more troublesome:

> In St. Louis a new cosmopolitan style had arisen that featured a staccato speed technique and brilliant display. . . . So it came about that many seized every opportunity to cajole Joplin into playing and then took delight in publicly topping him.[18]

This description could well be true and may have been related to the authors by a witness of such scenes. But the failure to attribute the testimony provides reason for doubt, especially as the passage ends with another sentence suggestive of a novelist's omniscience:

> It is strange that this should have disturbed Joplin so deeply, but he came from the playing school himself, and he took it harder than anyone knew.[19]

In defense of the book, it must be stated that however the scholar may protest at these shortcomings, *They All Played Ragtime* was not written to satisfy academic tastes; it was designed as a rhapsodic, partisan, and—for many—inspiring popular history. By these criteria the book has been supremely successful and is deservedly referred to as "the bible of ragtime."

In the 1950s the ragtime song was no longer considered *real* ragtime; its primacy was lost as piano music (or instrumental versions of piano music) became the main concern of performers and writers. A "rinky tink" piano style, frequently played upon an instrument that was doctored to create a brittle sound, attained some popular success at that time, but for those seriously concerned with the style, the true spirit of ragtime was revealed in jazz renditions. Significantly, the most important articles on the subject—interviews with figures from the period and biographical sketches—appeared in jazz magazines. Increasingly, also, there was a general acceptance of the historical interpretations and aesthetic positions of *They All Played Ragtime*: assumptions that the Midwest was both ragtime's birthplace and center of activity; that "classic ragtime" was the genre's major expression; that ragtime by whites was—with a few notable exceptions—a markedly inferior and decadent imitation of the authentic music written by blacks. These views were more than a simple shift in opinion; ideas formulated in the 1940s and consolidated during the 1950s were diametrically opposed to commonly held views of earlier decades.

The influence of *They All Played Ragtime* became even more apparent during the 1960s with the formation of the *Ragtime Review* (1962–1967), the Ragtime Society (1962– ), and the Maple Leaf Club (1967– ), all dedicated to the "interest" or "preservation" of "classic ragtime." (Actually, these organizations have exceeded the narrow confines of "classic ragtime" and promote all kinds of piano ragtime, occasionally touching upon vocal ragtime as well.) It is evident that these groups emerged in answer to a need within the community of ragtime enthusiasts, for the two fan clubs have flourished now for more than a decade. Their newsletters or journals (*Ragtime Society/Ragtimer* and *Rag Times*) have been particularly valuable as mediums for the exchange of ideas and have published, in addition to gossip and trivia, articles of scholarly interest and value (interviews, speculative essays), reprints of music, and important newly discovered documents. In helping to preserve and distribute the materials and lore of ragtime, these clubs, composed primarily of amateurs (in the best sense of the word), have provided an invaluable service to students of American culture.

The activities and accomplishments of the ragtime clubs were known primarily to aficionados; the larger American public, though, was reached by many fine performers in the 1950s and 1960s, including Max Morath, who to a rare degree combines the attributes of entertainer and historian. Morath emerged in 1960 on the first of many "turn-of-the-century" television broadcasts, captivating his audience with bits of history and sociology told through ragtime piano-music and song. Still active on TV and the stage, he strikes a fine balance between entertainment values and historical veracity, a quality he pursues assiduously. As an outgrowth of his scholarly activities he published, in 1963, *One Hundred Ragtime Classics*, the first (and still one of the best) extensive ragtime anthology in modern times. (It is now out of print.) He has since issued several music collections and written some articles, but his major contribution to ragtime studies has been as an entertainer. More than any other personality, Morath has demonstrated ragtime's links with its era and its ability to reflect social values that are otherwise often elusive.

RAGTIME AS CLASSICAL MUSIC;
OR, HOW RAGTIME BECAME BIGTIME

Rudi Blesh had long maintained that Scott Joplin and his colleagues were actually "classical" composers, the American counterparts of European art composers of the eighteenth and nineteenth centuries. Whatever the merits or deficiencies of this position, in the 1970s Joplin came to be treated as if he *were* "classical." He was accorded both mass acclaim and critical attention; his work was regarded as "classical" by scholars and *The Entertainer* became a "classic" to the public. Blesh could not have envisioned the wide acceptance now enjoyed by Joplin, the result of a confluence of events that created a new public for the composer and a new image for ragtime.

In 1970 Joshua Rifkin, a musicologist, strayed from his usual Renaissance-Baroque interests to record some of Joplin's pieces on Nonesuch Records, a company that frequently ventures into the more esoteric realms of classical music.[20] Unlike the jazzed, heavily improvised, or "rinky-tink" versions that were standard for ragtime, Rifkin performed the music as written, and on a concert grand piano. Exceeding the most optimistic expectations, the record became a "best seller" among classical discs. (Rifkin fought vigorously to have Joplin accepted as "classical" by the music industry.) Some critics branded the performance as lacking in spirit and authenticity, but they were judging it by what may be a corrupt tradition; undeniably, Rifkin was following Joplin's notation, playing the music as, according to reports, Joplin himself performed it. In addition, this undoctored rendering, in highlighting Joplin's music rather than a performer's improvisatory skills, revealed to many listeners an unsuspected musical sophistication. One reviewer, convinced of the recording's integrity, wrote that Joplin's pieces "are the precise American equivalent, in terms of a native style of dance music, of minuets by Mozart, mazurkas by Chopin, or waltzes by Brahms."[21]

At approximately the same time that the Rifkin recording was attracting interest, the New York Public Library (with a subvention from the Rockefeller Foundation) issued *The Collected Works of Scott Joplin*, the first in a projected series of American music collections.[22] Emanating from one of the great repositories of scholarship, this collection brought to ragtime the dignity that had long been sought by Joplin supporters, and probably by Joplin himself. In this impressive format Joplin's music reached musicians who had been untouched by the burgeoning activities of enthusiasts during the previous three decades. The combination of Rifkin's concert-style reading and the Joplin edition produced a startling change in attitude: Joplin's music (and the music of a few other ragtimers) began appearing on piano recital programs, and ragtime suddenly became a subject suitable for musicological investigation.

A wave of full-length studies began in 1973 and continues to the time of this writing. Among the overviews of ragtime are Schafer and Riedel's *Art of Ragtime* (1973), Terry Waldo's *This Is Ragtime* (1976), the earlier version of the present book, the author's doctoral dissertation (1976), and Jasen and Tichenor's *Rags and Ragtime* (1978).[23] While the books propose analytic and stylistic interpretations with which the present writer disagrees,[24] they are provocative works that approach the subject responsibly. They articulate many of today's views and expand upon some, if not to the satisfaction of all readers, at least in a manner that demands rebuttal. *Art of Ragtime* is strongest in nonmusical discussions, interpretations of social commentary underlying many ragtime sheet-music covers, and such tangential matters as the contemporary vogue for "Indian songs."[25] *This Is Ragtime*'s most significant contribution to ragtime scholarship is its splendid presentation of the ragtime revival from the performers' point of view (as opposed to the historiography of the present chapter), carefully documented by interviews with many of the major participants.[26] *Rags and Ragtime* is a hybrid, combining essays on history and style with encyclopedia-styled biographies and annotated listings of works.

In the area of biography and studies of individual composers there are four new works of importance. Addison Reed's dissertation "The Life and Works of Scott Joplin" (1973)[27] and James Haskins's *Scott Joplin* (1978)[28] necessarily rely upon *They All Played Ragtime* for basic structure, but enhance our understanding of the composer by revealing a considerable amount of newly discovered information. Marjorie Freilich Den's master's thesis, "Joseph F. Lamb: A Ragtime Composer Recalled" (1976),[29] and Joseph R. Scotti's doctoral dissertation, "Joe Lamb: A Study of Ragtime's Paradox" (1977),[30] both make extensive use of interviews and communications with individuals acquainted with Lamb to add depth to what is known of the composer. In addition, Scotti's paper, a meticulous, scholarly work, evaluates every earlier commentary as it relates to Lamb, and makes the first substantive assessment of Lamb's music.

David Jasen's *Recorded Ragtime, 1897–1958* is a carefully prepared discography of some 2,200 78 r.p.m. recordings of about 900 rags.[31] One may not entirely agree with the compiler's basis of selection, with his inclusion of novelty piano and of jazz improvisations on ragtime pieces, or with his exclusion of certain works, but the book is still unique and is an indispensable reference tool.[32]

RAGTIME RECLAIMED

Through most of the revival period ragtime was sustained by a coterie of diehard fans, record collectors, and devotees of traditional jazz and honky-tonk piano. In 1971 it conquered a segment of the classical public, a public already disposed to value the art of past eras. For most Americans, however, those whose grandparents had once been the music's major support, ragtime was only a quaint, old-fashioned novelty. Before the mid-seventies were reached, though, ragtime was reclaimed by the masses.

Ragtime's return to the public is no less remarkable than its acceptance by the classical world, and the phenomena are linked. Shortly after the Rifkin recording and the Scott Joplin edition stirred interest in ragtime, Gunther Schuller—composer, performer of classical music and jazz, and director of the New England Conservatory—obtained a copy of the *Red Back Book*, a ragtime-era collection of stock band arrangements of piano rags by Joplin and several others. After editing the parts (to reduce the thick doublings common to such arrangements), in 1973 Schuller performed and recorded selections with some of his students, a group called the New England Conservatory Ragtime Ensemble.[33] A movie producer, hearing the Schuller and Rifkin recordings, was intrigued by the fresh "new" sound and decided to use Joplin rags in his film *The Sting*—a fortuitous, if inappropriate, decision. ("Inappropriate" because the music evokes the atmosphere of a period quite different from the film's 1936 scenario. A result has been that to most people today ragtime represents the late 1920s and 1930s). The film won numerous awards in 1974, including "Best Picture of the Year" and "Best Musical Score," and with the awards came an undreamed-of mass acclaim for Scott Joplin's music.[34] For much of 1974 Joplin's *The Entertainer* was on the popular best-selling charts, anachronistically appearing alongside the current rock hits. It was heard everywhere—on radio, in supermarkets, in TV commercials, on concert stages, from the practice room of virtually every piano student in America. In its wake came a host of other rags, performed on piano, harpsichord, organ, synthesizer, by classical violin-piano duos, string quartets, bands, and symphony orchestras. For a while in the 1970s, they *all* played ragtime.

## Notes

1. Isaac Goldberg, *Tin Pan Alley: A Chronicle of the American Popular Music Racket* (New York: John Day, 1930), pp. 139–77.

2. Ibid., pp. 147, 174.

3. Alain L. Locke, *The Negro and His Music* (Washington, D.C.: Associates in Negro Folk Education, 1936), pp. 57–69.

4. Ibid., p. 62.

5. Helen L. Kaufman, *From Jehovah to Jazz: Music in America from Psalmody to the Present Day* (New York: Dodd, Mead, 1937), pp. 240–54.

6. *Jazz: Hot and Hybrid* (New York: Arrow Editions, 1938; 3d ed., enl., New York: Da Capo Press, 1975). The third edition of this book has been cited above in Chapters Four and Seven. As the present chapter is concerned with the historical sequence of commentary, the original edition will be used. For reference, corresponding pages of the current edition are placed in parentheses.

7. Ibid., p. 111 (p. 136).

8. Ibid., pp. 37–46, 104–119 (pp. 58–64, 128–46).

9. Isidore Witmark and Isaac Goldberg, *The Story of the House of Witmark: From Ragtime to Swingtime* (New York: Lee Furman, 1939).

10. Sterling Brown, "Negro Producers of Ragtime" in *The Negro in Music and Art*, International Library of Negro Life and History, vol. 16 (New York: Publishers Co., 1967), pp. 49–50.

11. Laura Pratt Howard, "Ragtime" (M.M. thesis, Eastman School of Music, University of Rochester, 1942).

12. For an outline of the performers and performing trends from the beginning of the revival to the present, see Terry Waldo, *This Is Ragtime* (New York: Hawthorn Books, 1976), pp. 133–98.

13. The following is a chronological list of important ragtime articles by Carew, or relating to him as a writer of ragtime history: Carew, "New Orleans Recollections," *Record Changer* (February 1943): 28–29; Jelly Roll Morton,

"A Fragment of an Autobiography" [a MS owned by Carew], *Record Changer* (March 1944): 15–16, (April 1944): 27–28; Carew and Don E. Fowler, "Scott Joplin: Overlooked Genius," *Record Changer* (September 1944): 12–14, (October 1944): 10–12, (December 1944): 10–11; Carew and S. Brunson Campbell, "Sedalia . . . Missouri, Cradle of Ragtime," *Record Changer* 4 (May 1945): 3; Carew, "Euphonic Sounds," *Record Changer* 4 (December 1945): 40–41; Carew, "Treemonisha," *Record Changer* 5 (October 1946): 17; Carew and Campbell, "How I Became . . . A Pioneer Rag Man of the 1890's," *Record Changer* 6 (April 1947): 12; Carew, "Scott Joplin," *Jazz Record*, no. 60 (November 1947): 6–7; Carew, "Shephard N. Edmonds," *Record Changer* (December 1947): 13–14; Carew, "Assorted Rags," *Record Changer* 8 (February 1949): 6; George W. Kay, "Basin Street Stroller [referring to Carew]: New Orleans and Tony Jackson," *Jazz Journal* 4 (June 1951): 1–3 (August 1951): 1–2, (September 1951): 1–2; Carew, "Hodge Podge," *Jazz Report* 2 (September 1961): 3–5; Kay, "Reminiscing in Ragtime: An Interview with Roy Carew," *Jazz Journal* 17 (November 1964): 8–9; [Carew], "A Tribute to Roy Carew: Not Forgetting Jelly Roll," *Jazz Journal* 21 (May 1968): 22–23.

14. Respectively: (New York: Duell, Sloan, and Pearse, 1950); (New York: Alfred A. Knopf, 1950).

15. For the contents of these recordings, see Lomax, *Mister Jelly Roll*, pp. 307–312.

16. Note Morton's self-proclaimed title, "Inventor of Jazz." As one example of how his contemporaries regarded his exaggerations, songwriter Shelton Brooks (1886–1975), who was acquainted with Morton, Jackson, Joplin, and other ragtimers, said upon hearing Morton's claim of having originated the *Tiger Rag*: "That Morton was the biggest liar of all time." See Ian Whitcomb, "Shelton Brooks Is

Alive & Strutting," *Jazz Report* 7, no. 2 [ca. 1970]: no pagination.

17. Blesh and Janis, *They All Played Ragtime*, p. 80.

18. Ibid., pp. 65–66.

19. Ibid., p. 66.

20. Joshua Rifkin, *Piano Rags by Scott Joplin* (Nonesuch H-71248). Two more recordings of Joplin rags, as played by Rifkin, were later issued: Nonesuch H-71264 in 1972, and Nonesuch H-71305 in 1974.

21. H. Wiley Hitchcock, "Ragtime of the Higher Class," *Stereo Review* (April 1971): 84.

22. Two vols., ed. Vera Brodsky Lawrence; Richard Jackson, Editorial Consultant; Introduction by Rudi Blesh (New York: New York Public Library, 1971).

23. William J. Schafer and Johannes Riedel, *The Art of Ragtime: Form and Meaning of an Original Black American Art* (Baton Rouge, La.: Louisiana State University Press, 1973); Terry Waldo, *This Is Ragtime* (New York: Hawthorn Books, 1976); Edward A. Berlin, "Piano Ragtime: A Musical and Cultural Study" (Ph.D. dissertation, City University of New York, 1976); David A. Jasen and Trebor Jay Tichenor, *Rags and Ragtime: A Musical History* (New York: The Seabury Press, 1978).

24. For some of my specific criticisms of *Art of Ragtime*, see review in *Black Perspective in Music* 3 (Spring 1975): 105–107; and my dissertation "Piano Ragtime," pp. 302–304, 317–19; see also below, pp. 191–92. For other assessments, mostly favorable, see Frank Conroy, *New York Times Book Review*, 3 February 1974, sec. 7, pp. 4–5; Dick Zimmerman, *Rag Times* 7 (September 1973): 4–5; Allen Mac-Innes, *Ragtimer* (September/October 1973): 8–9; Bill Long, *Ragtimer* (November/December 1973): 6–8; Wolfgang Suppan, *Jazzforschung* 6/7 (1974/75): 279–80. My review of *This Is Ragtime* is in *Notes* 33 (June 1977): 838–40; other opinions are of Ross Russell, *New York Times Book Review*,

24 October 1976, pp. 37–39, and Dick Zimmerman, *Rag Times* 10 (November 1976): 1–3. My review of *Rags and Ragtime* is in *Notes* 35 (March 1979): 616–19; other views are of Dick Zimmerman, *Rag Times* 12 (May 1978): 1–2, and Butch Thompson, *Mississippi Rag* (August 1978): 13.

25. Schafer and Riedel, *Art of Ragtime*, pp. 161–75.

26. Waldo, *This Is Ragtime*, pp. 133–98.

27. University of North Carolina at Chapel Hill, 1973.

28. With Kathleen Benson (Garden City, N.Y.: Doubleday, 1978); reviewed by me in *Notes* 35 (March 1979): 616–19.

29. M. A. thesis, Brooklyn College, 1976.

30. Ph.D. dissertation, University of Cincinnati, 1977.

31. (Hamden, Conn.: Archon Books, Shoe String Press, 1973).

32. Two books that need not concern the serious investigator are Mark Evans's *Scott Joplin and the Ragtime Years* (New York: Dodd, Mead, 1976), a fictional biography for juveniles, and Peter Gammond's *Scott Joplin and the Ragtime Era* (New York: St. Martin's Press, 1975). The latter, a completely derivative work for the popular market, is reviewed by me in *Journal of Research in Music Education* 24 (Fall 1976): 155–56.

33. *The Red Back Book* (Angel S-36060).

34. But not necessarily for Joplin himself. The film credits state that the musical score is based on the music of Scott Joplin, implying a significant reworking by the music director, Marvin Hamlisch. Actually, the music is presented in the film essentially as performed by Rifkin and Schuller, but Hamlisch won an Academy Award and considerable fame for his part in the production, and is even thought by many to be the music's composer.

CHAPTER X

# A Consideration of Style

For most commentators during the ragtime era, all ragtime was a single phenomenon, a single style; all was "syncopation." There were some who made distinctions, and they will be noted below, but it is primarily the modern writers who have concerned themselves with ragtime style, with the subdivision of ragtime into a variety of categories.

Ragtime categories, as perceived by modern writers, tend to reflect subjective impressions and prejudices rather than musical analysis. Consequently, there is considerable vagueness as to the meaning and scope of each category, and a notable lack of uniformity in their use by various writers. Still, the instinct is sound; concurrent with the evolutionary scheme, outlined in Part Two, are secondary levels of ragtime style, which further studies should bring into sharper focus. While there is reason to be dissatisfied with the generalities that today pose as categories of style, consideration of these categories may be a suitable beginning for the development of a more critical terminology.

## The Perception of Style

When James P. Johnson recognized that the ragtime he heard in Jersey City differed from the "real" ragtime he later learned in New York, and that the New York pianists played differently from those working in other parts of the country, he was acknowledging the existence of stylistic divisions within the ragtime genre. A similar conclusion was drawn by Jelly Roll Morton, as illustrated by his contrasting performances of *Maple Leaf Rag*, designed to show the respective mannerisms of New Orleans and Saint Louis musicians.[1] While these distinctions were made in

regard to performed music, stylistic divergences also exist in published ragtime.

Historical consideration of ragtime styles seems to have received its major impetus from Blesh and Janis in *They All Played
Ragtime*,[2] but some essential concepts may also be traced back to
Sargeant's *Jazz: Hot and Hybrid*.[3] Most important in this regard
are Sargeant's statements that the best ragtime came from outside
New York, and that Tin Pan Alley's role was as a later, and cor-
rupting, imitator:

> Few of the best rags even issued from New York. On the covers of
> the earliest and most imaginative of them the names of such pub-
> lishing houses as Victor Kremer, McKinley and W. C. Polla of
> Chicago, Herzer and Brown of San Francisco, Howard and
> Browne of St. Louis, Darrow and Sharp of Denver, appear quite as
> often, or oftener, than those of the New York publishers. . . .
> Exploitation by Tin Pan Alley came later, and with it came a
> cheapening of the product.[4]

Both of these attitudes are accepted and further developed by
Blesh and Janis. Tin Pan Alley—that is, New York—ragtime is
portrayed as an inferior product, a poor counterfeit of the authentic Midwestern strain, which they refer to as "classic ragtime." As this term is central to the modern ragtime cult, it is
important to understand the various transformations its meaning
has undergone.

### Classic Ragtime: Stark and Joplin

The term "classic ragtime" had its origins in the ragtime
period and was used by publisher John Stark and composer Scott
Joplin to denote a music of superior artistic quality, a ragtime
worthy of serious consideration. Stark referred to his publishing
company as "The House of Classic Rags," and his flamboyant and
whimsical advertisements are the source of some of the attitudes
that are today associated with the term, especially the comparisons with European classical music, and the classic–Tin Pan
Alley dichotomy:

### CLASSIC RAGS

> As Pike's Peak to a mole hill, so are our rag classics to the slush
> that fills the jobbers' bulletins. . . .
> St. Louis is the Galileo of classic rags. It is a pity that they did
> not originate in New York or Paree so that the understudy musi-
> cians and camp followers could tip toe and rave about them.[5]

Tell me ye winged winds that 'round my pathway roar.
—We know one house of classic rags—pray are there any more?
The answer filtered through the leaves and whispered 'long the
shore:
　"There's only one classic Rag House." . . . ,
　We know what we say when we call these instrumental rags classic.
　They are the perfection of type.[6]

Since we forced the conviction on this country that what we
called a rag may possibly contain more genius and psychic advance
thought than a Chopin nocturne or a Bach fugue, writers of di-
luted and attenuated imitations have sprung up from Maine's fro-
zen hills to the boiling bogs of Louisiana.[7]

　　Stark's use of the term "classic" was more than an advertising
ploy. The term reflects his sincere effort to avoid the hackneyed
and his willingness to print music of uncommon patterns and
technical difficulties. Nor did his high standards go unrecognized:
such connoisseurs of piano ragtime as Axel Christensen and Jelly
Roll Morton praised his publications.[8]
　　It is not known who originated the term "classic ragtime."
While Stark used the word "classic" in this context in his advertisements by 1910, if not earlier, the word did not appear in his
published titles until very late: James Scott's *Modesty Rag. A
Classic* (1920), *Pegasus. A Classic Rag* (1920), *Broadway Rag. A
Classic* (1922). Much earlier, some of Joplin's pieces issued by
other publishers began to refer to the classic concept: *The Sycamore. A Concert Rag* (1904), *Sugar Cane. A Ragtime Classic Two
Step* (1908). His two operas, *A Guest of Honor* (1903) and
*Treemonisha* (1911), also signify classical aims.
　　Although "classic ragtime" as a concept, or even as a term,
seems to have achieved little contemporaneous recognition or use
beyond the Stark/Joplin circle, there are a few other references to
it. In an interview in 1909, composer May Aufderheide, whose
rags were published in Indianapolis by her father, applied the
term to her own music.[9] She did not explain what she meant by
classic ragtime, but since she cited her piece *The Thriller* (1909),
which contains suggestions of Joplin's *Maple Leaf Rag* and
*Gladiolus*, it would seem that her adoption of the expression was
in emulation of Joplin. In a second instance, in 1911, the term
was used by an editorial writer praising the score of Joplin's
*Treemonisha*. The reference is somewhat mysterious and the
phraseology—"Scott Joplin, well known as a writer of music, and

especially of what a certain musician has classified as 'classic rag-time'"[10]—suggests that the term was not generally known.

Axel Christensen also used the expression,[11] but he was per-sonally acquainted with Stark. The evidence suggests, then, that "classic ragtime" had a severely restricted currency. It was used by Joplin to refer to his compositions, in a single known instance by May Aufderheide, and by Stark to characterize his entire catalogue. In all these cases the term signifies music of superior quality, supposedly the equal of European "classics." It does not imply either a stylistic unity among classic rags or a common source of inspiration, propositions that would be difficult to dem-onstrate in view of the diversity of Stark's publications. As later adapted by Blesh and Janis, though, and then by following com-mentators, "classic ragtime" assumed these properties and others as its coverage became increasingly broad and complex.

## Classic Ragtime: Blesh and Janis

*They All Played Ragtime*, emphasizing Joplin and other Stark-associated composers, very appropriately discusses the music as "classic ragtime." Due to these authors' persuasive nar-rative, the term then became the dominant slogan of ragtime en-thusiasts. But after having established organizations "dedicated to the preservation of Classic Ragtime," it occurred to some mem-bers to ask, "What *is* 'classic ragtime'?"

> The expression "classic ragtime" is a rather recently-introduced one so far as I know. . . . The term's meaning has escaped me. . . .
> [We] await enlightenment as to just what it is about a specimen of syncopation that makes it "classic ragtime" while countless of the world's old ragtime numbers apparently go rejected by the modernists.[12]

> Most ragtime fans (myself included) don't seem to know what's "classic" and what isn't, once they get away from a small body of pre-labelled "classic" compositions. Being committed to the propa-gation and preservation of "Classic Ragtime" and not knowing what you're talking about is embarrassing. What's worse, it tends to limit your range of ragtime interest to those few rags that some-body else has called "classic."[13]

> Just what the hell *is* classic ragtime, anyway?
> Drop that one in a crowd of twenty rag buffs, and you'll get forty different answers. Everyone seems to agree that there's a certain something called "classic ragtime," but they can't seem to agree on what it is.[14]

This confusion has been created by the extension of the original bounds of classic ragtime. Instead of simply referring to the music composed by associates of Stark, it has come to denote the music, first, of a specific geographic region:

> The scene of classic ragtime was the Missouri Valley area of Missouri and Kansas, with the adjacent fringes of Arkansas, Tennessee, Texas and the Oklahoma and Indiana territories. Its focal points were, successively, Sedalia and St. Louis.[15]

Second, a continuous undercurrent suggests that classic ragtime was derived from black folk music of the region:

> Piano ragtime was developed by the Negro from folk melodies. . . .
> Although ragtime originated on the folk level, several outstandingly gifted composers of both races carried the music to a creative level that can only be termed classical.

> Joplin's *Maple Leaf Rag* is only one of scores of richly folksy rags that got published. . . . But *Maple Leaf* was the one incomparable fusion of folk music and art music.

> The classicism that in *Original Rags* and *Maple Leaf* had already lifted folk melody to a serious, syncopated level . . .[16]

Third, classic ragtime also signifies a stylistic consistency, as implied by the inclusion of Joe Lamb, a white Easterner:

> Joe Lamb, the white ragtime composer nearest to the Joplin classicism, is the exception that proves the rule. This New Jersey phenomenon is the only one not born or brought up in the folk-rag area.[17]

Difficulties arise in attempts to apply the term "classic ragtime" uniformly. In *Classic Piano Rags*, a companion anthology to *They All Played Ragtime*,[18] Blesh gives concrete examples of his conception of classic ragtime. Stark publications are generously, and rightfully, represented; Joe Lamb is the only Easterner included, but his presence is justified by his having been published regularly by Stark and by his having consciously modeled his music after Joplin's. The admission of Percy Wenrich, Clarence Woods, and Charles Johnson is more questionable; these composers were not associated with Stark and do not bear real stylistic resemblances to Joplin or to any other composer who is justifiably called "classic." There is certainly little in common between the almost Chopinesque chromatics in Joplin's *Gladiolus*

*Rag* and the relatively static harmonies of Woods's *Slippery Elm Rag* (Example X–1). These additional composers were apparently included simply on the basis of their Missouri/Midwestern birth. (Jasen, in contrast, places these composers in the Tin Pan Alley category, although he concedes the geographic contradiction inherent in Johnson's preference for living in Kansas City rather than New York.)[19] Through such accretions to the domain of classic ragtime the term has been overextended, losing whatever precision and usefulness it had.[20]

EXAMPLE X–1. (a) S. Joplin, *Gladiolus Rag*, C 5–8; (b) Clarence Woods, *Slippery Elm Rag* (Dallas, Tx.: Bush and Gerts Piano Co., 1912), C 9–16.

(a)

© Edward B. Marks Music Corporation.
Used by permission.

(b)

Despite these difficulties and despite its vagueness, the Blesh/Janis conception of classic ragtime is, in general, the one most widely accepted today. Adding to the perplexity, though, is the expansion of the Blesh/Janis version by Schafer and Riedel in their favorably received *The Art of Ragtime*. Taking one further step away from the Stark/Joplin conception of classic ragtime,

Schafer and Riedel imbue the term with even more doubtful qualities.

### Classic Ragtime: Schafer and Riedel

One of the main tenets Schafer and Riedel adopt from Blesh and Janis is the tie between classic ragtime and folk music. They assert repeatedly that piano rags are nothing more than folk tunes collected and arranged into dance suites, thereby denying any melodic originality to the composers of record:

> Basically it is a formation, an organization of folk melodies and musical techniques. . . . In a sense, ragtime composers served as folk collectors or musicologists, collecting music in the air around them in the black communities and organizing it into brief suites or anthologies which they called piano rags.

> Classic ragtime can be defined very simply as the piano rags of Scott Joplin, James Scott, Joseph Lamb, and their immediate collaborators, students, and followers. . . . These three composers collected the materials of early folk ragtime, codified the style of a generation of folk players, and defined the structure of classic rag.

> Essentially all three men were as much collectors as composers, assembling and synthesizing the works of itinerant ragtime stylists who were too unskilled, or too indifferent, to write down their own creations.

> Joplin's first task was to create from a widely known folk *style* an actual *genre* of scored music. (This is roughly analogous to the manner in which Bela Bartok and Zoltan Kodaly collected and organized Hungarian folk music.) To do this he had to invent and perfect a set of conventions of structure and form.

> [James] Scott came closest to capturing Joplin's sensitive handling of Missouri folk materials.

> Joplin and his peers had folk inspiration aplenty but no form into which to cast it.[21]

With all of the claims of a derivative relationship between classic ragtime and folk music, there is not one suggestion of a specific folk melody being the source of a published classic rag, not a single statement from Joplin, Scott, or Lamb that they were collecting Missouri folk materials, and no explanation of how Joe Lamb managed to absorb the black folk tunes of Missouri without leaving Brooklyn. Also questionable are the statements that Joplin "had to invent and perfect a set of conventions of structure and form" and that he had "no form into which to cast" his music, for they completely ignore the rag literature in print before his first rag publication and the hundreds of earlier two-step dance compositions that provided the formal and structural model for ragtime.

The concept of classic ragtime has been stretched beyond recognition. What was originally a fairly well-defined and select category has been made to embrace a host of composers of various stylistic orientations, has been made to include an embryonic ethnomusicology, and has been made dependent upon a supposedly existing—but never displayed—body of folk music. If the term is ever to have any useful critical application, it must be pared down to sensible, definable dimensions.

### Toward a Definition of Classic Ragtime

There has been one recent effort to rescue the classic ragtime concept from extravagant verbiage. In his study of Joe Lamb, Joseph Scotti proposes that a musical definition of classic ragtime be attempted. Although he greatly facilitates his task by considering only three composers—Lamb, Joplin, and Scott—he still falls short of his goal, as he readily concedes. Instead of a definitive proposition he formulates a tentative working list of the traits of classic ragtime: (1) the music is conceived as a notated art (i.e., it is not improvised); (2) it is idiomatic to the piano; (3) syncopation is but one of several equal musical parameters; (4) it is absolute music, intended primarily for listening; (5) it is newly composed (i.e., no medley/pastiches); (6) there is a conscious manipulation of the macroform and tonal plan.[22]

This list probably raises more questions than it answers (and this may be one of its virtues). Are any of these traits more essential than others? Could some works by classic-ragtime composers be judged non-classic for failing to meet these criteria? Could the rags of a non-classic composer, exhibiting these traits, be considered classic? Item (5) seems to divest classic ragtime of its reliance on folk music, but the author is reluctant to make a complete break with this fashionable idea: "Although some of the rags of Joplin may have vestiges of black folk song in their melodic contours, each is conceived as an autonomous musical entity rather than an arrangement or "ragged" version of pre-existent material."[23] Number (4) is a new hypothesis. As Scotti elaborates: "Al-

though many classic rags may have been used for dancing, singing, etc., they are not functional in intent as, for example, ragtime songs and cakewalks. They are meant to be listened to and
appreciated by the initiated."[24] Lamb's nonprofessional attitude
toward composition might incline him toward this interpretation.
One also wonders if this is the meaning behind the subtitle "A
Concert Rag" appended to Joplin's *The Sycamore*. But there is
also evidence to the contrary, evidence of Joplin's concern with
dance music. It is also clear that from the earliest days of the era
ragtime dance-music was played by concert bands, thereby functioning as listening music. It seems that this distinction made by
Scotti simply did not exist, that *all* ragtime could be listening
music as well as dance music. Certainly, more evidence is needed
to substantiate the proposition.

Regardless of differences of opinion, Scotti's approach is
generally one of analysis rather than of platitudes, and his efforts
contribute to divesting classic ragtime of its almost mystical
shroud. His guidelines were offered as a point of departure for
future investigators, and they could well be put to this use.

## Other Ragtime Classifications

Various other categories of ragtime styles are mentioned in
the recent literature: cakewalk, folk, Tin Pan Alley, Eastern,
stride, Saint Louis, Midwestern, Chicago, Louisville, New Orleans, and novelty. In view of the perfunctory reasoning that has
gone into the claims for most of these categories, a close scrutiny
would not be very fruitful. In general, the literature promoting
these classifications is almost entirely lacking in musical discussion, musical examples, or efforts to isolate and define specific
traits characterizing a style. The following, then, is limited to a
few clarifications and comments.

The *cakewalk rag* designation is the least confusing; it refers
simply to the early rags that are characterized by untied and augmented syncopations, as discussed in Chapters Five and Seven.
The term is suitable, as most rags during the 1890s bore
"cakewalk" subtitles and utilized untied syncopation. Although a
few tied-syncopation rags (as well as unsyncopated marches) were
also labeled "cakewalk" at that time, the dance became associated
most closely with the untied-syncopation rag. Thus, when anach-
ronistic untied-syncopation rags were published later in the era

(such as Charles Johnson's *Fun on the Levee*, 1917), they were usually subtitled "cakewalk."

The so-called *folk rag* is more problematic. It is described by several writers as a style which was centered in Nashville, Tennessee, and which drew upon local folk material:

> ﹨ This early kind of ragtime utilized the simple syncopations coming from the songs and dances of the working people in the rural midwest and south. The outstanding member of the Folk Rag composers was Charles Hunter [1878–c. 1907] of Tennessee.[25]

> The extraordinary ragtime at Nashville could well be called a *school* of folk rag composition. There is a consistent style here—an inspired spontaneity and an unfettered approach characteristic of good folk rag, and an ebullient mix of both Black folk sources and White Tennessee hill music, a distinctly "southern-fried" concoction. The leading composer was blind pianist Charles Hunter.[26]

In an earlier writing, I had noted that only one individual other than Hunter, Thomas Broady, also of Nashville, had ever been identified as a folk-rag composer—hardly an auspicious make-up for "a school of composition."[27] Since then, Jasen and Tichenor have amplified their thoughts in what is the most ambitious treatment of folk ragtime to date.[28] Many more composers are introduced into the category, and the folk rag is proposed as the inspiration for all other ragtime (and novelty piano) styles. Supportive evidence, though, is lacking. While Tichenor is a self-proclaimed folk-ragtime composer,[29] and presumably possesses some insight into the subject, he offers no musical definition or description of the style. Essentially, the reader is told that folk ragtime is what, to the authors, sounds folksy.

*Tin Pan Alley ragtime* is a much maligned category. It is usually presented as the antithesis of classic ragtime, the result of the crass, exploitative commercialism of New York publishers (as if publishers in other parts of the country were innocent of these traits) and inferior workmanship. The category is generally applied to composers who lived and published in New York, but should such an individual demonstrate some talent, a reason is found to place him in another group, thereby denying Tin Pan Alley any merit. Thus Eubie Blake, despite his commercial success as a popular composer connected with New York publishers, is not given the Tin Pan Alley label. Instead, he is placed variously in the *Eastern* (referring to the Eastern seacoast from Baltimore to New York) or in the *stride* school. For Blesh and Janis, the reason for Blake's reclassification is the inherently high quality of his music, an attribute that stems from an undefined "folk strain" in his work.[30]

There is no intention here of defending what has been vaguely referred to as Tin Pan Alley ragtime, for, undeniably, an enormous amount of poor-quality music has emanated from New York presses, as well as those in other parts of the country; but an unbiased perspective, a view clear of the myths perpetuated in the literature, is needed. One such myth is that Tin Pan Alley ragtime is a late and corrupt form, a poor copy of classic and other superior styles:

> Exploitation by Tin Pan Alley came later, and with it came a cheapening of the product.[31]

> A handful of creative spirits, some black, some white—James Scott, Joseph F. Lamb and a few others, led by Scott Joplin—went on composing serious ragtime, getting it published when and where they could, but composing it nonetheless. Finally the decisive factor, commercialization, entered. Tin Pan Alley, reaching for the quick buck, flooded the market with an inundation of ragtime.[32]

But this appraisal is inaccurate. By the 1880s New York publishers were issuing rag-like compositions, such as *Patrol Comique* and *Hottentots Patrol*, and the first instrumental rag in print, Krell's *Mississippi Rag*, came from a New York firm; by the end of 1899, when classic ragtime was just getting started, hundreds of rags had already come off the New York presses. However artless the Tin Pan Alley product may be (and this point is also debatable), it was not a late arrival in ragtime publication.

The other styles listed can be described in a few words. *Saint Louis ragtime* is approximately the same as classic ragtime, but with the recognition that not all of the Saint Louis composers were associated with Stark.[33] *Midwestern ragtimers* were those of that region who were active mostly in the second decade of the twentieth century. Some were published by Stark, but there is no suggestion of stylistic unity. *Chicago* and *Louisville ragtime* are rarely used terms and refer simply to musicians working in those areas. Both Joe Jordan and Percy Wenrich have been named as members of the "Chicago School,"[34] although they are also, and more frequently, placed in the classic, Midwestern, and Tin Pan Alley groups. *New Orleans ragtime* has two outstanding exponents, Jelly Roll Morton and Tony Jackson. Morton, however, did not publish his rags until the 1920s, and Jackson published only songs. Few publications from New Orleans have come to light and, in view of the attention devoted to early New Orleans jazz, surprisingly little has been written about the piano ragtime from that city.[35] A final style, *novelty ragtime*, referring to the novelty piano of the 1920s, is discussed in Chapter Eight; as was indicated, this is not a true ragtime style, and use of the term should be reconsidered.

The question of stylistic diversity is one of the central issues in ragtime studies today. This book has provided an evolutionary view of ragtime styles, a view which, by providing a background for the evaluation of specific musical gestures, should facilitate investigations of individual composers. It is only after we have consolidated the data from such investigations that we will be able to determine, with some accuracy and on the basis of specific musical traits, how the composers fall into stylistic groupings.

The issue of regional styles is more problematic. Such a theory would have to consider, among other matters, how these indigenous group characteristics differed from general chronological and stylistic groupings; how, in an age when musicians traveled extensively and published and recorded music had wide distribution, localities avoided outside influences, preserving their stylistic purity and insularity. In addition, all stylistic formulations must be drawn up in exacting musical terms; whatever validity the strictly intuitive approach may have, it is too limited and personal to be applied to critical historical studies.

Ultimately, ragtime is more than a musical style; it is the achievement of cultural independence and identity. At a time when many American art composers were seeking to loosen the ties of European musical dominance in order to find and assert a recognizable national language, the ragtime composer had already attained this end. Significantly, the defining element of this language emerged not from the European-American heritage, but from the Afro-American; it represented, despite considerable opposition, the first widespread acceptance of a black cultural influence into the mainstream of American life.

The importance of ragtime transcends any individual work, composer, or group. Viewed in perspective, it is the rhythmic impulse of ragtime that is of greatest consequence, an impulse which, through its characteristic "swing," has made its impact on Western music. Whatever the fate of ragtime music, whether it remains in the public focus or again recedes to historical obscurity, it leaves a legacy of rhythmic vitality.

## Notes

1. Recordings re-released on *They All Played the Maple Leaf Rag* (Herwin 401).

2. (4th ed., rev., New York: Oak Publications, 1971).

3. (New York: Arrow Editions, 1938; 3d ed., enl., New York: Da Capo Press, 1975).

4. Ibid., p. 117 (p. 142).

5. Advertisement from 1916, as printed in facsimile in William J. Schafer and Johannes Riedel, *The Art of Ragtime: Form and Meaning of an Original Black American Art* (Baton Rouge, La.: Louisiana State University Press, 1973), frontispiece.

6. As reproduced in facsimile, without date, in *Ragtimer* 6 (April 1967): 23.

7. Advertisement on the back cover of Scott Joplin and Scott Hayden, *Felicity Rag* (St. Louis: Stark Music, 1911).

8. See above, p. 74; see also Axel Christensen, "Chicago Syncopations: Is Ragtime Respectable?" *Melody* 2 (August 1918): 8; idem, "Chicago Syncopations: Ragtime Demoralizing," *Melody* 2 (November 1918): 22; and Alan Lomax, *Mister Jelly Roll: The Fortunes of Jelly Roll Morton, New Orleans Creole and "Inventor of Jazz"* (2d ed., Berkeley, Ca.: University of California Press, 1973), pp. 148–49.

9. "'Classic Rags' Composed by May Aufderheide," *American Musician and Art Journal* 25 (13 August 1909): 20.

10. "A Musical Novelty," *American Musician and Art Journal* 27 (24 June 1911): 7.

11. See Axel Christensen, "Chicago Syncopations: John Stark, Pioneer Publisher," *Melody* 2 (October 1918): 8.

12. Russ Cole, untitled letter, *Ragtime Society* 4 (March/April 1965): 19–20.

13. Tom Shea, "Winging It with Tom Shea," *Ragtimer* 6 (April 1967): 3.

14. Bob Ashforth, "On Classic Ragtime," *Ragtimer* (March/April 1970): 7.

15. Rudi Blesh, Introduction to *Classic Piano Rags: Complete Original Music for 81 Rags* (New York: Dover, 1973), p. vi.

16. These three quotations are from Blesh and Janis, *They All Played Ragtime*: in order, pp. 7–8, 52, 66.

17. Ibid., p. 107.

18. Although the anthology was published twenty-three years later, Blesh considers the two volumes as a set. (Private communication from Blesh to the author, 22 January 1975.)

19. David Jasen, *Recorded Ragtime, 1897–1957* (Hamden, Conn.: Archon Books, Shoe String Press, 1973), p. 4.

20. A similar suggestion was made by the author in a review of *Classic Piano Rags* in *Black Perspective in Music* 2 (Fall 1974): 218–19. In response Blesh wrote on 22 January 1975: "Pressed by you, I must admit that not all midwest ragtime of the period is classic or of an even creative quality, but I had in mind something like what happened in, say, 18th century music: even minor composers are 'classic' because they are of the period."

Blesh's analogy is apt if restricted simply to time and place. But just as Lamb is admitted to the classic category, there should be sufficient flexibility for Midwestern composers to be placed in groups as dictated by stylistic affinity. Also ignored in Blesh's explanation is the original conception of classic ragtime as music of outstanding quality.

21. These six quotations are from Schafer and Riedel, *Art of Ragtime*: in order, pp. 5, 49, 51, 54, 75, 97.

22. Joseph R. Scotti, "Joe Lamb: A Study of Ragtime's Paradox" (Ph.D. dissertation, University of Cincinnati, 1977), pp. 177–79.

23. Ibid., p. 178.

24. Ibid.

25. Jasen, *Recorded Ragtime*, p. 3.

26. Trebor J. Tichenor, Introduction, *Ragtime Rarities: Complete Original Music for 63 Piano Rags* (New York: Dover, 1975), p. vii.

27. Edward A. Berlin, "Piano Ragtime: A Musical and Cultural Study"

(Ph.D. dissertation, The City University of New York, 1976), p. 324.

28. David A. Jasen and Trebor Jay Tichenor, *Rags and Ragtime: A Musical History* (New York: The Seabury Press, 1978), pp. 21–27.

29. Ibid., p. 278.

30. Blesh and Janis, *They All Played Ragtime*, p. 199.

31. Sargeant, *Jazz*, p. 117 (p. 142).

32. Rudi Blesh, "Scott Joplin: Black-American Classicist," Introduction to *The Collected Works of Scott Joplin*, ed. Vera Brodsky Lawrence; Richard Jackson, Editorial Consultant

(New York: New York Public Library, 1971), p. xiii.

33. Jasen, *Recorded Ragtime*, p. 3.

34. See Walter N. H. Harding, untitled letter, *Ragtime Society* 3 (April 1964): 25, and Bartlett D. Simms and Ernest Borneman, "Ragtime: History and Analysis," *Record Changer* 4 (October 1945): 7.

35. Author Al Rose reports having made significant discoveries in early ragtime publications from New Orleans, but has not yet published his findings and has declined my request for specifics.

# Appendix

## LOCATION INDEX FOR PIANO RAGS
## IN SELECTED ANTHOLOGIES

    Original ragtime sheet music is becoming increasingly rare and difficult to obtain, but there is ready access to many works in published anthologies. The following table indicates the location of piano rags in some of the more interesting and reliable collections. In addition to current anthologies, two important out-of-print collections are included.

BeR   *The Best of Ragtime Favorites and How to Play Them*. New York: Charles Hansen, n.d.

BlC   Blesh, Rudi, comp. *Classic Piano Rags: Complete Original Music for 81 Rags*. New York: Dover, 1973.

BrR   *Brainard's Ragtime Collection, Being a Collection of Characteristic Two-Steps, Cake Walks, Plantation Dances, Etc.* New York: S. Brainard's Sons, 1899. Out of print.

GEn   *Golden Encyclopedia of Ragtime, 1900 to 1974*. New York: Charles Hansen, 1974.

JCW   Joplin, Scott. *The Collected Works of Scott Joplin*. Ed. Vera Brodsky Lawrence; Richard Jackson, Editorial Consultant; Introduction by Rudi Blesh. Vol. 1, *Works for Piano*. New York: New York Public Library, 1971.

MMG   Morath, Max. *Max Morath's Giants of Ragtime*. New York: Edward B. Marks, 1971.

MOH   Morath, Max, ed. *One Hundred Ragtime Classics*. Denver: Donn Printing, 1963. Out of print.

PTR   *Play Them Rags: A Piano Album of Authentic Rag-Time Solos*. New York: Mills Music, 1961.

RtP   *Ragtime Piano: A Collection of Standard Rags for Piano*. New York: Mills Music, 1963.

SWF   Shealy, Alexander, ed. *World's Favorite Music and Songs: Ragtime*. Carlstadt, N.J.: Ashley Publications, 1973.

TFR   *34 Ragtime Jazz Classics for Piano*. New York: Melrose Music, 1964.

TRR  Tichenor, Trebor Jay, comp. *Ragtime Rarities: Complete Original Music for 63 Piano Rags*. New York: Dover, 1975.

ZTr  Zimmerman, Richard, comp. *A Tribute to Scott Joplin and the Giants of Ragtime*. New York: Sattinger-International Music, Charles Hansen, 1975.

PIANO RAGS IN SELECTED ANTHOLOGIES

| Composer | Composition | | | | | | | Anthologies | | | | | | |
|---|---|---|---|---|---|---|---|---|---|---|---|---|---|---|
| | | BeR | BlC | BrR | GEn | JCW | MMG | MOH | PTR | RtP | SWF | TFR | TRR | ZTr |
| Anderson, O. H. | Dakota Rag (1899) | | | | | | | | | | | | 1 | |
| Aufderheide, M. | Dusty Rag (1908) | | | 14 | | | | | | | 16 | | 5 | |
| | Thriller (1909) | | | | | | | | | | | | 9 | 33 |
| Barnard, G. D. | Alabama Dreams (1899) | | | | | | | | | | | | | |
| Barney & Seymore | St. Louis Tickle (1904) | | | | | | | 97 | | | | | 14 | |
| Bay, W. J. | Seben Come Eleben (1899) | | | | | | | | | | 29 | | | |
| Bayler, A. E. | Rastus Johnson's Cake Walk (1899) | | | 49 | | | | | | | | | | |
| [Bennett, T. C.], cf. Florence, G. E. | | | | | | | | | | | | | | |
| Bernard, M. | Sweet Pickles (1907) | | | | | | | | | | | | 19 | |
| Birch, R. | Stinging Bee (1908) | | 51 | | | | | | | | | | 24 | |
| [Johnson, C. L.] Blake, E. | Blue Goose Rag (1916) | | | | | | 20 | | | | | | | |
| | Chevy Chase (1914) | | | | | | 40 | 235 | | | | | | |
| | Dictys on 7th Avenue (ca. 1942)[a] | | | | | | 24 | 209 | | | | | | |
| | Fizz Water (1914) | | | | | | | | | | | | | |
| | Tricky Fingers (ca. 1907–1909)[a] | | | | | | 34 | | | | | | | |
| | Troublesome Ivories (ca. 1909–1914)[a] | | | | | | 28 | | | | | | | |
| Bolen, G. M. | Smoky Topaz (1901) | | | | | | | | | | | | 29 | |
| Boone, J. W. | Rag Medley No. 1 (1908) | | | | | | | | | | | | 33 | |
| | Rag Medley No. 2 (1909) | | | | | | | | | | | | 38 | |
| Botsford, G. | Black and White Rag (1908) | | | | | | | | 16[b] | | | | | |
| | Grizzly Bear (1910) | | | | | | | | | 38 | | | | |

[a] Published 1971.
[b] This is not the original, but a revision by Lou Leaman, 1940.

| Composer | Composition | BeR | BlC | BrR | GEn | JCW | MMG | MOH | PTR | RtP | SWF | TFR | TRR | ZTr |
|---|---|---|---|---|---|---|---|---|---|---|---|---|---|---|
| Broady, T. G. | Mandy's Broadway Stroll (1899) | | | | | | | | | | | | | |
| | Tennessee Jubilee (1898) | | | | | | | | | | | | 45 | |
| | Whittling Remus (1900) | | | | | | | | | | | | 50 | |
| | Florida Cracker (1899) | | | 10 | | | | | | | | | 55 | 126 |
| Brooks, E. | Suwanee Echoes | | | | | | | | | | 4 | | | |
| Brown, A. W. | Manhattan Rag (1901) | | | | | | | | | | | | | 102 |
| Brownold, F. | Rag-Time Joke (1905) | | | | | | | | | | | | | |
| Burke, A. L. | Rag La Joie (1918) | | | | | | | | | | | | 60 | |
| Cammack, J. | One o' Them Things (1904) | | | | | | | | | | | | 63 | |
| Chapman, J. & Smith, L. | | | | | | | | | | | | | | |
| Chauvin, L. & Joplin, S. | Heliotrope Bouquet (1907) | 86 | | | | | | | | | | 78 | | |
| Claypoole, E. B. | Alabama Jigger (1913) | | 156 | | 290 | 263 | | 172 | | | | | | |
| | Ragging the Scale (1915) | | | | 88 92 | | | 231 | | | | | | |
| Cobb, G. L. | Russian Rag (1918) | | | | | | | 30 | | | | | | |
| Cohan, G. M. | Popularity (1906) | | | | | | | | | | | | | |
| Cohen, C. | Fashion Rag (1912) | | | | | | | | | 22 | | | | 47 |
| | Riverside Rag | | | | | | | | 9 | | | | | 68 |
| Connor, R. W. | Carpet Rags (1903) | | | | | | | | | | | | | |
| Crabbe, C. D. | Klassicle Rag (1911) | | | | | | | | | | | | 68 | |
| Denney, H. | Chimes (1910) | | | | | | | | | | 36 | | | |
| Emerson, I. & Howard, J. E. | Hello! Ma Baby (1899) | | | | | | | | | | | | | |
| English, G. W. | Sweet Dreams of Youth (1905) | | | | | | 58 | 217 | | | | | | 106 |
| Europe, J. R. | Castle House Rag (1914) | 30 | | | | | | | | | | | | |
| Finzel, G. H. | Manila Belle (1899) | | | | | | | | | | | | | |
| Fischer, T. | Encore Rag (1912) | | | | | | | | | | | | | |
| Fischler, H. A. | Chili-Sauce (1910) | | | | | | | | 34 | | | | | |
| | Hot Scotch Rag (1911) | | | | | | | | | 18 | | | 73 | |

| Composer | Composition | BeR | BIC | BrR | GEn | JCW | MMG | MOH | PTR | RtP | SWF | TFR | TRR | ZTr |
|---|---|---|---|---|---|---|---|---|---|---|---|---|---|---|
| Florence, G. E. [Bennett, T. C.] | Pepper Sauce (1910) | | | | | | | | | 34 | | | | |
| | Weeping Willow Rag (1911) | | | | | | | | | 14 | | | | |
| Gearen, J. | Sweet Pickles (1907) | | | | | | | | | | | | 19 | |
| Gibson, L. P. | Big Foot Lou (1899) | | | | | | | | | | | | 77 | |
| | Cactus Rag (1916) | | | | | | | | | | | | 87 | |
| | Jinx Rag (1911) | | | | | | | | | | | | 82 | |
| Gillis, F. R. | Coon Hollow Capers (1899) | | | | | | | | | | | | 91 | |
| Gould, G. | Whoa! Nellie! (1915) | | | | | | | | | | | | 95 | |
| Guy, H. P. | Cleanin' Up in Georgia (1899) | | | | | | | | | | | | 105 | |
| | Echoes from the Snowball Club (1898) | | | | | | | 167 | | | | | 100 | |
| Hamilton, R. J. | Alabama Hoe Down (1899) | | | 34 | | | | | | | 52 | | | |
| Hampton, R. | Agitation Rag (1915) | | 6 | | | | | | | | | | | |
| | Cataract Rag (1914) | | 2 | | 100 | | | | | | | 34 | | |
| Harney, B. | Cake Walk in the Sky (1899) | 28 | | | | | | | | | | | | |
| | Rag Time Instructor (1897) | | | | | | | 358 | | | | | | 58 |
| Harris, S. P. | Virginia Rag (1907) | | | | | | | | | | | | | 120 |
| Harrison, W. | Bran Dance Shuffle (1902) | | | | | | | | | | | | | 136 |

| Composer | Composition | BeR | BlC | BrR | GEn | JCW | MMG | MOH | PTR | RtP | SWF | TFR | TRR | ZTr |
|---|---|---|---|---|---|---|---|---|---|---|---|---|---|---|
| Hayden, S. & Joplin, S. | Felicity Rag (1911) | | | | | 269 | | 179 | | | | | | |
| | Kismet Rag (1913) | | 151 | | 340 | 275 | | 195 | | | | | | |
| | Something Doing (1903) | | | | | 251 | | 262 | 46 | | 122 | | | |
| | Sunflower Slow Drag (1901) | 78 | | | | | | | | | | 70 | | |
| Held, W. | Chromatic Rag (1916) | 32 | 146 | | 238 | 245 | | 8 | | | | 24 | | |
| Hoffmann, M. | Rag Medley (1897) | | | | 100 | | | | | | | | | |
| | Ragtown Rags (1898) | | | | | | | 183 | | | 74 | | | |
| Holzmann, A. | Bunch o' Blackberries (1899) | | | | | | | | | | | | 110 | |
| | Flying Arrow (1906) | | | | | | | | | | | | 117 | 140 |
| | Smoky Mokes (1899) | | | | | | | 109 | | | | | 121 | 92 |
| | Polar Bear Rag (1910) | | | | | | | | | | | | | 54 |
| Howard, G. P. | Hello! Ma Baby (1899) | | | | | | | | | | 36 | | | |
| Howard, J. E. & Emerson, I. | My Filipino Princess (1899) | | | 42 | | | | | | | | | | |
| Hubbell, J. R. | Sandella (1921) | | | | | | | | | | | | | 44 |
| Hudson, E. | Back to Life (1905) | | 37 | | | | | | | | | | | |
| Hunter, C. | Cotton Bolls (1901) | | 27 | | | | | | | | | | | |
| | Just Ask Me (1902) | | | | | | | | | | | | | |
| | Possum and Taters (1900) | | 16 | | | | | 159 | | | | | 126 | |
| | Tennessee Tantalizer (1900) | | 22 | | | | | 304 | | | | | | |
| | Tickled to Death (1899) | | 11 | | | | | 82 | | | | | | |
| | Why We Smile (1903) | | | | | | | | | | | | | 143 |

| *Composer* | *Composition* | BeR | BIC | BrR | GEn | JCW | MMG | MOH | PTR | RtP | SWF | TFR | TRR | ZTr |
|---|---|---|---|---|---|---|---|---|---|---|---|---|---|---|
| Ingraham, R. G. | Mando Rag (1914) | | | | | | | | | | | | | 152 |
| Janza, M. | Lion Tamer (1913) | | 42 | | | | | | | | | | 130 | |
| Jentes, H. | Bantam Step (1916) | | 51 | | | | | | | | | | 135 | |
| Johnson, C. L. | Black Smoke (1902) | | 47 | | | | | | | | | | | |
| | Blue Goose Rag (1916) | | | | | | | | | | | | | |
| | Cum-Bac Rag (1911) | | | | | | | | | | | | | |
| | Dill Pickles (1906) | | | | | | | | 6 | | | | | |
| | Doc Brown's Cake Walk (1899) | | | | | | | | | | | | 140 | |
| | Tar Babies (1911) | | | | | | | | | | | | | |
| Johnson, J. P. | Caprice Rag (ca. 1914–1917)c | | | | | | | | | 62 | | | | 40 |
| | Daintiness Rag (ca. 1916–1917)c | | | | | | | | | 58 | | | | |
| Johnston, J. H. | Cake-Walkers (1899) | | | 60 | | | | | | | | | | |
| Joplin, S. | Bethena (1905) | | | | 304 | 113 | | 64 | | | | | | |
| | Breeze from Alabama (1902) | 24 | 75 | | 242 | 53 | | 251 | | | 82 | | | |
| | Cascades (1904) | | 109 | | 264 | 101 | | 38 | | | 86 | 16 | | |
| | Chrysanthemum (1904) | | 114 | | 268 | 107 | | 4 | | | | | | |
| | Cleopha (1902) | | 80 | | 328 | 47 | | | | | | | | |
| | Country Club (1909) | | | | | 197 | | | | 10 | | | | |
| | Easy Winners (1901) | 90 | 65 | | 234 | 41 | | 227 | | | 90 | 82 | | |
| | Elite Syncopations (1902) | | 85 | | 246 | 59 | | 75 | | | 94 | | | |
| | Entertainer (1902) | 82 | 70 | | 206 | 65 | | 203 | | | 98 | 74 | | 8 |
| | Eugenia (1906) | | 123 | | 282 | 139 | | 45 | | | | | | |
| | Euphonic Sounds (1909) | | | | | 203 | | | | 2 | 102 | | | |
| | Favorite (1904) | | | | 258 | 93 | | 88 | | | | | | |
| | Fig Leaf Rag (1908) | 98 | 119 | | | | | | | | | 40 | | |

cPublished 1963.

| Composer | Composition | BeR | BIC | BrR | GEn | JCW | MMG | MOH | PTR | RtP | SWF | TFR | TRR | ZTr |
|---|---|---|---|---|---|---|---|---|---|---|---|---|---|---|
| Joplin, S. (cont.) | Gladiolus Rag (1907) | | | | | 157 | 16 | 239 | | | | | | |
| | Leola (1905) | | | | 278 | 125 | | | | | | | | 5 |
| | Magnetic Rag (1914) | | | | | 227 | | | | | | | | |
| | Maple Leaf Rag (1899) | 129 | 56 | | 212 | 25 | | 1 | | 47 | 105 | 13 | | |
| | Nonpareil (1907) | 110 | | | 286 | 163 | | | | | | 102 | | |
| | Original Rags (1899) | | 60 | | 222 | 19 | | 19 | | | | | | |
| | Palm Leaf Rag (1903) | | 100 | | 261 | 89 | | 94 | | | 108 | | | |
| | Paragon Rag (1909) | | | | | 209 | | | | 42 | | | | |
| | Peacherine Rag (1901) | | 70 | | 230 | 29 | | 105 | | | 114 | | | |
| | Pineapple Rag (1908) | | 133 | | | 175 | | | | | | | | |
| | Pleasant Moments (1909) | | | | | 191 | | | 26 | | | | | |
| | Rag-Time Dance (1906) | 94 | 128 | | 218 | 151 | | | | | 118 | 86 | | |
| | Reflection Rag (1917) | | 138 | | 298 | 233 | | | | | | | | |
| | School of Ragtime (1908) | | | | | 283 | | | | | | | | |
| | Scott Joplin's New Rag (1912) | | | | | 221 | 8 | 221 | | | | | | |
| | Search-Light Rag (1907) | | | | | 291 | | 354 | | | | | | |
| | Silver Swan Rag[d] | | | | | 185 | | | | | | | | |
| | Solace (1909) | | | | | 215 | | | | | | | | |
| | Stoptime Rag (1910) | | 95 | | 250 | 77 | | 255 | | | 126 | | | |
| | Strenuous Life (1902) | | | | | 169 | 12 | 322 | | | | | | |
| | Sugar Cane (1908) | | | | 272 | 97 | | | 12 | | 111 | | | |
| | Sycamore (1904) | | | | | | | 153 | | | | | | |
| | Wall Street Rag (1909) | | | | | 181 | | | | | | | | |
| | Weeping Willow (1903) | | 104 | | 254 | 83 | | 138 | | | 134 | | | |
| Joplin, S. & Chauvin, L. | Heliotrope Bouquet (1907) | 86 | 156 | | 290 | 263 | | 172 | | | | 78 | | |
| Joplin, S. & Hayden, S. | Felicity Rag (1911) | | | | | 269 | | 179 | | | | | | |

[d] Attributed to Scott Joplin; published 1971.

| Composer | Composition | BeR | BIC | BrR | GEn | JCW | MMG | MOH | PTR | RtP | SWF | TFR | TRR | ZTr |
|---|---|---|---|---|---|---|---|---|---|---|---|---|---|---|
| Joplin, S. & Marshall, A. | Kismet Rag (1913) |  | 151 |  | 340 · | 275 |  | 195 | 46 |  | 122 |  |  |  |
|  | Something Doing (1903) |  | 146 |  |  | 251 |  | 262 |  |  |  |  |  |  |
|  | Sunflower Slow Drag (1901) | 78 |  |  | 238 | 245 |  | 8 |  |  |  | 70 |  |  |
| Jordan, J. | Lily Queen (1907) |  |  |  | 294 | 257 |  |  |  |  |  |  |  |  |
|  | Swipesy (1900) |  | 141 |  | 226 | 239 |  |  |  |  | 130 |  |  |  |
|  | Double Fudge (1902) |  |  |  |  |  |  | 112 |  |  |  |  |  | 95 |
|  | Nappy Lee (1905) |  |  |  |  |  |  | 120 |  |  |  |  |  |  |
|  | Pekin Rag (1904) |  | 162 |  |  |  |  | 271 |  |  |  |  |  | 123 |
| Kelly, E. H. | Peaceful Henry (1901) |  |  |  |  |  |  | 156 |  |  | 70 |  | 146 |  |
| Kirwin, M. | African Pas' (1902) |  |  |  |  |  |  |  |  |  |  |  | 151 |  |
| Klickman, F. H. | Smiles and Chuckles (1917) |  |  |  |  |  |  |  |  |  |  |  |  | 28 |
| Koninsky, S. | Eli Green's Cake Walk (1898) |  |  |  |  |  |  |  |  |  |  |  | 156 |  |
| Krell, W. H. | Cake-Walk Patrol (1895) | 140 |  | 56 |  |  |  |  |  |  |  |  |  |  |
|  | Mississippi Rag (1897) |  |  |  | 186 |  |  |  |  |  |  |  |  |  |
|  | Shake Yo' Dusters! (1898) |  |  | 69 |  |  |  | 51 |  |  |  | 134 | 161 |  |
| Lamb, J. F. | American Beauty Rag (1913) | 122 | 184 |  | 108 |  |  | 149 |  |  |  | 114 |  |  |
|  | Bohemia Rag (1919) | 20 | 202 |  | 112 |  |  | 86 |  |  |  | 9 |  |  |
|  | Champagne Rag (1910) |  | 179 |  | 124 |  |  | 300 |  |  |  | 125 |  |  |
|  | Cleopatra Rag (1915) | 16 |  |  | 116 |  |  | 134 |  |  |  | 5 |  |  |
|  | Contentment Rag (1915) | 74 |  |  | 120 |  |  | 101 |  |  |  | 66 |  |  |
|  | Ethiopia Rag (1909) | 54 | 170 |  | 132 |  |  | 307 |  |  |  | 46 |  |  |
|  | Excelsior Rag (1909) | 48 | 175 |  | 129 |  |  | 311 |  |  |  | 40 |  |  |
|  | Patricia Rag (1916) |  | 199 |  |  |  |  | 49 |  |  |  |  |  |  |
|  | Ragtime Nightingale (1915) | 106 | 189 |  | 136 |  |  | 34 |  |  |  | 98 |  |  |

| Composer | Composition | BeR | BIC | BrR | GEn | JCW | MMG | MOH | PTR | RtP | SWF | TFR | TRR | ZTr |
|---|---|---|---|---|---|---|---|---|---|---|---|---|---|---|
| Lamb, J. F. (Cont.) | Reindeer Rag (1915) | 70 | 194 | | 140 | | | 123 | | | | 62 | | |
| | Sensation (1908) | 136 | 166 | | 148 | | | 79 | | | | 130 | | |
| | Top Liner Rag (1916) | 118 | | | 144 | | | | | | | 110 | | 30 |
| Lampe, J. B. | Creole Belles (1900) | | | | | | | 130 | | | | | | |
| Lincoln, H. | Beeswax Rag (1911) | | | | | | | | 38 | | | | | |
| | Dixie (1911) | | | | | | | | 42 | | | | | |
| | Rag Bag Rag (1909) | | | | | | | | | | | | | |
| Livernash, W. | Georgia Giggle (1918) | | | | | | | | | 26 | | | | 150 |
| Lodge, H. | Oh You Turkey (1914) | | | | | | | | | | | | | 78 |
| | Sure Fire Rag (1910) | | | | | | | | | | | | 167 | |
| | Temptation Rag (1909) | | | | | | | | 2 | | | | | |
| Losey, F. H. | Rag Baby Rag (1909) | | | | | | | | | 30 | | | | |
| | Sumthin' Doin' (1907) | | | | | | | | | 55 | | | | |
| Lowell, G. L. | Tanglefoot Rag (1910) | | | | | | | | 30 | | | | | |
| | Darktown Diversion (1899) | | | 7 | | | | | | | | | | |
| | Dusky Doings in Darktown (1899) | | | 26 | | | | | | | | | | |
| | Turkey Walk (1899) | | | 79 | | | | | | | 64 | | | |
| McFadden, F. X. | Rags To Burn (1899) | | | | | | | 281 | | | | | | |
| McSkimming, H. H. | Felix Rag (1910) | | | | | | | | | | | | 172 | |
| Marshall, A. | Ham and! (1908) | | 210 | | | | | 345 | | | | | | |
| | Kinklets (1906) | | 205 | | | | | 116 | | | | | | |
| | Peach (1908) | | 215 | | | | | 336 | | | | | | |
| | Pippin (1908) | | 220 | | | | | 188 | | | | | | |
| Marshall, A. & Joplin, S. | Lily Queen (1907) | | 141 | | 294 | 257 | | 112 | | | | | | |
| Martin, J. | Swipesy (1900) | | | | 226 | 239 | | | | | 130 | | | |
| | 'Possum Barbecue (1899) | | | 22 | | | | | | | 56 | | | |

| Composer | Composition | BeR | BIC | BrR | GEn | JCW | MMG | MOH | PTR | RtP | SWF | TFR | TRR | ZTr |
|---|---|---|---|---|---|---|---|---|---|---|---|---|---|---|
| Matthews, A. | Pastime Rag No. 1 (1913) | | 225 | | | | | | | | | | | |
| | Pastime Rag No. 2 (1913) | | 230 | | | | | | | | | | | |
| | Pastime Rag No. 3 (1916) | | 235 | | | | | | | | | | | |
| | Pastime Rag No. 4 (1920) | | 240 | | | | | | | | | | | |
| | Pastime Rag No. 5 (1918) | | 243 | | | | | | | | | | | |
| Mills, K. | At a Georgia Camp-meeting (1897) | | | | | | | 287 | | | | | | 12 |
| | Happy Days in Dixie (1896) | | | | | | | 91 | | | | | | |
| | Impecunious Davis (1899) | | | | | | | 142 | | | | | | |
| | Kerry Mills Rag Time Dance (1909) | | | | | | | | | | | | 177 | |
| | 'Leven Forty-Five from the Hotel (1903) | | | | | | | 333 | | | | | | |
| | Whistling Rufus (1899) | | | | | | | 27 | | | | | | 74 |
| | Glad Cat Rags (1905) | | | | | | | | | | | | 182 | 110 |
| Nash, W. | Majestic Rag (1914) | | | | | | | | | | | | 198 | 98 |
| Neel, R. & Rawls, B. | Hoosier Rag (1907) | | | | | | | | | | 40 | | 187 | 156 |
| Niebergall, J. L. | Louisiana Rag (1897) | | | | | | | | | | | | 193 | 62 |
| Northrup, T. H. | Cannon Ball (1905) | | | | | | | 59 | | | | | | |
| Northup, J. | Rag Pickers Rag (1901) | | | | | | | | | | | | | |
| O'Brian, R. J. | Town Talk (1917) | | | | | | | | | | | | | |
| Olson, E. | Echoes from Old Mobile (1899) | | | 18 | | | | | | | | | | |
| Petry, W. E. | On a Southern Plantation (1899) | | | 38 | | | | | | | | | | |
| | Ragtown Guards (1899) | | | 52 | | | | | | | | | | |
| Phelps, E. A. | Darkies' Patrol (1892) | | | 82 | | | | | | | | | | |

| Composer | Composition | BeR | BIC | BrR | GEn | JCW | MMG | MOH | PTR | RtP | SWF | TFR | TRR | ZTr |
|---|---|---|---|---|---|---|---|---|---|---|---|---|---|---|
| Pitts, T. | Meadow Lark Rag (1916) | | | | | | | | | | | | | 18 |
| Pollock, M. | Rooster Rag (1917) | | | | | | | | | | | | | 116 |
| Porcelain, M. | Bric-A-Brac Rag (1906) | | | | | | | | | | | | | 25 |
| | Missouri Rag (1907) | | | | | | | | | | | | | 132 |
| Powell, W. C. | Colonial Glide (1910) | | | | | | | 247 | | | | 94 | | |
| Pratt, P. | Hot-House Rag (1914) | 102 | | | 104 | | | | | | | | | 113 |
| | Vanity (1909) | | | | | | | | | | | | | |
| Rawls, B. & Neel, R. | Majestic Rag (1914) | | | | | | | | | | | | 198 | |
| Roberts, C. L. | Junk Man (1913) | | | | | | 50 | 243 | | | | | | |
| | Music Box Rag (1914) | | | | | | 54 | | | | | | | |
| | Pork and Beans (1913) | | | | | | 46 | 213 | | | | | | |
| Roberts, J. | Entertainer's Rag (1910) | | | | | | | | | | | | | 82 |
| Rockwell, C. J. | Aunt Jemima's Cake Walk | | | | | | | | | | | | | 146 |
| Rubens, P. | Rag-Time Pasmala (1899) | | | | | | | | | | 44 | | | |
| St. John, C. H. | Cole Smoak (1906) | | | | | | | | | | | | 203 | |
| Schroeder, A. | Rag-Time Medley No. 1 (1899) | | | 46 | | | | | | | 79 | | | |
| | Rag-Time Medley No. 2 (1899) | | | 74 | | | | | | | | | | |
| Scott, J. | Broadway Rag (1922) | | | | | | | | | | | 32 | | |
| | Climax Rag (1914) | 40 | 313 | | 154 | | | 192 | | | | | | |
| | Dixie Dimples (1918) | | | | | | | | | | | | | 90 |
| | Don't Jazz Me Rag (1921) | | 306 | | | | | 259 | | | | | | |
| | Efficiency Rag (1917) | | 282 | | | | | 352 | | | | | | |
| | Evergreen Rag (1915) | 127 | 227 | | 151 | | | 314 | | | | 118 | | |
| | Fascinator (1903) | | | | | | | 277 | | | | | | |
| | Frog Legs Rag (1906) | 36 | 246 | | 158 | | | | | | 20 | 28 | 213 | 36 |
| | Grace and Beauty (1907) | 44 | | | 162 | | | | | | | 36 | | |

| Composer | Composition | BeR | BIC | BrR | GEn | JCW | MMG | MOH | PTR | RtP | SWF | TFR | TRR | ZTr |
|---|---|---|---|---|---|---|---|---|---|---|---|---|---|---|
| Scott, J. (Cont.) | Great Scott Rag (1909) | 51 | 255 | | 190 | | | 349 | | | | | | |
| | Hilarity Rag (1910) | 58 | 268 | | 166 | | | 326 | | | | 43 | | |
| | Honey Moon Rag (1916) | | | | | | | | | | | 50 | | |
| | Kansas City Rag (1907) | | 251 | | | | | 294 | | | | | | 22 |
| | Modesty Rag (1920) | | 300 | | | | | 199 | | | | | | |
| | New Era Rag (1919) | | 291 | | | | | 201 | | | | | | |
| | On the Pike (1904) | | | | | | | | | | | | 218 | |
| | Ophelia Rag (1910) | | 285 | | | | | 318 | | | | | | |
| | Paramount Rag (1917) | | | | | | | 340 | | | | | | |
| | Peace and Plenty Rag (1919) | | | | | | | 207 | | | | | | |
| | Pegasus (1920) | 132 | 294 | | 170 | | | 225 | | | | | | |
| | Prosperity Rag (1916) | 62 | 303 | | 174 | | | | | | | 121 | | |
| | Quality Rag (1911) | | | | | | | | | | | 54 | | |
| | Rag Sentimental (1918) | | 288 | | | | | 275 | | | | | | |
| | Ragtime Betty (1909) | | 259 | | | | | 342 | | | | | | |
| | Ragtime Oriole (1911) | 66 | 272 | | 178 | | | 23 | | | | 58 | | |
| | Summer Breeze (1903) | | | | | | | | | | | | 208 | |
| | Sunburst Rag (1909) | | 263 | | | | | 329 | | | | | | |
| | Troubadour Rag (1919) | | 297 | | | | | 266 | | | | | 228 | |
| | Victory Rag (1921) | 114 | 310 | | 182 | | | | | | | 106 | 222 | |
| Settle, L. E. | X. L. Rag (1903) | | | | | | | | | | | | | |
| Severin, E. P. | Jungle Time (1909) | | | | | | | | | | | | | |
| Seymore & Barney | | | | | | | | | | | | | | |
| Seymore, C. | St. Louis Tickle (1904) | | | | | | | 97 | | | | | 14 | |
| Shepherd, A. | Black Laugh (1904) | | | | | | | | | | | | | 86 |
| | Pickles and Peppers (1906) | | | | | | | 70 | | | | | | |
| Silverman, D. H. & Ward, A. R. | That "Hand-Played" Rag (1914) | | | | | | | | | | | | 232 | |

| *Composer* | *Composition* | BeR | BIC | BrR | GEn | JCW | MMG | MOH | PTR | RtP | SWF | TFR | TRR | ZTr |
|---|---|---|---|---|---|---|---|---|---|---|---|---|---|---|
| Simon, W. C. | Sponge (1911) | | | | | | | | | | | | 237 | |
| Sizemore, A. | Climbers Rag (1911) | | | | | | | | | | | | 242 | |
| Smith, E. B. & Wooster, F. | Black Cat Rag (1905) | | | | | | | | | | | | 300 | |
| Smith, L. & Chapman, J. | One o' Them Things (1904) | | | | | | | | | | | | 63 | |
| Smith, R. | That Demon Rag (1912) | | | | | | | | | | | | 246 | |
| Stone, F. S. | Belle of the Philippines (1903) | | | | | | | | | | | | | 64 |
| | Ma Ragtime Baby (1898) | | | | | | | | | | | | 250 | |
| Taylor, B. | Dogzigity Rag (1910) | | 317 | | | | | | | 52 | | | | |
| Thompson, C. | Lily Rag (1914) | | | | | | | | | | | | 254 | |
| Thompson, H. C. | Watermelon Trust (1906) | | | | | | | | | | | | | |
| Turpin, T. | Bowery Buck (1899) | | 328 | | | | | 12 | | | 32 | | | |
| | Buffalo Rag (1904) | | 342 | | | | | 127 | | | | | | |
| | Harlem Rag (1897) | | 322 | | | | | | | | 24 | | | |
| | Harlem Rag (1899) | | | | | | 62 | 176 | | | | | | |
| | Rag-Time Nightmare (1900) | | 333 | | | | | 163 | | | 8 | | | |
| | St. Louis Rag (1903) | | 338 | | | | | 16 | | | 67 | | | |
| Tyler, C. A. | Cotton Patch (1902) | | | | | | | | | | | | 258 | |
| Von Tilzer, H. | Ragtime Dance (1898) | | | | | | | | | | 48 | | | |
| Ward, A. R. & Silverman, D. H. | That "Hand-Played" Rag (1914) | | | | | | | | | | | | 232 | |
| Wayburn, N. | Ragtime Jimmie's Jamboree (1899) | | | | | | | | | | 60 | | | |
| Weigel, W. E. | Sheath (1908) | | | | | | | | | | | | 263 | |
| Wenrich, P. | Ashy Africa (1903) | | 347 | | | | | 268 | | | | | | |
| | Dixie Blossoms (1906) | | | | | | | | | | | | 272 | |
| | Fun-Bob (1907) | | | | | | | | | | | | | 71 |

| Composer | Composition | BeR | BIC | BrR | GEn | JCW | MMG | MOH | PTR | RtP | SWF | TFR | TRR | ZTr |
|---|---|---|---|---|---|---|---|---|---|---|---|---|---|---|
| Wenrich, P. (Cont.) | Peaches and Cream (1905) | | | | | | | | | | | | 268 | |
| | Smiler (1907) | | 351 | | | | | 42 | | | | | | 15 |
| | Sweetmeats (1907) | | | | | | | 291 | | | | | | 50 |
| Wilcockson, J. M. | Pride of the Smoky Row (1911) | | | | | | | | | | | | | |
| Wiley, C. | Car-Barlick-Acid (1903) | | 359 | | | | | 55 | | | | | 281 | |
| Willis, F. | Queen Rag (1911) | | 355 | | | | | | | | | | 286 | |
| Woods, C. | Sleepy Hollow Rag (1918) | | | | | | | 297 | | | | | | |
| | Slippery Elm Rag (1912) | | | | | | | | | | | | | |
| Woolsey, C. L. | Mashed Potatoes (1911) | | | | | | | | | | | | 296 | |
| | Medic Rag (1910) | | | | | | | | | | | | 291 | |
| Wooster, F. & Smith, E. B. | Black Cat Rag (1905) | | | | | | | | | | | | 301 | |

# Selected Bibliography

Since writings contemporary with the ragtime era and the years immediately following have a different historical perspective from later commentary, it is helpful to keep these sources separate. An arbitrary division between the materials is made at the year 1930.

### Sources: 1886–1929

"Again the Origin of Ragtime." *Melody* 2 (December 1918): 4.

"American Music." *American Musician and Art Journal* 27 (28 October 1911): 9.

"American Music and Ragtime." *Music Trade Review* 37 (3 October 1903): 8.

Amstead, W. H. "'Rag-Time': The Music of the Hour." *Metronome* 15 (May 1899): 4.

"Another Defender of Ragtime." *Christensen's Ragtime Review* 1 (April 1915): 3.

Ansermet, Ernest. "Sur un orchestre nègre." *Revue romande* 3 (15 October 1919): 10–13. Facsimile reprint in "Ein Jazzbericht aus dem Jahre 1919" by Jan Slawe, in *Jazzforschung* 3/4 (1971/72): 162–65. Translated by Walter J. Shaap as "Bechet and Jazz Visit Europe, 1919" in *Frontiers of Jazz*, ed. Ralph de Toledano, pp. 115–22. 2d ed. New York: Ungar Publishing, Co., 1962.

Autolycus. "'Rag-Time' on Parnassus." *Musical Opinion* 36 (February 1913): 328–29.

Bell, Clive. "Plus de jazz." *New Republic* (21 September 1921): 92–96.

Berlin, Irving, and Justus Dickinson. "Words and Music." *Green Book Magazine* (July 1915): 98–105.

"Berlin Calls Jazz American Folk Music." *New York Times*, 10 January 1925, p. 2.

"Bernard Is King of Rag-Timers." *New York Dramatic Mirror*, 3 February 1900, pp. 18–19. Reprinted in *Ragtime Review* 1 (October 1962): 10–11.

"Best Songs Never Make Hit." *Christensen's Ragtime Review* 1 (June 1915): 12.

Bickford, Myron A. "Something about Ragtime." *Cadenza* 20 (September 1913): 13; (November 1913): 10–11.

Bickford, Zarh Myron. "Ragtime as an Introduction and Aid to Better Music." *Melody* 2 (January 1918): 7.

"'Black America' at the Garden." *New York Times*, 17 September 1895, p. 10.

Boblitz, Sherwood K. "Where Movie Playing Needs Reform." *Musician* 25 (June 1920): 8.

Bowman, James Cloyd. "Anti-Ragtime." *New Republic* 5 (6 November 1915): 19; reprinted in *Ragtimer* 7, no. 1 (1968): 6–7.

Boyd, George C. "Ragtime Is Rhythm." *Melody* 3 (June 1919): 5.

Buchanan, Charles L. "The National Music Fallacy: Is American Music to Rest on a Foundation of Ragtime and Jazz?" *Arts and Decoration* 20 (February 1924): 26.

———. "The Prodigal Popular Composer: Some Reflections upon Possible Development in the Writers of American Light Music." *Opera Magazine* 2 (July 1915): 15.

———. "Ragtime and American Music." *Opera Magazine* 3 (February 1916): 17–19.

———. "Ragtime and American Music." *Seven Arts* 2 (July 1917): 376–83.

Burk, John N. "Ragtime and Its Possibilities." *Harvard Musical Review* 2 (January 1914): 11–13. Reprinted in *Opera Magazine* 2 (June 1915): 24–26.

Cable, George W. "The Dance in Place Congo." *Century Magazine* (February 1886): 517–32.

Cadman, Charles Wakefield. "Cadman on Rag-Time." *Musical Courier* 69 (12 August 1914): 31.

"Der Cake Walk." *Illustrierte Zeitung* (Leipzig), 5 February 1903, pp. 202–203.

"The Cake Walk." *New York Times*, 28 February 1892, p. 4.

"The Cake Walk a 'Fake' Walk." *New York Times*, 28 February 1892, p. 5.

"Cake Walk Broken Up." *New York Times*, 13 February 1898, p. 2.

"The Cake Walk in Vienna." *New York Times*, 1 February 1903, p. 5.

"Cakewalk Trust the Latest." *New York Times*, 26 November 1900, p. 3.

"Canon Assails Our New Dances." *New York Times*, 25 August 1913, p. 3.

"Canon Newboldt's Warning." *New York Times*, 26 August 1913, p. 8.

Carr, Paul G. "Abuses of Music." *Musician* 6 (October 1901): 299.

"Charles E. Trevathan Dead." *American Musician and Art Journal* 23 (28 March 1907): 5.

"Charles L. Johnson." *American Musician and Art Journal* 25 (11 June 1909): 19.

Chase, F. E. "The Decay of the Popular Song." *Musical Record*, no. 455 (1 December 1899): 530–35.

Christensen, Axel. "Can Ragtime Be Suppressed?" *Christensen's Ragtime Review* 1 (June 1915): 3. Reprinted in *Melody* 2 (May 1918): 2; reprinted in *Rag Times* 5 (January 1972): 8.

————. "Chicago Syncopations: Is Ragtime Respectable?" *Melody* 2 (August 1918): 8.

————. "Chicago Syncopations: John Stark, Pioneer Publisher." *Melody* 2 (October 1918): 8.

————. "Chicago Syncopations: May Garden Says Ragtime Is Typical of American Life." *Melody* 3 (February 1919): 21.

————. "Chicago Syncopations: An Open Letter to Orpheus on Ragtime." *Melody* 3 (January 1919): 21.

————. "Chicago Syncopations: Ragtime Demoralizing." *Melody* 2 (November 1918): 22.

————. "A Course in Vaudeville Piano Playing." Arrangements by John S. Meck. *Christensen's Ragtime Review* 1–2 (December 1914– March 1916): passim.

————. "The Popularity of Ragtime." *Christensen's Ragtime Review* 1 (December 1914): 1–2; reprinted in *Melody* 2 (January 1918): 8.

————. "Popular Music an Absolute Necessity." *Melody* 2 (October 1918): 6.

————. "Ragtime: A Few Remarks in Its Favor." *Christensen's Ragtime Review* 1 (December 1914): 20.

————. "Ragtime Pianists I Have Known." *Melody* 2 (December 1918): 5.

————. "A Talk on Ragtime." *Melody* 2 (September 1918): 2. Reprinted in *Rag Times* 9 (November 1975): 4–5.

————. "Teasing the Ivories. How I Broke In." *Melody* 3 (March 1919): 4.

————. "Teasing the Ivories, No. 2." *Melody* 3 (May 1919): 5.

Christiani, Courtland. "Ragtime in A.D. 2017." *Ragtime Review* 3 (February 1917): 7.

"'Classic Rags' Composed by Max Aufderheide." *American Musician and Art Journal* 25 (13 August 1909): 20.

"Classic's Loss Is Ragtime's Gain." *Melody* 3 (December 1919): 6.

Collier, Adèle. "Feldman's How to Dance the Fox-Trot." London: B. Feldman, n.d.. Reprinted in *Rag Times* 9 (November 1975): insert, 4 pp.

Collins, Treve, Jr. "Concerning Harry Jentes." *Melody* 2 (September 1918): 4–6.

"Concerning Ragtime." *Musical Monitor* 8 (September 1919): 619.

"Consular Aid for Ragtime." *Literary Digest* (11 April 1914): 825.

Converse, C. Crozat. "Rag-Time Music." *Etude* 17 (June 1899): 185; (August 1899): 256.

"'Coon Songs' on the Wane." *American Musician and Art Journal* 22 (12 June 1906): 26a.

Copland, Aaron. "Jazz Structure and Influence on Modern Music." *Modern Music* 4 (January/February 1927): 9–14.

Curtis, Natalie. "The Music America Buys." *Craftsman* 23 (January 1913): 390–400.

———. "The Negro's Contribution to the Music of America." *Craftsman* 23 (15 March 1913): 660–69.

Damon, S. Foster. "American Influence on Modern French Music." *Dial* (15 August 1918): 93–95.

"Dance Puzzle Stirs Teachers to Action." *New York Times*, 20 April 1914, p. 9.

Davidson, Harry. "What Has 'Ragtime' to Do with 'American Music'?" *Ragtime Review* 2 (August 1916): 3.

"Decadence of the Waltz: Sousa's Marches Held Responsible by Dancing Masters for the Reign of the Two-Step." *New York Times*, 10 September 1899, p. 16.

"Degenerate Music." *Musical Courier* 39 (13 September 1899): 14.

Dett, R. Nathaniel. Program notes to *In the Bottoms: Characteristic Suite*. Chicago: Clayton F. Summy, 1913. Reprinted in *The Collected Piano Works of R. Nathaniel Dett*, p. 33. Introductions by Dominique-René de Lerma and Vivan Flagg McBrier. Evanston, Ill.: Summy-Birchard, 1973.

Downes, Olin. "An American Composer." *Musical Quarterly* 4 (January 1918): 23–36.

"Ducasse Uses Ragtime in New Tone Poem." *Musical America* 37 (10 March 1923): 15.

Dunbar, Paul Laurence. "The Colored Band." In *Lyrics of Love and Laughter*. New York: Dodd, Mead, 1903. Reprinted in *The Complete Poems of Paul Laurence Dunbar*, pp. 286–87. New York: Dodd, Mead, 1958.

Dvořák, Antonin. "Music in America." *Harper's New Monthly Magazine* (February 1895): 429–34.

[Editorial]. *American Musician and Art Journal* 26 (13 August 1910): 19.

"Editorials." *New Music Review and Church Music Review* 22 (December 1923): 542; (October 1924): 464.

Eliot, T. S. "Fragment of an Agon." *Criterion* 4 (January 1927): 74–80. Reprinted in *The Complete Poems and Plays: 1909–1950*, pp. 79–85. New York: Harcourt, Brace, 1952.

———. *The Waste Land*. New York: Boni and Liveright, 1922. Reprinted in *The Complete Poems and Plays: 1909–1950*, pp. 37–55. New York: Harcourt, Brace, 1952.

Engel, Carl. "Jazz: A Musical Discussion." *Atlantic Monthly* (August 1922): 182–89.

"The Ethics of Ragtime." *Jacobs' Orchestra Monthly* 3 (August 1912): 27–29.

"Ethics of Ragtime." *Literary Digest* (10 August 1912): 225.

Farjeon, Harry. "Rag-Time." *Musical Times* 65 (1 September 1924): 795–97. Reprinted in *New Music Review and Church Music Review* 23 (November 1924): 513–15.

"The Farrells Took the Cake." *New York Times*, 3 March 1895, p. 5.

Farwell, Arthur. "Apaches, Mollycoddles and Highbrows." *Musical America* 16 (17 August 1912): 2.

———. "The Popular Song Bugaboo." *Musical America* 16 (6 July 1912): 2.

———. "The Popular Song Bugaboo: No. 2." *Musical America* 16 (27 July 1912): 2.

———. "Where Professors and Socialists Fail to Understand Music." *Musical America* 16 (31 August 1912): 26–27.

"The Father of Ragtime Has Another Big Idea." *New York Times*, 12 September 1915, sec. 6, p. 3.

"Flays Rag-Time as Not Reflecting Americanism." *Musical America* 28 (20 July 1918): 22.

"Fun at the Cake Walk." *New York Times*, 4 May 1895, p. 6.

Gardner, Carl E. "Ragging and Jazzing." *Metronome* 35 (October/November 1919): 34.

Gates, W. F. "Ethiopian Syncopation—The Decline of Rag-Time." *Musician* 7 (October 1902): 341.

Gilbert, Henry F. "Folk-Music in Art Music—A Discussion and a Theory." *Musical Quarterly* 3 (October 1917): 577–601.

Gleason, W. T. "Answering the Critics." *Ragtime Review* 3 (March 1917): 22–23. Reprinted in *Melody* 3 (February 1919): 22–23; reprinted in *Ragtimer* (November/December 1968): 4–5.

Gluck, Alma, "America and Good Music." *Musical Courier* 66 (28 May 1913): 22–23.

Goodrich, A. J. "Syncopated Rhythm vs. 'Rag-Time.'" *Musician* 6 (November 1901): 336.

Gordon, Philip. "Ragtime, the Folk Song and the Music Teacher." *Musical Observer* 6 (November 1912): 724–25. Reprinted in *Rag Times* 6 (September 1972): 12–13; reprinted in *Ragtimer* (May/June 1973): 8–10.

"Great American Composer—Will He Speak in the Accent of Broadway?" *Current Opinion* 63 (November 1917): 316–17.

*Grove's Dictionary of Music and Musicians.* New York: Macmillan, 1908. S.v. "Rag Time," by Frank Kidson.

"Heard about Town." *New York Times*, 13 February 1900, p. 12.

"He Has No Scorn for Jazz." *New York Times*, 28 January 1925, p. 16.

Henderson, W. J. "Ragtime, Jazz, and High Art." *Scribner's Magazine* (February 1925): 200–203.

"'A Hot Time' Is War Song." *American Musician and Art Journal* 24 (14 February 1908): 4.

"How to Dance the Fox Trot." *Christensen's Ragtime Review* 1 (March 1915): 8.

Hubbard, W. L. "A Hopeful View of the Ragtime Roll." *Musician* 25 (August 1920): 6.

Hubbs, Harold. "What Is Ragtime?" *Outlook* 118 (27 February 1918): 345. Reprinted in *Ragtime Society* 3 (February 1964): 8.

Hughes, Rupert. "A Eulogy of Rag-Time." *Musical Record*, no. 447 (1 April 1899): pp. 157–59.

——. "Will Ragtime Turn to Symphonic Poems?" *Etude* 38 (May 1920): 305.

"The Interviewer Talks with . . . Stark Music Company." *American Musician and Art Journal* 24 (11 December 1908): 13.

"The Interviewer Talks with . . . 'Ted' Snyder." *American Musician and Art Journal* 24 (9 October 1908): 15.

"Is the Coon Craze Dying Out?" *New York Dramatic Mirror*, 12 November 1898. Reprinted in part in *Black Perspective in Music* (July 1976): 264.

Ives, Charles. *Essays before a Sonata*. New York: Knickerbocker Press, 1920. Reprinted in *Essays before a Sonata and Other Writings*, ed. Howard Boatwright. New York: W. W. Norton, 1961.

"J. Bodewalt Lampe." *American Musician and Art Journal* 28 (27 April 1912): 3.

Jackson, J. H. Smither. "Rag-Time." *Musical Times* 65 (November 1924): 1022.

"Jazz and Ragtime Are the Preludes to a Great American Music." *Current Opinion* (August 1920): 199–201.

"John S. Zamecnik." *American Musician and Art Journal* 24 (23 October 1908): 7.

Johnson, J. Rosamond. "Why They Call American Music Ragtime." *Colored American Magazine* 15 (January 1909): 636–39. Reprinted in *Black Perspective in Music* 4 (July 1976): 260–64.

Johnson, James Weldon. *The Autobiography of an Ex-Colored Man*. Boston: Sherman, French, 1912. Reprinted in *Three Negro Classics*, pp. 391–511. New York: Avon Books, Discus Books, 1965.

——. "The Negro of To-Day in Music." *Charities* 15 (7 October 1905): 58–59.

——, ed. and Preface. *The Book of American Negro Poetry*. New York: Harcourt, Brace, 1922; rev. ed., 1931.

——, ed. and Introduction. *The Book of American Negro Spirituals*. Musical arrangements by J. Rosamond Johnson and Lawrence Brown. New York: Viking Press, 1925.

——, ed. and Introduction. *The Second Book of Negro Spirituals*. Musical arrangements by J. Rosamond Johnson. New York: Viking Press, 1926.

Joplin, Scott, *School of Ragtime*. New York: Scott Joplin, 1908.

Judson, Arthur L. "Works of American Composers Reveal Relation of Ragtime to Art-Song." *Musical America* 15 (2 December 1911): 29.

Kenilworth, Walter Winston. "Demoralizing Rag Time Music." *Musical Courier* 66 (28 May 1913): 22–23.

Knowlton, Don. "The Anatomy of Jazz." *Harper's Magazine* 152 (April 1926): 578–85.

Kramer, W. Walter. "Extols Ragtime Article." *New Republic* 5 (4 December 1915): 122.

Krehbiel, Henry Edward. *Afro-American Folksongs: A Study in Racial and National Music*. New York: G. Schirmer, 1914. Reprint ed., New York: Frederick Ungar Publishing, 1962.

Kühl, Gustav. "Rag Time." *Die Musik* 1 (August 1902): 1972–76. Reprinted as "The Musical Possibilities of Rag-Time," trans. Gustav Saenger. *Metronome* 19 (March 1903): 11; (April 1903): 8.

Lampe, J. Bodewalt. "The Art of Arranging Music." *Tuneful Yankee* 1 (1917). Reprinted in *Rag Times* 7 (January 1974): 4–5.

Lanseer-MacKenzie, J. "Ragtime as National Music." *Musical Monitor* 8 (May 1919): 401–402.

"Leo Feist: Ragtime Publisher." *Metronome* (September 1923). Reprinted in *Rag Times* 6 (March 1973): 10–11.

Liebich, Rudolph Bismark von. "The Benighted Lover of Ragtime as a Musical 'Man and the Hoe.'" *Musical America* 16 (31 August 1912): 26.

Liebling, Leonard. "The Crime of Ragtime." *Musical Courier* 72 (20 January 1916): 21–22.

"Lieut. James Reese Europe: Master of Syncopated Rhythm." *Melody* 3 (July 1919): 3.

Lowry, Helen Bullitt. "Putting the Music into the Jazz." *New York Times*, 19 February 1922, sec. 3, p. 8.

M. H. R. "German Composer Who Writes American Cakewalk Music." *New York Herald*, 13 January 1901, sec. 6, p. 3.

"Martin Ballmann's Rag-Time Philosophy." *American Musician and Art Journal* 28 (28 September 1912): 5.

Mason, Daniel Gregory. "Concerning Ragtime." *New Music Review and Church Music Review* 17 (March 1918): 112–16.

———. "Folk-Song and American Music (A Plea for the Unpopular Point of View)." *Musical Quarterly* 4 (July 1918): 323–32.

———. "Prefers Demonstration to Cheers." *New Republic* 5 (4 December 1915): 122.

Mendl, R. W. S. *The Appeal of Jazz*. London: Philip Allan, 1927.

"Mission of Popular Music." *American Musician and Art Journal* 26 (11 March 1910): 23.

Moderwell, Hiram Kelly. "A Modest Proposal." *Seven Arts* 2 (July 1917): 368–76.

———. "Ragtime." *New Republic* 4 (16 October 1915): 284–86.

————. Reply to a letter. *New Republic* 4 (6 November 1915): 19.

Morgan, William J. "A Defense of Jazz and Ragtime." *Melody* 6 (September 1922): 5.

Muck, Karl. "The Music of Democracy." *Craftsman* 29 (December 1915): 270–79.

"Musical Gossip." *New-York Daily Tribune*, 15 April 1900, sec. 3, p. 1.

"Musical Impurity." *Etude* 18 (January 1900): 16.

"A Musical Novelty." *American Musician and Art Journal* 27 (24 June 1911): 7.

"Music for Piers and Parks." *New York Times*, 29 May 1902, p. 8.

"Music in America." *New York Times*, 9 October 1911, p. 10.

"Music of Today." *American Musician and Art Journal* 26 (25 March 1910): 23.

"Must Avoid Ragtime." *Musical Courier* 69 (12 August 1914): 10.

Narodny, Ivan. "The Birth Process of Ragtime." *Musical America* 17 (29 March 1913): 27.

"A Negro Explains Jazz." *Literary Digest* 41 (26 April 1919): 28–29. Reprinted in *Readings in Black American Music*, ed. Eileen Southern, pp. 224–27. New York: W. W. Norton, 1971.

"Negro Music in the Land of Freedom." *Outlook* 106 (21 March 1914): p. 611.

"The Negro's Contribution to American Art." *Literary Digest* (20 October 1917): 26–27.

"Negro's Contribution to Music of America." *New York Age*, 10 April 1913, p. 6.

"Not a Ragtime Band This Nation of Ours." *American Musician and Art Journal* 27 (28 October 1911): 12.

Oehmler, Leo. "'Ragtime': A Pernicious Evil and Enemy of True Art." *Musical Observer* 11 (September 1914): 14–15.

"An Old-Time Cake Walk." *New York Times*, 2 March 1895, p. 6.

"Original Cakewalk Man." *New York Times*, 6 February 1905, p. 8.

"Origin of Rag-Time." *Metronome* 17 (August 1901): 7.

"Origin of Rag Time." *Musician* 6 (September 1901): 227.

"The Origin of Ragtime." *New York Times*, 23 March 1924, sec. 9, p. 2.

"Origin of the Cakewalk." *Metronome* 17 (September 1901): 8.

Osgood, Henry O. *So This Is Jazz*. Boston: Little, Brown, 1926.

"Our Musical Condition." *Negro Music Journal* 1 (March 1903): 137–38: Reprint ed., Westport, Conn.: Negro Universities Press, 1970.

"Our 'One' Superior Art." *Literary Digest* 46 (1 February 1913): 281.

"Passing of the Coon and Degrading Dance." *Gazette and Land Bulletin* (Waycross, Ga.), 27 January 1900, p. 2.

Pemberton, Ralph Brock. "The Ragtime King: Author of Famous Popular Songs." *American Magazine* 78 (October 1914): 57–58.

Perry, Edward Baxter. "Ragging Good Music." *Etude* 36 (June 1918): 372. Reprinted in *Rag Times* 9 (September 1975): 3.

"Philosophizing Rag-Time." *Literary Digest* 46 (15 March 1913): 574–75.

"Pickles and Peppers." *American Musician and Art Journal* 23 (13 September 1907): 11; 24 (8 May 1908): 11; 24 (10 July 1908): 14.

"Playing Ragtime Abroad." *American Musician and Art Journal* 23 (11 October 1907): 8.

"Primitive Folk Songs of Broadway." *Outlook* 117 (7 November 1917): 365–66.

"Psychological and Socialistic Aspects of the Problems of Ragtime." *Musical America* 16 (13 August 1912): 26–27. (A blanket title covering articles by Arthur Farwell, Rudolph von Liebich, and Alexander Thompson.)

"Questions and Answers." *Etude* 16 (October 1898): 285; (December 1898): 349; 17 (March 1899): 69; (August 1899): 245; 18 (February 1900): 52.

"Rag-Time." *Musician* 5 (March 1900): 83.

"Ragtime." *Ragtime Review* 2 (May 1916): 4.

"Rag-Time." *Times* (London), 8 February 1913, p. 11. Reprinted in *Boston Symphony Orchestra Programmes* 32 (19 February 1913): 1186–96.

"Rag Time and Program Making." *American Musician and Art Journal* 28 (10 August 1912): 10–11.

"Rag Time and Royalty." *New York Times*, 10 October 1903, p. 6.

"Ragtime as Source of National Music." *Musical America* 17 (15 February 1913): 37.

"A Rag-Time Communication." *Musical Courier* 40 (30 May 1900): 20.

"Rag-Time Hurts Classics." *American Musician and Art Journal* 28 (13 July 1912): 3.

"Ragtime in the Trenches." *Literary Digest* 52 (8 April 1916): 997.

"Rag-Time Loses Favor." *American Musician and Art Journal* 28 (27 July 1912): 11.

"The Ragtime Queen Has Abdicated." *New York Times*, 24 May 1925, sec. 4, p. 21.

"The Ragtime Rage." *Musical Courier* 40 (23 May 1900): 20.

"Ragtime Wrangling." *Literary Digest* 52 (8 January 1916): 68–70.

"Real Art in Ragtime." *Ragtime Review* 3 (March 1917): 5.

"Remarks on Rag-Time." *Musical Courier* 66 (28 May 1913): 22–23.

"Requiescat, Ragtime!" *American Musician and Art Journal* 26 (13 August 1910): 19.

"Robert (Bob) Cole, Actor, Dead." *Chicago Defender*, 12 August 1911, p. 1.

Rosenfeld, Monroe H. "'Ragtime'—A Musical Mystery: What It Is and Its Origin." *Tuneful Yankee* 1 (January 1917): 9–10. Reprinted in *Rag Times* 6 (March 1973): 6–7.

Sachs-Hirsch, Herbert. "Dangers That Lie in Ragtime." *Musical America* 16 (21 September 1912): 8.

Sadler, Basil. "Teaching Popular Music." *Tuneful Yankee* 1 (December 1917): 7.

Saroni, H. S. "Sousa's March Form." *Etude* 16 (November 1898): 330.

Scoggins, Charles H. "The Ragtime Menace." *Musical Progress* 2 (April 1914): 3–4.

"Scores of Popular Songs Coming Out." *American Musician and Art Journal* 23 (14 March 1907): 26.

"Scott Joplin." *American Musician and Art Journal* 23 (17 June 1907): 35.

"Scott Joplin Dies of Mental Troubles." *New York Age*, 5 April 1917, p. 1.

"Sees National Music Created by Ragtime." *New York Times*, 9 February 1913, sec. 4, p. 5.

Seldes, Gilbert. "Jazz in American Musical Development." *Arts and Decoration* 20 (April 1924): 21.

————. *The Seven Lively Arts*. New York: Harper and Bros., 1924; rev. ed., New York: Sagamore Press, 1957.

Sherlock, Charles Reginald. "From Breakdown to Ragtime." *Cosmopolitan* (October 1901): 631–39.

Smith, Frederick James. "Irving Berlin and Modern Ragtime." *New York Dramatic Mirror*, 14 January 1914, p. 38.

Smith, Wilson G. "The Vagrant Philosopher." *Negro Music Journal* 1 (May 1903): 181–83. Reprint ed., Westport, Conn.: Negro Universities Press, 1970.

"Something about Popular Songs." *Musician* 5 (May 1900): 153.

"Songs without History." *American Musician and Art Journal* 26 (22 April 1910): 23.

Sousa, John Philip. "A Letter from Sousa." *Etude* 16 (August 1898): 231.

"Sousa at the Hippodrome." *New York Times*, 15 January 1906, p. 9.

"Stark Music Printing Company's New Home." *American Musician and Art Journal* 20 (26 June 1906): 6.

Stults, R. M. "Something about the Popular Music of Today." *Etude* 18 (March 1900): 97.

"Syncopated Melody Not Negro Music." *Music Trade Review* 48 (20 February 1909): 15.

"Ted Snyder Talks about the Old Days." *Metronome Orchestral Monthly* (1923). Reprinted in *Rag Times* 10 (September 1976): 4–5.

"Theatrical Comment." *New York Age*, 3 April 1913, p. 6.

"Theatrical Gossip." *New York Times*, 26 April 1892, p. 8.

"Theatrical Jottings." *New York Age*, 7 August 1913, p. 6; 14 August 1913, p. 6.

Thompson, Alexander S. "A Critical Answer to the Theory of 'Apaches, Mollycoddles and Highbrows.'" *Musical America* 16 (31 August 1912): 26.

Thomson, Virgil. "Jazz." *American Mercury* 2 (August 1924): 465–67.

"'To Jazz' or 'To Rag.'" *Literary Digest* 73 (6 May 1922): 37.

"To Replace Rag-Time." *Literary Digest* 66 (22 March 1913): 641.

Toye, Francis. "Ragtime: The New Tarantism." *English Review* 13 (March 1913): 654–58.

"The Truth about Jazz Bands and Jazzus." *Tuneful Yankee* 1 (October 1917): 2–3.

Turner, Chittenden. "Dance, the Foe of American Song." *Arts and Decoration* 20 (November 1923): 21.

"Two Views of Ragtime." *Seven Arts* 2 (July 1917): 368–83. (A blanket title covering articles by Hiram K. Moderwell and Charles L. Buchanan.)

Van Vechten, Carl. "Communications." *Seven Arts* 2 (September 1917): 669–70.

———. "The Great American Composer." *Vanity Fair* (April 1917). Reprinted in Van Vechten, *Red: Papers on Musical Subjects*. New York: Alfred A. Knopf, 1925; reprinted in *Rag Times* 8 (July 1974): 2–3.

Walker, George W. "The Real 'Coon' on the American Stage." *Theatre* 6 (August 1906): 224.

"Walking for a Cake." *New York Times*, 7 February 1897, p. 2.

Walton, Lester A. "Music and the Stage: Composer of Ragtime Now Writing Grand Opera." *New York Age*, 5 March 1908, p. 6.

———. "Music and the Stage: President Bans Ragtime." *New York Age*, 6 February 1908, p. 10.

"War on Rag-Time." *American Musician* 5 (July 1901): 4.

Weld, Arthur. "The Invasion of Vulgarity in Music." *Etude* 17 (February 1899): 52.

"What Is American Music?" *Musical America* 3 (24 February 1906): 8.

"What 'The Concert Goer' Says of 'The Negro Music Journal.'" *Negro Music Journal* 1 (October 1902): 28. Reprint ed., Westport, Conn.: Negro Universities Press, 1970.

"The Whence and What of Jazz." *Melody* 3 (April 1919): 4–5.

"Who Was Sponsor?" *Melody* 2 (December 1918): 4.

"Why Ragtime Is the True Music of 'Hustlers.'" *Christensen's Ragtime Review* 1 (December 1914): 3–4.

"Will Livernash's Remarkable Success." *American Musician and Art Journal* 25 (8 January 1909): 43.

"Will Ragtime Save the Soul of the Native American Composer?" *Current Opinion* (December 1915): 406–407.

Winn, Edward R. *How to Play Ragtime (Uneven Rhythm)*. Edward R. Winn, 1915.

———. "'Ragging' the Popular Song Hits." *Melody* 2 (January–September 1918): passim.

———. "Ragtime Piano Playing." *Cadenza* 21–23 (March 1915–October 1916): passim.

————. "Ragtime Piano Playing: A Practical Course of Instruction for Pianists." *Tuneful Yankee/Melody* 1–2 (January 1917–June 1918): passim.

Wise, C. Stanley. "'American Music Is True Art,' Says Stravinsky." *New York Tribune*, 16 January 1916, sec. 5, p. 3.

Young, Filson. "Tango." *Living Age* (23 August 1913): 509–511.

### Sources: 1930–1975

Allen, Frederick Lewis. "When America Learned to Dance." *Scribner's Magazine* 102 (September 1937): 11–17.

Arnold, Elliott. *Deep in My Heart*. New York: Duell, Sloan and Pearce, 1949.

Ashforth, Bob. "On Classic Ragtime." *Ragtimer* (March/April 1970): 7.

Atkins, Jerry L. "Early Days in Texas: New Notes on Scott Joplin's Youth." *Rag Times* 6 (September 1972): 1–3.

Balliet, Whitney. "The Ragtime Game." *New Yorker* (2 July 1960): 20–21. Reprinted in *Ragtime Society* 2 (September 1963): 3.

Baskerville, David. "The Influence of Jazz on Art Music to Mid-Century." Ph.D. dissertation, University of California at Los Angeles, 1965.

Berlin, Edward A. "Piano Ragtime: A Musical and Cultural Study." Ph.D. dissertation, The City University of New York, 1976.

————. "Ragtime and Improvised Piano: Another View." *Journal of Jazz Studies* 4 (June 1977): 4–10.

————. Review of *The Art of Ragtime*, by William J. Schafer and Johannes Riedel. *Black Perspective in Music* 3 (Spring 1975): 105–107.

————. Review of *Classic Piano Rags*, compiled by Rudi Blesh. *Black Perspective in Music* 2 (Fall 1974): 218–19.

————. Review of *Rags and Ragtime: A Musical History*, by David A. Jasen and Trebor Jay Tichenor, and *Scott Joplin*, by James Haskins with Kathleen Benson. *Notes* 35 (March 1979): 616–19.

————. Review of *Scott Joplin and the Ragtime Era*, by Peter Gammond. *Journal of Research in Music Education* 24 (Fall 1976): 155–56.

————. Review of *This Is Ragtime*, by Terry Waldo. *Notes* 33 (June 1977): 838–40.

Bierly, Paul E. *John Philip Sousa: America Phenomenon*. New York: Appleton-Century-Crofts, 1973.

Blesh, Rudi. "Ragtime Revaluated." *Playback* 2 (May 1949): 5–6.

————. "Scott Joplin: Black-American Classicist." Introduction to *The Collected Works of Scott Joplin*, vols. 1 and 2. Edited by Vera Brodsky Lawrence. Richard Jackson, editorial consultant. New York: New York Public Library, 1971.

————, comp. and Introduction. *Classic Piano Rags: Complete Original Music for 81 Rags*. New York: Dover, 1973.

————, and Harriet Janis. *They All Played Ragtime*. New York: Alfred A. Knopf, 1950; 4th ed., rev. New York: Oak Publications, 1971.

"Bob Darch Unearths Treasures." *Ragtimer* (September/October 1970): 8.

Borneman, Ernest. "From Minstrelsy to Jazz." *Record Changer* (January 1945): 3.

Bourne, Dave. "The Ben Harney Years (A Continuing Interview with George Orendorff)." *Rag Times* 4 (November 1970): 11–12.

————. "L. Wolfe Gilbert: 1886–1970." *Rag Times* 3 (September 1970): 3.

Bowers, Q. David. *Encyclopedia of Automatic Musical Instruments*. Vestal, N.Y.: Vestal Press, 1972.

————. *A Guidebook of Automatic Musical Instruments*. Vol. I: *Player Pianos, Coin Pianos, Orchestrions, Reproducing Pianos, Etc*. Vestal, N.Y.: Vestal Press, 1967.

————. *Put Another Nickel In: A History of Coin-Operated Pianos and Orchestrions*. Vestal, N.Y.: Vestal Press, 1966.

Bradford, Robert Allen. "Arthur Marshall—Last of the Sedalia Ragtimers." *Rag Times* 2 (May 1968): 5.

"Brief Encounter." *Ragtimer* (January/February 1975): 14.

Brown, Sterling. "Negro Producers of Ragtime" in *The Negro in Music and Art*, pp. 49–50. Ed. Lindsay Patterson. International Library of Negro Life and History, vol. 16. New York: Publishers Co., 1967.

Campbell, S. Brunson. "Euday Bowman and the '12th Street Rag.'" *Jazz Journal* 4 (January 1951): 14.

————. "From Rags to Ragtime: A Eulogy." *Jazz Report* 5 [ca. 1967]: 5–6.

————. "More on Ragtime." *Jazz Journal* 4 (May 1951): 4.

————. "Ragtime Begins." *Record Changer* 7 (March 1948): 8. Reprinted in *Ragtime Society* 2 (November 1963): 4–5.

————. "The Ragtime Kid (An Autobiography)." *Jazz Report* 6 [ca. 1967–68]: 7–12.

————, and Roy J. Carew. "How I became . . . A Pioneer Rag Man of the 1890's." *Record Changer* 6 (April 1947): 12.

————. "Sedalia . . . Missouri, Cradle of Ragtime." *Record Changer* 4 (May 1945): 3.

Carew, Roy J. "Assorted Rags." *Record Changer* 8 (February 1949): 6. Reprinted in *Ragtime Society* 3 (November 1964): 75.

————. "Euphonic Sounds." *Record Changer* 4 (December 1945): 40–41.

————. "Historic Corner." *Jazz Forum*, no. 3 (April 1947): 9.

————. "Hodge Podge." *Jazz Report* 2 (September 1961): 3–5.

————. "New Orleans Recollections." *Record Changer* (February 1943): 28–29. Reprinted in *Record Changer* 6 (July 1947): 9; reprinted in *Ragtime Society* 3 (March 1964): 22.

————. "New Orleans Recollections." *Record Changer* 7 (December 1948): 12; reprinted in *Ragtime Society* 3 (May 1964): 36.

————. "Random Recollections." *Jazz Forum*, no. 3 (January 1947): 1–2.

————. "Scott Joplin." *Jazz Record*, no. 60 (November 1947): 6–7.

————. "Shephard N. Edmonds." *Record Changer* (December 1947): 13–14.

————. "Treemonisha." *Record Changer* 5 (October 1946): 17.

————. "A Tribute to Roy Carew: Not Forgetting Jelly Roll." Introduction by George W. Kay. *Jazz Journal* 21 (May 1968): 22–23.

————, and Don E. Fowler. "Scott Joplin: Overlooked Genius." *Record Changer* (September 1944): 12–14; (October 1944): 10–12; (December 1944): 10–11.

Cassidy, Russ. "Joseph Lamb—Last of the Ragtime Composers." *Jazz Report* 1 (January, February, March, April, August 1961). Reprinted in *Jazz Monthly* 7 (August 1961): 4–7; (October 1961): 13–15; (November 1961): 9–10; (December 1961): 15–16; reprinted as "Joseph F. Lamb: A Biography," *Ragtime Society* 5 (Summer 1966): 29–42.

————. Obituary of Etilman J. Stark. *Ragtime Review* 1 (January 1962): 3–4.

"Charles Luckeyeth (Luckey) Roberts (1893–1968)." *Ragtimer* 6, nos. 5–6 (1967): 13.

Charters, A. R. Danberg. "Negro Folk Elements in Classic Ragtime." *Ethnomusicology* 5 (September 1961): 174–83. Reprinted in *Ragtime Review* 4 (July 1965): 7–12.

Charters, Ann. *Nobody: The Story of Bert Williams*. New York: Macmillan, 1970.

————, ed. and Introduction. *The Ragtime Songbook*. New York: Oak Publications, 1965.

Charters, Samuel B. "Red Backed Book of Rags." *Jazz Report* 2 (July 1962): 7–8.

————, and Leonard Konstadt. *Jazz: A History of the New York Scene*. Garden City, N.Y.: Doubleday, 1962.

Chase, Gilbert. *America's Music from the Pilgrims to the Present*. 2d ed., rev. New York: McGraw-Hill, 1966.

Coats, Dorothy. "Clarence Woods. It Might Have Been . . ." *Rag Times* 9 (March 1976): 5.

Cole, Russ. Untitled letter. *Ragtime Society* 4 (March/April 1965): 19–20.

Collier, James Lincoln. "The Scott Joplin Rag." *New York Times Magazine*, 21 September 1975, pp. 18ff.

"The Compositions of Joseph F. Lamb." *Ragtime Society* 2 (January 1963): 5–6.

Conroy, Frank. Review of *The Art of Ragtime*, by William J. Schafer and Johannes Riedel. *New York Times Book Review*, 3 February 1974, sec. 7, pp. 4–5.

Cook, Will Marion. "Clorindy, the Origin of the Cakewalk." *Theatre Arts* 31 (September 1947): 61–65. Reprinted in *Readings in Black American Music*, ed. Eileen Southern, pp. 217–23. New York: W. W. Norton, 1971.

Cuney-Hare, Maud. *Negro Musicians and Their Music*. Washington, D.C.: Associated Publishers, 1936.

Darch, Robert R. "'Blind' Boone: A Sensational Missourian Forgotten." *Ragtimer* 6, nos. 5–6 (1967): 9–13.

Davin, Tom. "Conversations with James P. Johnson." *Jazz Review* 2 (June 1959): 14–17; (July 1959): 10–13; (August 1959): 13–15; (September 1959): 26–27. Reprinted in *Jazz Panorama*, ed. by Martin Williams. New York: Collier Books, 1962.

Den, Marjorie Freilich. "Joseph F. Lamb: A Ragtime Composer Recalled." M. A. thesis, Brooklyn College, 1976.

Elderry, R. B., Jr. "Eliot's Shakespeherian Rag." *American Quarterly* 9 (Summer 1957): 185–86.

Emery, Lynne Fauley. *Black Dance in the United States from 1619 to 1970*. Foreword by Katherine Dunham. Palo Alto, Ca.: National Press Books, 1972.

Ewen, David. *The Life and Death of Tin Pan Alley: The Golden Age of American Popular Music*. New York: Funk and Wagnalls, 1964.

Fletcher, Tom. *The Tom Fletcher Story: 100 Years of the Negro in Show Business*. New York: Burdge, 1954.

Franks, Percy. Untitled letter. *Ragtime Review* 4 (January 1965): 4.

———. Untitled letter. *Ragtimer* (January/February 1971): 12.

Freedland, Michael. *Irving Berlin*. New York: Stein and Day, 1974.

Gammond, Peter. *Scott Joplin and the Ragtime Era*. New York: St. Martin's Press, 1975.

Geil, Jean. "American Sheet Music in the Walter N. H. Harding Collection at the Bodleian Library, Oxford University." *Notes* 34 (June 1978): 805–813.

Gillis, Frank. "Hot Rhythm in Piano Ragtime" in *Music in the Americas*, pp. 91–104. Ed. George List and Juan Orrego-Salas. Bloomington, Ind.: Indiana University Research Center in Anthropology, Folklore, and Linguistics, 1967.

Goldberg, Isaac. *Tin Pan Alley: A Chronicle of the American Popular Music Racket*. Introduction by George Gershwin. New York: John Day, 1930. Reprinted as *Tin Pan Alley: A Chronicle of American Popular Music*, Supplement "From Sweet and Swing to Rock 'n' Roll," by Edward Jablonski. New York: Frederick Ungar Publishing, 1961.

Goodman, Solomon. "Henry Lodge." *Rag Times* 10 (March 1977): 9.

Grove, Thurman, and Mary Grove. "St. Louis Piano: The Story of Charles Thompson." *Playback* 3 (January 1950): 3–6.

Guentner, Francis J. "The Billiken in Ragtime." *Universitas* (January 1977). Reprinted in *Rag Times* 11 (July 1977): 8.

————. "The Stark's First Decade in St. Louis." *Rag Times* 10 (January 1977): 1–2.

Handy, W. C. *Father of the Blues: An Autobiography*. Ed. Arna Bontemps; Foreword by Abbe Niles. New York: Macmillan, 1941.

Hankins, Rogers. "Familiar Chord Patterns." *Ragtimer* 6 (April 1967): 6–7.

————. "Sounds Familiar." *Ragtime Society* 5 (November 1966): 53–54.

————. "Sounds Familiar." *Ragtimer* 6, no. 2 (1967): 6–8.

————. "Sounds Familiar." *Ragtimer* (October 1968): 9–10.

————. "Sounds Familiar: The Cycle of 5ths." *Ragtimer* 6, no. 3 (1967): 7–8.

————. "Sounds Familiar: From the Scrap Heap." *Ragtimer* 6, no. 4 (1967): 6–7.

————. "Sounds Familiar: The Preludes to the Maple Leaf Rag." *Ragtimer* (July/August 1972): 10–12.

————. "Sounds Familiar: The Preludes to the Maple Leaf Rag." *Ragtimer* (July/August 1972): 10–12.

————. "Sounds Familiar: Those Bill Bailey Songs. Part I. Classic Ballad Structure." *Ragtimer* (September/October 1970): 10–14; " . . . Part 2. Sounds and Symbols." (November/December 1970): 4–8; " . . . Part 3. Transition Songs." (January/February 1971): 7–11; " . . . Part 4. Those Bill Bailey Blues." (May/June 1971): 4–12.

————. "Sounds Familiar: Those Indian Songs." *Ragtimer* (May/June 1970): 5–9.

Harding, Walter N. H. Untitled letter. *Ragtime Society* 3 (April 1964): 24–25.

Harrah, Madge. "The Incomparable Blind Boone." *Ragtimer* (July/August 1969): 9–12.

————. "Wayne B. Allen: 'Blind' Boone's Last Manager." *Ragtimer* (September/October 1969): 10–15.

Haskins, James, and Kathleen Benson. *Scott Joplin*. Garden City, N.Y.: Doubleday, 1978.

Heermans, Jerry. "Mike Bernard: The Ragtime King." *Rag Times* 6 (November 1972): 6–8.

Hentoff, Nat. "Garvin Bushell and New York Jazz in the 1920's." *Jazz Review* 2 (January 1959): 11–12; (February 1959): 9–10.

Hertzberg, Dan. "One Last Hand for the Entertainer." *Newsday*, 1 August 1974, p. 4.

Hitchcock, H. Wiley. *Music in the United States: A Historical Introduction*. 2d ed. Englewood Cliffs, N.J.: Prentice-Hall, 1974.

————. "Ragtime of the Higher Class." *Stereo Review* (April 1971): 84. Reprinted in *Ragtimer* (July/August 1972): 13–15.

Howard, Laura Pratt. "Ragtime." M.M. thesis, Eastman School of Music, University of Rochester, 1942.

"In Memoriam: J. Russel Robinson." *Ragtime Review* 2 (October 1963): 6.

Ives, Charles. *Memos*, ed. John Kirkpatrick. New York: W. W. Norton, 1972.

"J. B. Lampe, 1869–1929." *Rag Times* 7 (January 1974): 5.

"J. Laurence Cook." *Rag Times* 10 (July 1976): 8.

Jasen, David. "Another Look at Ragtime." *Rag Times* 3 (August/September 1969): 6–7.

———. "Ragtime—A Re-Evaluation." *Ragtimer* 6, nos. 5–6 (1967): 26–28. Reprinted in *Jazz Journal* 21 (April 1968): 22–23.

———. "Ragtime Explained." *Storyville*, no. 37 (October/November 1971): 4–7.

———. *Recorded Ragtime, 1897–1958*. Hamden, Conn.: Archon Books, Shoe String Press, 1973.

———. "Zez Confrey: Creator of the Novelty Rag." *Rag Times* 5 (September 1971): 4–5.

———, and Trebor Jay Tichenor. *Rags and Ragtime: A Musical History*. New York: Seabury Press, 1978.

"Joe Jordan (1882–1971)." *Rag Times* 5 (November 1971): 1.

"Joe Jordan: Mr. Music Officer." *Ragtimer* (July/August 1970): 9–11.

Johnson, James Weldon. *Along This Way*. New York: Viking Press, 1933.

———. *Black Manhattan*. New York: Alfred A. Knopf, 1930; reprint ed., New York: Arno Press and New York Times, 1968.

Kaufmann, Helen L. *From Jehovah to Jazz: Music in America from Psalmody to the Present Day*. New York: Dodd, Mead, 1937; reprint ed., Port Washington, N.Y.: Kennikat Press, 1969.

Kay, George W. "Basin Street Stroller: New Orleans and Tony Jackson." *Jazz Journal* 4 (June 1951): 1–3; (August 1951): 1–2; (September 1951): 1–2.

———. "Final Years of Frustration (1939–1941) as Told by Jelly Roll Morton in His Letters to Roy J. Carew." *Jazz Journal* 21 (November 1968): 2–5; (December 1968): 8–9.

———. "Ragged but Right." *Record Changer* 9 (March 1950): 5. Reprinted in *Ragtime Society* 3 (January 1964): 7–8.

———. "Reminiscing in Ragtime: An Interview with Roy Carew." *Jazz Journal* 17 (November 1964): 8–9. Reprinted in *Ragtime Society* 5 (December 1966): 67–69.

Keepnews, Orrin. "Sweet Papa Jelly Roll." *Record Changer* 7 (February 1948): 6–7.

Kimball, Robert, and William Bolcom. *Reminiscing with Sissle and Blake*. New York: Viking Press, 1973.

King, Bobbi. "Conversation with Eubie Blake (continued): A Legend in His Own Lifetime." *Black Perspective in Music* 1 (Fall 1973): 151–56.

Koenigsberg, Allen. *Edison Cylinder Records, 1889–1912: With an Illus-trated History of the Phonograph*. New York: Stellar Productions, 1969.

Kramer, Karl. "Influence of Ragtime on Stage Music." *Ragtime Society* 4 (January 1965): 4–5.

———. "Jelly Roll in Chicago: The Missing Chapter." *Ragtimer* 6 (April 1967): 15–22.

Laurie, Joe, Jr. "The Ragtime Kids." *Variety*, 9 August 1950, p. 51.

Levin, Floyd. "The American Scene." *Jazz Journal* 3 (February 1950): 13.

Levy, Eugene. *James Weldon Johnson: Black Leader, Black Voice*. Chicago: University of Chicago Press, 1973.

Locke, Alain L. *The Negro and His Music*. Washington, D.C.: Associates in Negro Folk Education, 1936.

Lomax, Alan. *Mister Jelly Roll: The Fortunes of Jelly Roll Morton, New Orleans Creole and "Inventor of Jazz."* New York: Duell, Sloan, and Pearse, 1950; 2d ed. Berkeley, Ca.: University of California Press, 1973.

Lucas, John. "Ragtime Revival." *Record Changer* 7 (December 1948): 8. Reprinted in *Ragtime Society* 3 (Summer 1964): 50.

McNeil, W. K. "Syncopated Slander: The 'Coon Song,' 1890–1900." *Keystone Folklore Quarterly* 17 (Summer 1972): 63–82.

"Maple Leaf Goals." *Rag Times* 1 (September 1967): 7.

Marcuse, Maxwell F. *Tin Pan Alley in Gaslight: A Saga of the Songs That Made the Gray Nineties "Gay."* Watkins Glen, N.Y.: Century House, 1959.

Marks, Edward Bennet. *They All Sang: From Tony Pastor to Rudy Val-lée*. As told to Abbott J. Liebling. New York: Viking Press, 1934.

Martin, Bill. "Ragtime Man—Cakewalk Man." *Record Changer* (February 1953): 7.

Mason, Daniel Gregory. *Tune in America: A Study of Our Coming Musical Independence*. New York: Alfred A. Knopf, 1931. Reprint ed., Freeport, N.Y.: Books for Libraries Press, 1969.

Melton, Larry. "Sedalia Addresses." *Rag Times* 10 (November 1976): 9.

Merriam, Alan P. *A Bibliography of Jazz*. Assisted by Robert J. Benford. Philadelphia: American Folklore Society, 1954; reprint ed., New York: Kraus Reprint, 1970.

Mitchell, Bill. "Elite Syncopations." *Rag Times* 1 (March 1968): 9.

———. "Elite Syncopations: An Open Letter from Roy Bargy." *Jazz Report* 4 (September/October 1965): [5].

———. "Nashville to St. Louis: A Tragic Odyssey." *Jazz Report* 4 (November/December 1965): [5–7].

———. "Virginia City Ragtime: A Visit with Harry Bruce, with Some New Light on Euday Bowman." *Jazz Report* 5, no. 3 (1966). Reprinted in *Rag Times* 1 (January 1968): 5–6.

Montgomery, Michael. "Joseph F. Lamb—A Ragtime Paradox, 1887–1960." *Second Line* 3/4 (1961): 17–18.

———. "Rags to Riches: The Odyssey of Player Piano Rolls." *American Life: A Collector's Annual* 4 (1964): 144–47.

———. "The Story of 'Ragging the Scale.' " *Ragtime Society* 5 (May/June 1963): 6–7.

———. "A Visit with Joseph Lamb." *Jazz Report* (December 1957).

Moore, Carman. "Notes on *Treemonisha*." Preface to *Works for Voice*. Vol. 2 of *The Collected Works of Scott Joplin*, ed. Vera Brodsky Lawrence; Richard Jackson, editorial consultant. Introduction by Rudi Blesh. New York: New York Public Library, 1971.

Morath, Max. "Any Rags Today?" *Music Journal Magazine* 18 (October 1960): 76–77. Reprinted as Introduction to *34 Ragtime Jazz Classics*. New York: Edwin H. Morris, Melrose Music, 1964.

———. "First There Was Ragtime." *Jazz Report* 2 (January 1962): 8–9.

———. "Ragtime—Folk Music of the City." *Music Journal* 22 (November 1964): 29–30.

———, comp. and Introduction. *Max Morath's Giants of Ragtime*. New York: Edward B. Marks, 1971.

———, ed. and Introduction. *Max Morath's Ragtime Guide*. New York: Hollis Music, 1972.

Morton, Jelly Roll. "A Fragment of an Autobiography." *Record Changer* (March 1944): 15–16; (April 1944); 27–28.

———. "I Discovered Jazz in 1902." *Downbeat* (August 1938). Reprinted in *Frontiers of Jazz*, ed. Ralph de Toledano, pp. 104–107. 2d ed. New York: Frederick Ungar Publishing, 1962.

Moynahan, James H. S. "Ragtime to Swing." *Saturday Evening Post* (13 February 1937): 14–15.

*Die Musik in Geschichte und Gegenwart*. S.v. "Gesellschaftstanz," by Alfred Baresel; "Jazz," by Werner Burkhardt; "Negermusik," by Bruno Nettl.

Nathan, Hans. *Dan Emmett and the Rise of Early Negro Minstrelsy*. Norman, Okla.: University of Oklahoma Press, 1962.

Newberger, Eli H. "The Transition from Ragtime to Improvised Piano Style." *Journal of Jazz Studies* 3 (Spring 1976): 3–18.

Niles, Abbe. Foreword to *Blues: An Anthology*, ed. W. C. Handy. 3d ed., rev., ed. Jerry Silverman; illustrated by Miguel Covarrubias. New York: Macmillan, Collier Books, 1972.

"Old Ragtimer." *Time*, 5 August 1935, p. 54.

"On 65 Note Piano Rolls." *Ragtime Review* 1 (July 1962): 8–9.

"Organist Dies at 90, Leaving Fortune in Rare Sheet Music." *New York Times*, 14 December 1973, p. 34.

"Original Maple Leaf Club Document Found." *Rag Times* 9 (March 1976): 1.

Parker, John W. (Knocky). "J. Russel Robinson . . . An Overdue Trib-
    ute." *Ragtime Review* 1 (October 1962): 4–5.
Pash, Dennis. "E. Harry Kelly." *Rag Times* 10, Part 1 (March 1976): 2–4;
    Part 2 (May 1976): 2–3.
"'Penniless' Ragtime Pianist Leaves Fortune in Books." *Ragtimer*
    (January/February 1975): 13.
"Percy Wenrich & Dolly Connolly." *Rag Times* 7 (September 1973): 6.
Powers, Frank. "Ragtime Stock Orchestrations." *Ragtime Society* 5
    (November 1966): 44–48.
"Ragtime." *Ragtime Review* 1 (January 1962): 2.
"Rare Rag Found." *Rag Times* 4 (May 1970): 1.
"'Record World' Features Joplin." *Rag Times* 8 (September 1974): 5.
Reed, Addison Walker. "The Life and Works of Scott Joplin." Ph.D.
    dissertation, University of North Carolina at Chapel Hill, 1973.
————. "Scott Joplin, Pioneer." *Black Perspective in Music* 3 (Spring
    1975): 45–52; (Fall 1975): 269–77.
Robinson, J. Russel. "Dixieland Piano." As told to Ralph auf der Heide.
    *Record Changer* (August 1947): 7–8.
Roehl, Harvey N. *Keys to a Musical Past*. Vestal, N.Y.: Vestal Press,
    1968.
————. *Player Piano Treasury*. 2d ed. Vestal, N.Y.: Vestal Press, 1973.
Rogers, Charles Payne. "Charles Thompson." *Record Changer* 9 (May
    1950): 13.
————. "Ragtime." *Jazz Forum*, no. 4 (April 1947): 5–8.
Rose, Al. "New Orleans Rags & Robert Hoffman." *Rag Times* 9 (Sep-
    tember 1975): 4–5.
"Roy J. Carew, 1884–1967." *Ragtimer* 6, no. 3 (1967): 19.
Russell, Ross. Review of *This Is Ragtime*, by Terry Waldo. *New York
    Times Book Review*, 24 October 1976, pp. 37–39.
Sargeant, Winthrop. *Jazz: Hot and Hybrid*. New York: Arrow Editions,
    1938; 3d ed., enl. New York: Da Capo Press, 1975.
Schafer, William J. "Ragtime Arranging for Fun and Profit: The Cases
    of Harry J. Alford and J. Bodewalt Lampe." *Journal of Jazz
    Studies* 3 (Fall 1975): 103–117.
————, and Johannes Riedel. *The Art of Ragtime: Form and Meaning of
    an Original Black American Art*. Baton Rouge, La.: Louisiana
    State University Press, 1973.
Schuller, Gunther. *Early Jazz: Its Roots and Musical Development*.
    New York: Oxford University Press, 1968.
Schwartz, H. W. *Bands of America*. Garden City, N.Y.: Doubleday,
    1957.
Scotti, Joseph Ralph. "Joe Lamb: A Study of Ragtime's Paradox." Ph.D.
    dissertation, University of Cincinnati, 1977.
Shapiro, Elliott. "'Ragtime' USA." *Notes* 8 (June 1951): 457–70.
Shea, Tom. "Bart Howard." *Ragtimer* 6, no. 3 (1967): 4–5.

————. "Finney's Orchestra." *Ragtime Society* 4 (July/August 1965): 34–38.

————. "Winging It with Tom Shea." *Ragtimer* 6 (April 1967): 3; 6, nos. 5–6 (1967): 23–25.

"Shelton Brooks, 1886–1975." *Rag Times* (November 1975): 8.

Simms, Bartlett D., and Ernest Borneman. "Ragtime: History and Analysis." *Record Changer* 4 (October 1945): 4–9.

Smart, James R. *The Sousa Band: A Discography*. Washington, D.C.: Library of Congress, 1970.

Smith, Charles Edward. "The Chicken and the Egg." *Record Changer* 8 (August 1949): 7.

————. "Oh, Mr. Jelly!" *Jazz Record*, no. 17 (February 1944): 8–10. Reprinted in *Jazz Piano*, no. 2 (1945): 17–19.

"Snoring Sampson: Reprint." *Rag Times* 8 (July 1974): 1.

Souchon, Edmond. "Doctor Bites Doctor Jazz (and Apologises)." *Record Changer* (February 1953): 6.

Southern, Eileen. "Conversation with Eubie Blake: A Legend in His Own Lifetime." *Black Perspective in Music* 1 (Spring 1973): 50–59.

————. *The Music of Black Americans: A History*. New York: W. W. Norton, 1971.

————, ed. *Readings in Black American Music*. New York: W. W. Norton, 1971.

Spaeth, Sigmund. *A History of Popular Music in America*. New York: Random House, 1948.

Spottswood, Richard, and David A. Jasen. "Discoveries concerning Recorded Ragtime." *Jazz Journal* 21 (February 1968): 7.

Stearns, Marshall. *The Story of Jazz*. London: Oxford University Press, 1956.

————, and Jean Stearns. *Jazz Dance*. New York: Macmillan, 1968.

Suppan, Wolfgang. Review of *The Art of Ragtime*, by William J. Schafer and Johannes Riedel. *Jazzforschung* 6/7 (1974/75): 279–80.

Thompson, Kay C. "Early Cakewalks: The Roots of Ragtime." *Jazz Journal* (March 1952). Reprinted in *Ragtime Society* 3 (February 1964): 7–8.

————. "The First Lady of Storyville: The Fabulous Countess Willie Piazza." *Record Changer* 10 (1951): 5. Reprinted in *Ragtimer* (May/June 1975): 13–15.

————. "Lottie Joplin." *Record Changer* 9 (October 1950): 8, 18.

————. "More on Ragtime." *Record Changer* 8 (October 1949): 9–10.

————. "The Pre-History of Ragtime." *Ragtimer* 6, no. 3 (1967): 16–19.

————. "Rag-Time and Jelly Roll." *Record Changer* 8 (April 1949): 8.

Tichenor, Trebor J. "The Rags of Scott Joplin." *Ragtime Review* 1 (July 1962): 2–3. Reprinted in *Rag Times* 11 (July 1977): 7.

————. "'The Real Thing' as Recalled by Charles Thompson." *Ragtime*

*Review* 2 (April 1963): 5–6. Reprinted in *Rag Times* 5 (November 1971): 3–4.

——. "Who *Really* Wrote the St. Louis Tickle?" *Ragtime Review* 3 (April 1964): 6. Reprinted in *Rag Times* 3 (January/March 1970): 4.

——. "The World of Joseph Lamb—An Exploration." *Jazz Report* 1 (January, February, March, April, August 1961). Reprinted in *Jazz Monthly* 7 (August 1961): 7–9; (October 1961): 15–16; (November 1961): 10–11; (December 1961): 16–17.

——, comp. and Introduction. *Ragtime Rarities: Complete Original Music for 63 Piano Rags.* New York: Dover, 1975.

Tick, Judith. "Ragtime and the Music of Charles Ives." *Current Musicology*, no. 18 (1974): 105–113.

Toll, Robert C. *Blacking Up: The Minstrel Shown in Nineteenth-Century America.* New York: Oxford University Press, 1974.

"Treemonisha Copyright Litigation." *Rag Times* 11 (July 1977): 4.

Vanderlee, Ann, and John Vanderlee. "The Early Life of Scott Joplin." *Rag Times* 7 (January 1974): 2–3.

——. "Scott Joplin's Childhood Days in Texas." *Rag Times* 7 (November 1973): 5–7.

Waldo, Terry. *This Is Ragtime.* New York: Hawthorn Books, 1976.

Waterman, Guy. "Joplin's Late Rags: An Analysis." *Record Changer* 14, no. 8 [ca. 1955–56]: 5–8. Reprinted as Part 2 of "Ragtime" in *The Art of Jazz: Essays on the Nature and Development of Jazz*, ed. Martin Williams, pp. 19–31. New York: Oxford University Press, 1959.

——. "Ragtime." In *Jazz*, Ed. Nat Hentoff and Albert J. McCarthy, pp. 43–58. New York: Rinehart, Holt and Winston, 1959.

——. "A Survey of Ragtime." *Record Changer* 14, no. 7 [ca. 1955–1956]: 7–9. Reprinted as Part 1 of "Ragtime" in *The Art of Jazz: Essays on the Nature and Development of Jazz*, ed. Martin Williams, pp. 11–18. New York: Oxford University Press, 1959.

Waterman, Richard A. "Hot Rhythm in Negro Music." *Journal of the American Musicological Society* 1 (Spring 1948): 24–37.

Whitcomb, Ian. "Britain Invaded!" *Rag Times* 8 (November 1974): 6–7.

——. "Shelton Brooks Is Alive & Strutting." *Jazz Report* 7, no. 2 [ca. 1970]: no pagination.

Wilder, Alec. *American Popular Song: The Great Innovators, 1900–1950.* Ed. and Introduction by James T. Maher. New York: Oxford University Press, 1972.

Wilford, Charles. "Ragtime: An Excavation." *Piano Jazz*, no. 2 (1945): 9–12.

Wilson, Olly. "The Significance of the Relationship between Afro-American Music and West African Music." *Black Perspective in Music* 2 (Spring 1974): 3–22.

Witmark, Isidore, and Isaac Goldberg. *The Story of the House of Witmark: From Ragtime to Swingtime*. New York: Lee Furman, 1939. Reprint ed., New York: Da Capo Press, 1976.

Wright, Bob, and Trebor J. Tichenor. "James Scott and C. L. Johnson—An Unlikely Musical Kinship." *Ragtime Review* 5 (January 1966): 7–8. Reprinted in *Rag Times* 6 (September 1972): 4.

Zimmerman, Dick. "C. L. Woolsey: The Ragtime Doctor." *Rag Times* 10 (May 1976): 4–5.

———. "Charles L. Johnson—The Happy Ragtimer: An Interview with His Nephew." *Rag Times* 2 (July 1968): 6–7.

———. "'El Cota': 60 Years Later." *Rag Times* 3 (March 1970): 4.

———. "F. Henri Klickman." *Rag Times* 7 (November 1973): 9.

———. "George Botsford: 1874–1949." *Rag Times* 7 (January 1974): 9.

———. "The Henry Lodge Story." *Rag Times* 9 (January 1976): 1–6.

———. "The Incredible Billy Eckstein: An Interview with Dai Vernon." *Rag Times* 1 (March 1968): 6A–6B.

———. "An Interview with John Stark." *Rag Times* 10 (September 1976): 5.

———. "Joe Jordan and Scott Joplin." *Rag Times* 2 (November 1968): 5.

———. "The Original Maple Leaf Club." *Rag Times* 8 (May 1974): 3.

———. "Ragtime Recollections: An Interview with Dai Vernon." *Rag Times* 2 (May 1968): 7–8.

———. "Saga of the Silver Swan." *Rag Times* 4 (July 1970): 1.

———. "A Visit with Joe Jordan." *Rag Times* 2 (September 1968): 6.

———. "A Visit with Mrs. Ted Snyder." *Rag Times* 4 (May 1970): 2–4.

———, comp. and Introduction. *A Tribute to Scott Joplin and the Giants of Ragtime*. New York: Shattinger-International Music, Charles Hansen, 1975.

# Index

The index includes persons, music, books, articles, and subjects. Music examples are in boldface type. The index to quoted passages includes the footnote numbers to facilitate location. Thus, the entry for Virgil Thomson's article "Jazz" is cited as "16(n49)," thereby distinguishing Thomson's quotation from the six others on page 16.

| | |
|---|---|
| Designer: | Dave Comstock |
| Compositor: | Advanced Typesetting Services |
| Printer: | Thomson-Shore |
| Binder: | Thomson-Shore |
| Text: | VIP Electra |
| Display: | Typositor DeVinne Ornamented, Gutenberg, & Koster |
| Cloth: | 55lb. P&S offset A69 |
| Paper: | Holliston Roxite B53556 |